ROUTLEDGE LIBRARY EDITIONS: INTERNATIONAL TRADE POLICY

I0028134

Volume 31

UNITED STATES FOREIGN ECONOMIC POLICY AND THE INTERNATIONAL CAPITAL MARKETS

UNITED STATES FOREIGN ECONOMIC POLICY AND THE INTERNATIONAL CAPITAL MARKETS

The Case of Capital Export Countries, 1963-1974

JOHN A. C. CONYBEARE

Routledge
Taylor & Francis Group

LONDON AND NEW YORK

First published in 1988 by Garland Publishing, Inc.

This edition first published in 2018
by Routledge
2 Park Square, Milton Park, Abingdon, Oxon OX14 4RN

and by Routledge
711 Third Avenue, New York, NY 10017

Routledge is an imprint of the Taylor & Francis Group, an informa business

© 1988 John A. C. Conybeare

All rights reserved. No part of this book may be reprinted or reproduced or utilised in any form or by any electronic, mechanical, or other means, now known or hereafter invented, including photocopying and recording, or in any information storage or retrieval system, without permission in writing from the publishers.

Trademark notice: Product or corporate names may be trademarks or registered trademarks, and are used only for identification and explanation without intent to infringe.

British Library Cataloguing in Publication Data
A catalogue record for this book is available from the British Library

ISBN: 978-1-138-06323-5 (Set)
ISBN: 978-1-315-14339-2 (Set) (ebk)
ISBN: 978-1-138-30573-1 (Volume 31) (hbk)
ISBN: 978-1-138-30576-2 (Volume 31) (pbk)
ISBN: 978-0-203-72877-2 (Volume 31) (ebk)

Publisher's Note
The publisher has gone to great lengths to ensure the quality of this reprint but points out that some imperfections in the original copies may be apparent.

Disclaimer
The publisher has made every effort to trace copyright holders and would welcome correspondence from those they have been unable to trace.

UNITED STATES FOREIGN ECONOMIC POLICY AND THE INTERNATIONAL CAPITAL MARKETS

THE CASE OF CAPITAL EXPORT COUNTRIES, 1963-1974

JOHN A. C. CONYBEARE

GARLAND PUBLISHING, INC.
NEW YORK & LONDON 1988

Copyright © 1988
John A. C. Conybeare
All Rights Reserved

Library of Congress Cataloging-in-Publication Data

Conybeare, John A. C.
United States foreign economic policy and the international
capital markets: the case of capital export countries, 1963-1974 /
John A. C. Conybeare.
p. cm. — (Harvard dissertations in American history and
political science)
Originally presented as the author's thesis (Ph. D. — Harvard
University, 1976).
Bibliography: p.
ISBN 0-8240-5119-X (alk. paper)
1. Balance of payments — United States. 2. Capital market —
United States. 3. Capital movements — United States. 4.
United States — Foreign Economic relations. I. Title. II. Series.
HG3883.U7C66 1988
332'.042'0973 — dc19
88-23520

Printed on acid-free, 250-year-life paper
Manufactured in the United States of America

TABLE OF CONTENTS

LIST OF TABLES AND FIGURES iii

Chapter

I. INTRODUCTION 1

II. THE POLICY BACKGROUND, ANALYSES, OPTIONS
AND CHOICES 13

III. ECONOMIC THEORY AND THE CONTROL OF CAPITAL
MOVEMENTS 34

IV. THE INDICES OF POWER AND THE LIMITS OF
CHOICE: PRESIDENTIAL POLITICS AND THE
BALANCE OF PAYMENTS, 1963-68 57

V. DOMESTIC INTEREST GROUP POLITICS AND THE
UNITED STATES' CAPITAL CONTROL PROGRAM 104

VI. BUREAUCRATIC POLITICS AND CAPITAL CONTROLS . . . 149

VII. THE INTERNATIONAL FRAMEWORK: FOREIGN
ATTITUDES AND REACTIONS TO UNITED STATES
POLICY 189

VIII. THE DENOUEMENT: THE 1968 PROGRAM AND THE
BALANCE OF PAYMENTS POLICY OF THE NIXON
ADMINISTRATION 231

IX. CONCLUSION 267

. . . .

NOTES 279

SELECTED BIBLIOGRAPHY 322

LIST OF TABLES AND FIGURES

Table
2.1   Government Transfers and Long-Term Private
       Capital Flows in the U.S. Balance of
       Payments   19
7.1   Selected Net Outflows of U.S. Private Capital
       Other than Direct Investment 193
7.2   U.S. Direct Investment in Selected European
       Countries   201
7.3   Public Long-Term Debt Offerings of Foreign
       Governments, Registered with the SEC,
       1 January 1961 to 15 July 1963 217

Figure
3.1   The Welfare Aspects of Home and Foreign
       Investment   39
3.2   Capital Outflow Restrictions Under Conditions
       of Equilibrium   53
3.3   Capital Outflow Restrictions to Correct a
       Payments Deficit   54
4.1   Power and Economics Under a Gold Exchange
       Standard   66
4.2   Internal and External Balance with a Flexible
       Exchange Rate   67
4.3   Internal and External Balance with a Fixed
       Exchange Rate   68
5.1   International Holding Company Organization . . . 118
5.2   The Financial Structure of Foreign Direct
       Investment   124

CHAPTER I

INTRODUCTION

. . . There still prevails, even in nations well
acquainted with commerce, a strong jealousy with
regard to the balance of trade, and a fear that all
their gold and silver may be leaving them. This
seems to me, almost in every case, a groundless
apprehension; . . .
> David Hume, "Of the Balance of Trade," 1752

. . . as a contribution to statecraft, which is concerned with the economic system as a whole and with
securing the optimum employment of the system's
entire resources, the methods of the early pioneers
of economic thinking in the sixteenth and seventeenth
centuries may have attained to fragments of practical
wisdom which the unrealistic abstractions of Ricardo
first forgot and then obliterated.
> J. M. Keynes, "Notes on Mercantilism," 1936

The external trade and capital transactions of a nation

have been subject to political intervention ever since govern-

ments were capable of doing so. Yet for the first fifteen

years following the Second World War the political dimension

of balance of payments policy, at least in the case of the

United States, was largely neglected by policy-makers and

academics alike. However, during the 1960's, their attention

was increasingly directed toward a confluence of issues associ-

ated with the decline of the international monetary system

established by the Bretton Woods Agreement of 1944, the rise

of the multinational corporation and the uncertain nature and

trend of economic interdependence between nations. For those

who had hitherto thought otherwise, "it became clear," as
Henry Kissinger recently told Business Week, "that every
economic policy had profound political implications, and
really required political inspiration and leadership to
make it effective."[1] This thesis is an attempt to explain
the political sources and implications of the policies of
one country toward an economic activity of critical importance in determining the nature and scope of the international financial system, the multinational corporation and
economic interdependence: the flows of capital across
national boundaries.[2]

 The Bretton Woods conference established a gold
exchange standard based on the United States dollar. Capital
outflows from the United States were vital to the provision
of liquidity in the system during its heyday in the 1950's.
However, as the supply of foreign held dollars grew, the stock
of gold held ready to redeem these dollars did not, and the
major participants in the Bretton Woods system found themselves
facing three new problems: lack of confidence in the convertibility of the dollar into gold, lack of symmetry in the process by which countries adjust to payments deficits or surpluses,
and the consequent need to find some method of reforming the
system upon which all major powers could agree. The regulation of capital flows, and in particular, in the case of the
United States, the control of long-term capital outflows, was

one of the principal methods of dealing with these problems.

Capital flows have also found a central place in the recent debate over whether and how the world is becoming more interdependent. At least one theorist on the subject holds long-term capital movements to be instrumental in equalizing the costs of production in different countries, and so rendering each country more sensitive to incremental economic changes in the rest of the world. However, the relationship between long-term capital flows and interdependence is not entirely self-evident; and where one writer can point to a decline in long-term capital movements as a percentage of world production between 1865 and 1965,[3] another can point to a doubling in foreign direct investment by the United States roughly over the decade of the 1960's.[4]

Both of these issues--the central role of capital flows in meeting the functional requisites of the postwar gold exchange standard and in influencing the extent of interdependence--have a common meeting place in the debate over the power of the multinational corporation as the primary mover of real capital across national boundaries. Much of this debate has focused on the explicitly political or "welfare" issues of direct foreign investment. This thesis will draw attention to a less dramatic aspect of international investment: the assessment and control of the effects of capital flows on the balance of payments of the capital

exporting country. During the first years of this decade it
appeared that the emergent trend was toward greater regulation
of capital inflows by host countries and less regulation of
capital outflows by home countries. However, despite the
demise of capital export controls by the United States, this
trend is no longer quite so clear, as capital-poor countries
compete for foreign capital in the wake of the rise in petroleum prices, and as the United States itself makes some
halting moves back to the discouragement of capital outflows--
although not necessarily for the same reasons that this was
done during the 1960's.

The problem of regulating world capital movements
is hardly unique to the post-World War Two era. After the
First World War, the long-term situation for the balance of
payments of the United States changed from that of a net
debtor to that of a net creditor in international capital
movements. Despite the turmoil in the capital markets of
the 1930's, and the passive acceptance of capital controls
at the Bretton Woods conference,[5] the United States resumed
this position in the postwar world. As a major exporter of
capital the United States was also the main advocate of
eliminating national controls on capital movements, although
recognition was given to the need for capital controls by the
recovering belligerents of the Second World War. Ironically,
capital markets only briefly conformed to this American

design, between the removal of Western controls and the establishment of currency convertibility in 1958, and the imposition of the first of the United States' controls in 1963. Thus while the norms of the system may explain why there was a general prediliction in favour of capital controls, a more detailed analysis is necessary to explain the pattern, emphasis and timing of the controls imposed by the United States.

The U.S. capital account was a neglected subject for some eighteen years after World War Two, until the last years of the Eisenhower Administration, when the U.S. balance of payments became a major policy problem. President Kennedy's comment, that the two major problems facing his Administration were nuclear weapons and the balance of payments, set the atmosphere for a long and protracted struggle to correct the balance of payments "deficit" as measured by the net liquidity concept.[6] For various reasons, U.S. policy makers directed their major efforts toward regulating long-term capital movements. In the terms by which the problems of the post-war international monetary system are usually described, these capital controls were the only major, direct adjustment measure pursued by the United States until the devaluation of 1971. Other adjustment measures pursued were either of minor significance (e.g., exhortations to American exporters), were not followed consistently (e.g., monetary restraint), or were

long-term measures whose benefits were not clearly apparent
(e.g., the Kennedy Round of trade negotiations). The other
balance of payments measures implemented or supported by
the United States were minor financing measures to help
maintain confidence in the dollar (e.g., the Gold Pool and
Roosa bonds), and long-term liquidity measures of no immediate benefit to the United States (e.g., Special Drawing Rights).
Thus, for almost ten years the task of eliminating the deficit
fell upon a series of measures to control long-term capital
outflows.

These measures were: the Interest Equalization Tax
of 1963, to make outflows of portfolio capital unprofitable;
the 1965 programs to curb bank lending (the Voluntary Foreign
Credit Restraint program) and impose "voluntary" curbs on
direct foreign investments; and, finally, the Foreign Direct
Investment Program of 1968, which set mandatory ceilings on
such direct foreign investment. All three measures were
terminated in January 1974. These were not the only policies
to affect long-term capital outflows, since other regulations
(such as foreign tax credits and domestic banking legislation)
are also important influences. However, these programs were
the only measures whose purpose was specifically directed
to the balance of payments.

The central role of the capital controls may seem surprising, considering that the United States has been the major

post-war advocate of an open international economic system.
Hence the major question of this thesis: why were measures
taken to selectively close the international markets for
long-term capital? The answer to this question must explain
why the other major policy options were rejected: (1) Ignore
(but finance) the deficit, a policy followed in the late
Eisenhower and early Kennedy Administrations, and again,
although for very different reasons, with the Nixon Administration's policy of "benign neglect" toward the balance of payments; (2) Fiscal and monetary restraint, a strategy followed
at various times, although not necessarily for balance of payments reasons; and (3) Devaluation, a strategy brought up
principally in academic circles but emphatically rejected by
successive Administrations until 1971.

The second major question of the thesis is: did the
controls actually work successfully? Were they intended to
work? While the answers to these questions may or may not
reflect on the reasons why the policy was chosen, it does help
give an answer (albeit a partial one) to the debate over whether
those who act in the name of the nation-state are losing control over international transactions, as Morse puts it, "to
an extent that may be historically unprecedented."[7]

Finally, one must explain why the controls were removed.

The answers to these questions will be framed in

terms of four different, but not mutually exclusive, ways
of thinking about policy-making:

(1) a priori economic theory,

(2) the state as a rational, strategic actor,

(3) domestic interest aggregation,

(4) international influences, from both state and
sub-state level actors.

Should it be found that the sources of decision-making changed
during the life of the policy, some attempt must be made to
specify the determinants of such change.

Two major problems arise in connection with this highly
eclectic approach to causal inference: overdetermination
and tautology. The first results when one attempts to explain
a unique event, or series of related events, with a number
of factors, any one of which could have been sufficient to
produce the phenomenon in question. Given the nature of the
subject matter of the non-experimental sciences generally
and non-quantifiable nature of the investigation at hand, it
is unlikely that this problem can be wholly overcome, except
in the intuitive sense of making a subjective judgment as to
which of the causal elements selected for analysis were most
important, and showing that one's causal reasoning in this
case is at least consistent with what is known about the
more general balance of payments and foreign policy objectives
of the United States.

The problem of tautology can hopefully be avoided by carefully specifying the key explanatory variable for each variety of explication, and constructing one's inferences in the form of predictive hypotheses of which the evidence selected can at least serve as a critical test if not a conclusive verification. In this case, the questions to be asked are: would it be predicted that the United States would have adopted capital controls (either the entire program or various parts thereof) on the basis of a consideration of a priori economic theory, the strategic interests of the national leadership, the interests of bureaucratic agencies, the interests of non-governmental interest groups, or the impact of international influences on policy-making or all of the above? Ideally, one of these factors would be a more convincing predictor than the others.

A further caution is warranted with regard to spurious correlation, the most likely cause of which would be a non-random relationship between several of the hypothetical causes. It may be, for example, that while the pattern of bureaucratic interests predicts that capital controls would have been adopted, that these interests were in turn determined by private interests--as a Marxist model might suggest. In a study where correlation analysis is hardly possible this problem can only be dealt with by careful explanation of the reasons for imputing interests and influence to the various sources of policy-making.

The wider rationale for this study is twofold. Firstly, there has been no previous study of this topic which could reasonably be called "political economy," the systematic study of the role of political structures and processes in determining both the framework within which economic activity occurs and the allocation of resources within that particular environment. Previous studies of this subject, such as those by Cairncross and Hogan,[8] do not treat political factors beyond specifying them as constraints on a rational policy determined by economic analysis. These analyses have generally restricted themselves to either one or both of two questions: do capital controls benefit national or global welfare, and do they help the balance of payments over a particular time period? Both questions assume a single-focus, rational decision-making process in pursuit of a pre-determined goal, and hence do not necessarily provide a good explanation of why policy decisions are taken, or even of why the policy was or was not a success, since the method inevitably requires that one make highly restrictive assumptions about the nature and relationship of the relevant variables.

Secondly, an analysis of this issue may shed light on issues which have been much discussed between political scientists in recent years. Among these are questions relating to the applicability of theories of foreign policy-making to

economic affairs', the position of the modern nation-state
in a world where it is allegedly losing its ability to
control activities nominally within its sovereign power,
and the nature and trends of economic and political interdependence between countries.

Two major sources of evidence will be used. Firstly,
what one might call "rational interest" speculation. For
example, assuming that the Federal Reserve Board feels that
one of its major interests is to maintain the efficacy of
monetary policy, it would seem reasonable to assume that the
Board would oppose capital controls if they could be shown
to jeopardize this goal while not significantly contributing
to any other major goal of the Board. This type of reasoning
can be supplemented with evidence of what the relevant actors
have said were their motives and what others have said about
their reasons for taking a particular policy stand. The
major sources of this kind of evidence are newspapers, Congressional testimonies and interviews.

The following chapter will outline the background of
United States balance of payments policy in the early 1960's
and describe the capital control programs as they evolved from
1963 to 1974. Chapter three will deal with capital controls
as a problem of a priori economic theory. Chapter four will
focus on the role of Presidential and White House politics
as representative of a strategic or single-focus explanation

of foreign economic policy as a response to a hierarchy of
political interests. Chapter five will draw attention to the
role of private domestic interests in shaping policy and the
usefulness of predicting policy on the basis of a presumed
pattern of interest group politics. Chapter six will continue the same theme into the realm of domestic, intra-governmental activities. Chapter seven will redirect attention
to the international influences on United States policy:
interstate, transgovernmental and transnational interactions.[9]
Chapter eight will deal with the economic consequences of
the controls, and explain the gradual removal of the controls
between 1969 and 1974. Finally, chapter ten will link
together the various influences on policy-making in terms of
a general concept of politicization and structural change in
the international monetary system.

CHAPTER II

THE POLICY BACKGROUND, ANALYSES,

OPTIONS AND CHOICES

The purpose of this chapter is to outline the nature
of the balance of payments "problem" as it was perceived
during the first half of the 1960's, the options which could
have been chosen and the mechanics of the various policies
which were adopted, and in particular, the capital outflow
restraints. There will be no explicit argument here, except
perhaps to reaffirm the introductory assertion that capital
restraint programs were the only balance of payments adjustment policy to be consistently pursued during the 1960's.

The Rise and Fall of the Bretton Woods System

At its worst, the international monetary system can
be considered a Prisoner's Dilemma game in which the dominating strategy is for each player to choose a non-cooperative
strategy regardless of what he thinks the other players will
do. At best, it may be seen as a series of halting moves,
by no means unilinear, towards some mutually acceptable
forms of public international financial management. The
Gold Standard, in its pure form, required the sacrificing of
national autonomy to an extent increasingly unacceptable in

the twentieth century, particularly in those countries whose political norms and values required the pursuit of full employment, ar at least an independent employment policy not determined by considerations of external balance. The Bretton Woods Agreement of 1944 was an attempt to preserve as much national autonomy as possible without sacrificing either sovereignty or stability of exchange rates.[1]

The basic rule of the system was to be a commitment to fixed exchange rates and to the dismantling of trade and exchange controls. In its implications for domestic policy the system was not very different from a Gold Standard insofar as the burden of adjustment appeared to fall primarily on monetary and fiscal policy, and hence on employment. The difference was that the Bretton Woods system accepted exchange rate changes under conditions of "fundamental disequilibrium" and also made provision for international borrowing facilities via the International Monetary Fund (IMF). For a variety of reasons, neither of these provisions has well served the international financial system, with the result that countries facing chronic payments imbalances have been forced to resort to essentially unilateral national measures.[2] It is in this context that one should view the efforts of the United States to eliminate its deficit during the 1960's and early 1970's.

However, the case of the American deficit was unique,

since the dollar was central to the structure of the system
itself.[3] The problems arising out of the role of the dollar
have been variously referred to as liquidity, confidence and
adjustment. The liquidity problem arises out of the
numeraire function of gold as the ultimate standard of value
whose price could not vary in terms of reserve currencies,
principally the dollar. However, if the supply of new
monetary gold to the reserve currency country cannot keep pace
with the demand for new reserves by the rest of the world,
there will be a shortage of international liquidity unless
the major holders of the reserve currencies are prepared to
accept a deterioration in the liquidity position of the
reserve currency country. Hence the confidence problem: as
the ratio of gold to reserve currency liabilities falls, holders
of these reserves may begin to doubt their redeemability at
par value. The adjustment problem refers generally to the
lack of any agreed distribution of the burdens of adjustment
under the Bretton Woods system, and more specifically, with
regard to the United States, it points to the basis of the
liquidity problem: in the absence of a sufficient quantity
of new monetary gold, the system actually requires that the
United States do not adjust to eliminate its balance of
payments deficit. Since the current account balance of the
United States remained in surplus until the late 1960's,
mechanics of the system dictated a relatively large outflow

of capital from the United States. The obvious dilemmas
involved in the operation of this kind of system directed
the attention of economists and politicians alike toward
the possibilities for structural reform.

The basic reform proposals discussed were: flexible
exchange rates (or some variant thereof), a return to the
gold standard (based on a rise in the price of gold) and
centrally created reserves. With the exception of the last
mentioned, none of these plans had been adopted by the end
of the 1960's. Centrally created reserves, the so-called
Special Drawing Rights, were agreed upon in 1967 but came
too late and in too small a quantity to affect the situation.
Thus, by the end of the decade, the problem of reforming
the international monetary system was still inextricably
linked to the balance of payments policies of the United
States, and the apparent need for unilateral national policies
had not been superseded.

These measures took the form of exchange rate changes
and direct restrictions on external transactions, particularly
merchandise trade and capital movements. Exchange rate
changes by Britain, France and West Germany, private speculation and possibly demands for conversion into gold by
official holders of dollars finally precipitated the suspension
of dollar-gold convertibility in August 1971 and the consequent
devaluation of the dollar in December of that year. Further

difficulties in maintaining these parities led to another
dollar devaluation in February 1973, and a managed "float"
by the major convertible currencies of the world.

The overall structure within which balance of payments
policy must be analysed is, then, one in which there has been
no effective international coordination of a type which
might obviate the need for national policies--such as the
capital export restraint programs administered by the
United States from 1963 to 1974.

The Post-War Balance of Payments Situation of the United States

The emphasis on liquidity creation in the international
negotiations of the 1960's was unfortunate not only because
they produced so little in the way of results, but also because they turned attention away from international agreement on modes of adjustment. However, this did not preclude attention to national adjustment, particularly with
regard to the United States after 1958, when foreign follar
liabilities first exceeded U.S. gold reserves. Yet the
implications of the deficit for international monetary reform were not entirely clear: it was taken by some to mean
that there was excess liquidity in the system and by others
as an indication of the need for more liquidity, since a
reduction of the deficit would deprive the rest of the
world of needed reserves.

Regardless of whether U.S. deficits were necessary for
the welfare of the system as a whole, pressure to take
action built up in the wake of European conversions of
dollar reserves into gold, a poor U.S. current account and
basic balance in 1958 and 1959, and speculation in the short-
term capital and gold markets. The critical year was 1960,
when the prospect of a Democratic Administration committed
to economic reflation helped produce the heavy speculation
in the London gold market which obliged the major official
holders of gold to establish a price support system known as
the Gold Pool.[4] During the next three years gold and short-
term capital outflows declined somewhat and the current
account improved. However, the balance on net private
long-term capital movements continued to deteriorate from
a deficit of $2.1 billion in 1960 to $3.4 billion in 1963.

Long-term private capital movements had become particularly salient as the largest negative item in the balance
of payments accounts since the mid-1950's. This may be
seen in the following table which shows how net long-term
capital movements began to outpace government transfers
as the largest negative items in the late 1950's and early
1960's, until the situation was again reversed in the latter
half of the decade:

TABLE 2.1

GOVERNMENT TRANSFERS AND LONG-TERM CAPITAL
FLOWS IN THE U.S. BALANCE OF PAYMENTS
(Four Year Averages, in Billions of Dollars)

	Government Transfers	Long-Term Private Capital Movements
1950-1953	-2.7	-0.73
1954-1957	-1.85	-1.58
1958-1961	-1.90	-2.13
1962-1965	-2.20	-3.78
1966-1969	-2.18	-1.10

SOURCE: Federal Reserve Bank of St. Louis, Balance of Payments Trends, October 18, 1973, p. 2.

This rising volume of capital flows was the source of some confusion in the interpretation of balance of payments accounts, namely the logical fallacy of matching debits and credits for the purpose of causal inference and the problem of choosing criteria for defining a deficit. The first problem is particularly important in this context since it relates to the labeling of capital flows as the "cause" of the U.S. deficit, and therefore the most appropriate item at which to direct government policy. Given an overall deficit situation, there is no logical basis for picking any one item as the "cause" of the deficit--to do so implies that every debit must have a matching credit of the same type. While debits and credits in the balance of payments must

balance in an overall sense (i.e. the accounts sum to
zero) there is no reason to infer, for example, that if a
long-term capital debit does not have a matching long-term
capital credit, then the debit is a "cause" of the deficit.
There is no necessary link between debits and credits,
except in aggregate summation. While there are many ways to
justify the restrictions of capital outflows, one cannot do
so by reference to the balance of payments accounts alone.
If one is to speculate about causes, one can only do so in
terms of explaining why each individual item is a net debit
or credit in the overall account, rather than fallaciously
imputing causal significance to debit items only.

The reasons for the widening deficit on long-term
capital at the beginning of the 1960's go beyond the classical
economist's comparison of rates of return on capital. To a
large extent the deficit here is a function of the multinational spread of American business, which itself has a
variety of causes ranging from the static microeconomic analysis
of marginal cost and marginal revenue, to more dynamic economic
theories of product cycles and technological or managerial
"gaps," and ultimately to socio-political explanations focusing
on the changing nature of interdependence between nations.
In addition to explanations based on the spread of the
multinational corporation, there were also special institutional
factors at work. Portfolio capital outflows were encouraged

by the rebirth of the international bond markets and possibly
by expectations of exchange rate changes. Direct foreign
investment may have responded to the establishment of the
European Economic Community (in particular, regional incentives and the desire to "jump over" the common external
tariff).

The second problem of methodology which deserves
mention is that of answering the question "What is a balance
of payments deficit?" There are two major sub-questions to
be dealt with: is the accounting balance the most appropriate format, and, if so, where does one draw the "line" to
distinquish between autonomous and accommodating transactions?

It has been argued by some that the United States did
not have a balance of payments problem, since the most
appropriate criterion is not the accounting or "flow"
balance, which is concerned with liquidity, but the balance
of international indebtedness or "stock" account (or at
least those items which are relatively liquid) of net worth
or solvency.[5] From this perspective the balance of payments
problem was merely a self-induced run on a bank whose asset
position was fundamentally sound. However, such arguments
are only marginally relevant to the questions posed by
this thesis, since for the purpose of explaining policy-
making what matters is that the general consensus was that

the United States did have a balance of payments deficit.
It was upon this assumption that the debate over policy choice
rested.

Given the general acceptance of the accounting balance
as the basis for policy-making, there remains the question
of which transactions to define as autonomous, a question
which aroused some debate in the mid-1960's. In 1965 a review
committee chaired by E. M. Bernstein recommended including
all short-term capital flows "above the line," rather than
including net changes in liquid liabilities to private
foreigners "below the line" as accommodating transactions,
which had been the practice of the Commerce Department.
These questions should not affect one's judgment of the role
of historical perceptions of the importance of long-term capital movements in the balance of payments, and hence the
significance of long-term capital flows for policy prescriptions, since all of the major measures of balance include
long-term capital flows as autonomous, "above the line" transactions.

What Is to be Done?

The variety of ways of approaching balance of payments accounting would also suggest that there are a number
of ways of defining the causes and prescribing solutions for
a situation of external disequilibrium. In the early part

of the 1960's, there were several influential studies of the
U.S. balance of payments which set the tone of the debate
for most of that decade. The studies selected for citation
below have been chosen not because they cover the full
range of analyses of the problem, but because they were the
most widely known expressions of the predominant lines of
thinking at the time. Since the devaluation and floating
of the dollar, one commonly hears influential economists declaring that they had known all along that the problem of the
dollar "glut" was a simple case of overvaluation of the exchange rate. Some even profess surprise that their colleagues
could have been so blind as to fall victim to ". . . a simple
oversight of the relevance of price to supply and demand. . ."[7]
However, a decade ago the nature of the problem and the best
solution were perhaps not quite so obvious as they may be with
the exercise of historical hindsight.

   . The views of Yale economist Robert Triffin on the
international liquidity problem, outlined in a book published in 1961,[8] were important insofar as they began a
trend of thinking which by implication analysed and made prescriptions relevant to the U.S. balance of payments.
Triffin's theme, in brief, was that the increasing unacceptability of the dollar as a reserve (given a relatively fixed
supply of monetary gold) would be the cause of a global liquidity
shortage. The cause of the U.S. deficit was, therefore, the

demand for reserves by the rest of the world, and the policy
prescription involved the control of reserve creation by
an international organization, which would in effect place
the United States in the same position as any other country
with regard to the need to adjust to a payments deficit.
Presumably this adjustment would occur by means of domestic
monetary and fiscal policy, since Triffin opposed exchange
rate changes and restrictions on trade and payments. While
the implications of the Triffin plan for U.S. policy may not
have been clear at the time (since the plan emphasized
liquidity rather than adjustment), the implied recommendation
that the U.S. must adjust by means of domestic policy was
widely accepted.

The published views of the Committee on Economic
Development, in surveys published in 1960 and 1961[9] are typical
of, albeit much more explicitly than the liquidity shortage
theorists, the emphasis on internal adjustment. However, the
CED has been concerned with a broader range of actions than
fiscal and monetary alone. In its 1960 report the CED
attributed the balance of payments deficit to the recession
of 1957-1958 (in particular, its effects on U.S. capital
goods exports); falling raw materials prices (reducing purchasing power in U.S. export markets); outflows of private
capital, especially portfolio capital, where the effect on
U.S. exports is less direct; and a general decline in the

competitiveness of U.S. exports. Its major policy recommendations were a strong anti-inflationary fiscal and monetary
policy, coupled with diplomatic pressure on other industrial
countries to remove current and capital account restrictions
directed against the United States. The general attitude was
one of optimism: "We are confident that an effective anti-
inflationary policy at home and non-discriminatory access to
markets abroad should permit the competition of American industry to succeed in restoring the United States balance of
payments to a sustainable position."[10]

While the 1961 report of the CED mentioned most of the
factors cited in the earlier study as the causes of the
deficit, the emphasis was more on secular trends rather than
temporary problems. The primary causes of the deficit, the
report claimed, were the post-war industrial recovery of
Europe and Japan (raising productivity and reducing American
exports, and attracting U.S. investment), and overseas
military expenditures by the U.S. government. Despite this
slight shift in emphasis, the policy recommendations were much
the same as in the previous study, although the addition of
more detailed proposals (e.g., tax incentives for investment,
wage restraint, export assistance) indicates less confidence
in general macroeconomic policy than in the previous year.
The major new proposal for 1961 was for a greater degree of
burden-sharing by other industrial countries of the expenses

associated with NATO and international development assistance.
Thus, the general attitude of the CED in 1960 and 1961 was
that no radical measures were necessary, particularly not
unilateral restrictions on international payments.

By the following year, however, proposals for measures
more severe than a mild dose of expenditure reduction were
at least being given a hearing in government circles. The
most well-known collection of such proposals was presented
to the Joint Economic Committee in 1962, in connection with
hearings then being held on balance of payments policy.[11]
While most of the studies followed Seymour Harris' introductory article recommending a continuation of general macroeconomic restraint plus selective microeconomic measures on
the current account, and most approved of proposals for more
international liquidity (with the exception of Robert Roosa,
Undersecretary of the Treasury for Monetary Affairs), other
contributors suggested two new directions. Professors
Jaroslav Vanek and H. S. Houthakker, of Harvard University,
both argued the case for devaluation of the dollar by
15 percent, although for different reasons--Houthakker
basing his case on the "purchasing power parity" theory and
Vanek on the idea of a full-employment external balance.
The second new line of argument was outlined in an essay by
Phillip W. Bell of Haverford College. In a wide-ranging survey of the role of capital flows in the balance of payments

deficit, Bell concludes that outflows of private capital
were the major cause of the deterioration since 1956, even
when one takes into account transfer effects onto the
current account (such as increased exports induced by direct
foreign investment). Although Bell was careful not to make
policy prescriptions, the general thrust of his study was
clear.[12]

However, such radical suggestions were as yet generally
unacceptable to both economists and policy-makers. In the
following year, two major studies were published which
appeared to support the advocates of moderation. One of
these, that conducted for the Council of Economic Advisors
under the auspices of the Brookings Institution,[13] received
wide publicity with its prediction that the United States would
have a basic balance surplus of $600 million to $2 billion
by 1968. In 1962 the basic balance deficit was -$2 billion.
The primary reason cited for this change was a faster rate
of inflation among the major trading partners of the United
States.

Another study appeared at the same time, under the
auspices of the National Bureau of Economic Research.[14]
Though agreeing with the conclusion of the Brookings study,
that the balance of payments deficit would gradually dis-
appear without the need for more severe measures than had
already been taken, author Hal Lary added the proviso that

the improvement would be slow and would therefore con-
strain domestic growth in the process. The book thus gave
ammunition to those who were arguing that the radical measures were necessary so that growth would not be constrained.
In any case, both studies were overtaken by events, namely
the imposition of the first capital control, the Interest
Equalization Tax in July 1963.

It seems clear, then, that the consensus of economic
opinion in the period 1960 to 1963 did not favour capital
controls or any other radical measure beyond general macroeconomic restraint, selective measures on the current account,
and possibly some moves toward the international creation of
liquidity. Why, then, were capital controls chosen as the
major instrument of adjustment from the middle of 1963? Before speculating on the answers to this question, it would
be useful to first establish that the capital control programs were the most important adjustment measure to be adopted
during the 1960's.

The Policy Measures

The major balance of payments policy measures undertaken by the Kennedy Administration in its first two years
were directed towards the liquidity and confidence
problems. These measures included the General Arrangements
to Borrow (to facilitate currency "swaps"), the Gold Pool (to
support the price of gold) and Roosa Bonds (giving an exchange

guarantee to foreign official dollar holders). The adjustment measures taken during this period were either not very successful or of relatively minor importance. Most of these measures followed from President Kennedy's Special Message to Congress on Gold and the Balance of Payments (delivered in February 1961) and suggested export promotion, cost and price stabilization, tied aid, tariff negotiations, tax reforms and a review of military expenditures abroad.[15] Other policies pursued were also either unsuccessful (e.g., Operation Twist, to raise short- but not long-term interest rates) or not followed with any consistency (e.g., monetary or fiscal deflation).

Kennedy's second balance of payments message of July 1963,[16] reiterated most of the policies announced in 1961 (export expansion, reduction of government expenditure overseas, etc.), but added a major new measure designed to halt the outflow of long-term portfolio capital: the Interest Equalization Tax (IET). The tax was imposed at a rate of 15 percent on the purchase of foreign stock, while on debt securities the rate varied depending on the period remaining to maturity, ranging from 2.75 percent for a three year security to 15 percent for a 28½ year security. Exemptions from the tax were provided for transactions in the following categories: foreign securities acquired from another U.S. citizen; export financing (assumed to include any debt of less than three

years duration); for reasons of "international monetary
stability" (under which Canada and Japan received exemptions); securities to be resold to foreigners; debt issues
of recognized international organizations; securities issued
by the governments designated as less developed by Presidential executive order; and direct investments (defined as having
10 percent or more of the voting power in a corporation). In
1965 the tax was broadened to cover non-bank credits of one
to three years maturity and to bank loans of one year or more,
the latter being known as the Gore Amendment. The Act was
renewed every two years until 1973.

The next major bundle of balance of payments measures
came with President Johnson's Special Message to the Congress
on International Balance of Payments in February 1965,[17]
which announced two "voluntary" programs to "enroll the
banking community in a major effort to limit their lending
abroad. . ." and to ". . . enlist the leaders of American
business in a national campaign to limit their direct
investments abroad, their deposits in foreign banks, and
their holding of foreign financial assets. . ."[18] The programs were the centerpiece of the Johnson Administration's
balance of payments policy until 1968. Both programs were
subject to modification in 1966 and 1967, primarily in the
direction of greater restraint. The program for banks, known
as the Voluntary Foreign Credit Restraint (VFCR) program, was

based on the general rule that outstanding bank credit to
nonresidents of the United States should not rise above the
amount outstanding at the end of 1964 by more than 5 percent,
although exceptions were made for certain classes of transactions, such as prior loan commitments and export
credits.[19]

The voluntary restraints on direct investors took the
form of a direct appeal by Secretary of Commerce John T.
Connor to the chief executives of 600 major corporations,
asking them to take the following measures: accelerate the
repatriation of income earned in developed countries; avoid
or postpone direct investment in marginal projects; and make
greater use of non-U.S. sources to finance investment.[20] The
results of these exhortations were sufficiently disappointing
to encourage the Commerce Department to set more specific
(though still voluntary) guidelines for individual companies.
Companies were asked to limit new foreign direct investment
during the two-year period 1965-1966 to 235 percent of
their annual average of direct capital outflows plus retained
earning of overseas subsidiaries for the years 1962-1964.
Furthermore, the number of corporations asked to comply with
the program was raised to 900.[21]

The next major innovation in balance of payments
policy was the New Year statement by President Johnson in
January 1968.[22] As with previous messages, it included rather

vague promises of action in the areas of wage and price restraint, tourism, exports, government expenditures abroad and trade negotiations; and again, the major target of the message was long-term capital outflows. The Executive order established the Foreign Direct Investment Program (FDIP), to be administered by the Department of Commerce, which would limit foreign direct investments according to a three-fold schedule. In order to reduce direct foreign investment by $1 billion from the 1967 level of $3 billion, companies' quotas for 1968 were limited to 110 percent of their 1965-1966 average for schedule C countries (most less developed countries), 65 percent for schedule B countries (mainly non-West European developed countries), and no net investment in schedule A countries (mainly Western Europe).

All of these programs--the IET, VFCR and FDIP--were gradually relaxed under the Nixon Administration. In his first message to Congress on the balance of payments, in April 1969, President Nixon repeated the concern of his predecessors for export expansion, trade negotiations, defense burden sharing, and tourism, but centered his message around a statement of intent to remove the capital controls: "I have begun, gradually but purposefully, to dismantle the direct controls which only mask the underlying problem."[23] The dismantling process played a major role in balance of payments strategy during the first two and a half years of the Administration.

CHAPTER III

ECONOMIC THEORY AND THE CONTROL OF

CAPITAL MOVEMENTS

Much of the current discussion about capital outflows
from the United States has focused on its allegedly detrimental effects on national economic welfare, concluding with
the recommendation that long-term capital outflows, particularly of direct investment, be restricted. An explanation
of U.S. policies toward long-term capital outflows should
begin by considering what would be, at least to many
economists, the most obvious hypothesis: that the capital
control programs were a "rational" economic policy. The
term is here used in the sense defined by Max Weber as "formal
rationality," or choosing the most efficient (or least cost)
means to achieve a given end.[1]

The question to be asked in this chapter is: are there
any generally accepted a priori grounds for the policy in
question?; does a consideration of the economic theory relating
to long-term capital flows tend to suggest that it is to
the advantage of a country to restrict such outflows? If
this is the case, one could make a plausible argument that
there is no need to resort to explicitly political explanations

of policy-making, since economic theory predicts that a
rational, unitary actor would choose to impose capital
controls.

Even if the literature did produce a consensus
policy prescription, there are two potential problems
relating to the use of economic theory as an explanation of
policy-making; namely, the assumption which the theory
makes about the objective economic situation and the motives
of the decision-makers. The pure theory of international
trade and investment generally assumes a situation of "pure
competition" (all economic units are price-takers with
perfect information about the market). Thus, the use of
theory as a basis for policy may be inappropriate insofar as
the real world is not one of pure competition. Yet this is
not really a problem for explaining the motives of policy-
makers, since what matters is whether or not they deliberately
acted according to the theory, not whether it was appropriate
to do so.

A more difficult cproblem occurs insofar as the
various economic theories relating to capital flows make
assumptions about the motives of the policy-makers, namely
that they are rational optimizers. The policy-makers may,
however, be choosing a rational policy for non-rational
reasons (i.e., choosing that polciy as an inefficient way of
achieving some other goal) and only acting "as if" they were

rational. If this were the case, the economic theory would
be a good predictor of policy but would not explain it in
the sense of isolating the causal motives of the actors
involved. However, if the general trend in the literature
were to suggest that capital controls were the most rational
policy to adopt, one could at least make a prior presumption
in favour of an economic theory of policy-making.

Ideally, a rational, unitary actor explanation of policy-
making should specify an ultimate value goal (e.g., growth,
employment, welfare, etc.), the balance of payments requirement of this goal (deficit, surplus, or balance) and
finally, the capital flow requirements of the balance of
payments goal. This would enable one to avoid the tautology
problem of taking whichever theory does predict capital
controls and presuming the ultimate goals to be those required
by the theory. However, the existing body of theoretical
literature in this field does not fall into such a neat
pattern. Rather, it dichotomizes into two groups of writings:
the welfare economics approach, which jumps directly from
the goal of welfare maximization to a judgment upon the
appropriateness of free capital outflows, and the balance of
payments approach, which makes no presumption about ultimate
value goals and simply asks whether or not capital controls
are an efficient means of dealing with problems of external
balance. A number of representative examples from each

school of analysis will be cited in order to show how theory of long-term international capital flows is of little use in attempting to explain why policy decisions are made.

This chapter will not make any systematic distinction between portfolio flows and direct investment abroad. The only difference between portfolio and direct investment is that the latter involves an equity participation high enough (10 percent, according to the Commerce Department) to be considered "ownership." The ownership of a capital asset does, of course, have a great deal of importance in considering the behavior aspects of capital flows (e.g., foreign direct investment has a much greater transfer effect onto the current account than do portfolio flows). However, the theoretical principles of analysis are the same for both types of investment, even though the empirical results may be quite different. The problems involved in assessing the results of the U.S. capital controls will be examined in chapter eight.

Welfare Economics

Welfare economics is concerned with the logic of choosing public policies which will efficiently maximize the welfare (usually defined as a set of indifference curves or an aggregate social welfare function) of a particular individual or social group, which may be sub-national, national or global in scope.[2] The welfare analyses of capital controls divide into two groups, depending on whether it is national or global welfare which is to be maximized. Both approaches can be either static or dynamic, although national welfare arguments are usually static, while global analyses tend to focus more on dynamic problems such as the cyclical or secular stability of the system as a whole.

National Welfare

The neo-classical theory of international capital movements emphasized differences in rates of return: capital flows from countries where the rate of return is low to where it is high. Under conditions of pure competition this would result in capital having an equal rate of return in all places and thus maximizing global welfare.

The argument for restrictions on capital exports in this context is analogous to the optimal tariff concept familiar to students of the pure theory of international trade: while free trade may maximize global welfare, it does not necessarily represent the optimal strategy for a single country. Similarly, free capital flows which equalize the marginal product of capital in all countries may not be the best national strategy where private and national (or social rates of return on capital differ. Most of the older writings on capital controls followed this line of reasoning and pointed to externalities as the main rationale for such

controls. This insight was the basis for a great deal of
literature on optimal rates of foreign investment.³ The
main points are illustrated diagrammatically in Figure 3.1,
with a two country model.

Figure 3.1. The Welfare Aspects of
Home and Foreign Investment

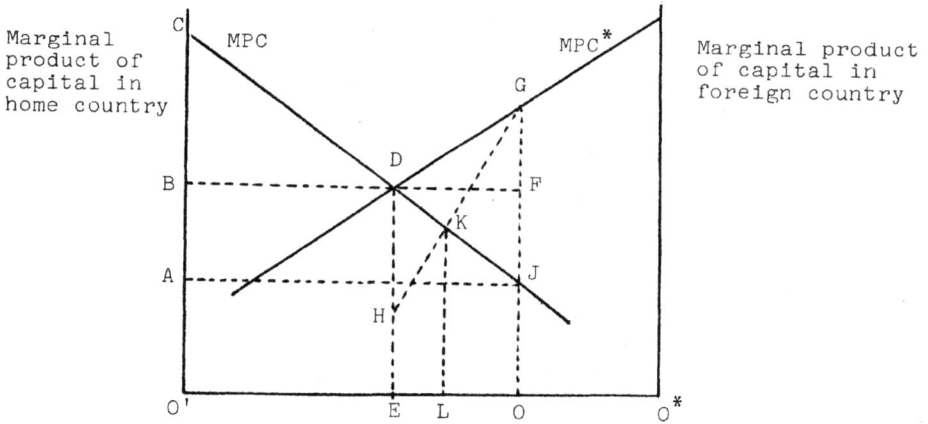

Given capital stocks of O'O and O*O, and marginal
product of capital curves MPC and MPC* for the home and foreign
countries respectively, the equilibrium situation for the
home country in the absence of capital flows is represented
by point J on the MPC curve. National income is thus equal
to the area O'CJO, with O'AJO going to capital and ACJ to

labor. Under conditions of free movement of capital, returns will be equalized at point D (MPC = MPC*) with the home country exporting EO of its capital stock, raising national income by amount DFJ over its previous level. However, the national return on this foreign investment is less than the private return, since domestic investment produces both labor and capital returns (BCD and O'BDE), while foreign investment produces only returns to capital (EDFO). Since the curve MPC* is a measure of average return on foreign investment (hence the contribution EDFO of foreign investment to home national income), one can derive a measure of marginal return to foreign investment by drawing a line GH to bisect angle DGF; and the area under GH is an identical measure of returns to foreign investment (i.e., EDFO = EHGO). Total national income for the home country can then be redefined as O'CDE plus EHGO (= O'CDFO). The point of this redefinition is that it is now clear that by reducing foreign investment from EO to LO (equating the marginal rate of return on foreign investment with the average return on home investment), national income is raised by amount HDK. Optimal foreign investment is thus amount LO. The same result could be obtained equally by taxing foreign investment or by quantitative controls.

This basic argument can be found in a variety of different forms. While some writers have denied the proposition

that one can establish the presumption of a general bias for
overseas investment to be too large,[4] the predominant trend
in the pure theory of trade is to accept the conclusion that
a capital abundant country will find its national interest
best served by limiting (preferably by a tax) its foreign
investments.[5]

There was some basis for presuming, in the early 1960's,
that the private rate of return on U.S. foreign investment
was greater than the national rate of return. Firstly,
the relatively lower rate of unemployment and faster rate
of growth in Europe vis-à-vis the U.S. in the early 1960's
has been cited as a factor causing greater than optimal
capital outflows from the U.S., insofar as the higher nominal
private rate of return in Europe was a cyclical phenomenon
rather than an indication of real national rates of
return. Secondly, the various incentives for U.S. capital
outflows created by the establishment of the EEC have been
held to be distortionary, since the flows were responses to
political rather than efficiency incentives. Thirdly,
there was the widely held belief that European capital
markets were relatively inefficient compared to those of the
U.S., and hence the large outflow of portfolio capital from
New York was responding to institutional rather than
efficiency criteria.[6] The argument here is slightly different
from the theoretical rationale outlined above: the three

points cited here rely on demonstrating that inefficiencies
in the capital markets cause a lack of equality between
national and private rates of return; whereas the diagrammatic
explanation shown above points out that even if capital
markets were free of inefficiencies, private and national
rates of return would still not be equal.

These externality arguments were fairly intuitive in
nature until quite recently, when Musgrave marshalled
a good deal of empirical evidence to show not only that U.S.
foreign investment has a higher private than national rate of
return, but that it has also lowered labor's share of
national income. Using data for 1968, she shows that the
net private rate of return on foreign direct investment by
non-financial U.S. corporations was 2.6 percent after tax,
compared with a national rate of return of -2.9 percent.[7]

Many of the static, national welfare arguments in
favour of restricting capital outflows also show attention
to the dynamic implications of foreign investment. The
tendency of foreign investment to weaken a country's industrial
base received some attention in the early 1960's, but has not
been systematically articulated outside the technical
literature until recently. Gilpin,[8] for example, argues
that foreign direct investment by the U.S. has been a second-
best solution to the challenge of foreign competition, since
the result has been to export the comparative advantage of

the United States. In his highly eclectic theme, Gilpin portrays foreign investment as both a cause of and a response to America's decline and loss of its innovative "product cycle" industries to other nations. The result is a secular trend in domestic capital formation towards the low productivity services and government sector. As evidence, Gilpin cites the deterioration in the U.S. trade balance between 1960 and 1971, the loss of America's technological lead and the declining U.S. share of world GNP. While Gilpin's case was not specifically directed to the issue at hand, but rather to the wealth of literature which asserts that foreign investment always benefits the home country and harms the host, the implication is clear: that foreign investment should be restricted on national welfare grounds.

It may be seen that theoretical arguments based on the maximization of national welfare can easily be made to produce a presumption in favour of restricting capital outflows, but that these arguments are by no means conclusive, although they are representative of a preponderant trend in the literature. Several empirical and historical studies appear to confirm this conclusion.

The major problem with static (and, to a lesser extent, dynamic) welfare theories is that they are highly dependent on assumptions made about the number of non-competitive distortions in the system. Indeed, the theory of the second-best suggests that in a world where disparities between rates of return, for example, are only one among a multitude of distortions, one cannot make any a priori presumption that the elimination of one or some (but not all) distortions will increase or reduce welfare.

Furthermore, theories of optimal foreign investment are vulnerable to the same criticism as are theories of an optimal tariff, that they ignore the possibility of retaliatory action by other nations. Optimal investment theory assumes that the "foreign" country is either passive or is an aggregate of many small countries unable to make any collective reaction against capital outflow restrictions. Manning has shown that, if reactions occur in the form of mutual taxation of capital outflows, there will be a new equilibrium point, but that it does not necessarily involve positive taxes by both countries.[9] Thus, if competitive retaliation is taken into account, a national welfare maximizing strategy does not necessarily call for the taxation of capital outflows.

Global Welfare

If one assumes the goal of policy to be the maximization of global rather than national welfare, a divergence between private and social returns might also be the basis for restricting long-term capital investments. If, for example, the real return on capital in country A is higher

than in country B, but because of domestic tax policies
nominal private returns are greater in B, a case might be
made for the restriction of capital movements from A to B on
grounds of world efficiency.

Fielecke[10] contends that this theoretical rationale
could not be applied to the situation of U.S. capital outflows.
Examining the major possible sources of externalities, he
concludes that none of them are convincing reasons to restrict
capital outflows from the U.S. The use of differing monetary-
fiscal policy mixes,[11] differences in rates of inflation, differing placement fees on securities issues, domestic controls
in foreign capital markets, and differing tax structures
are all either not conclusive sources of externalities or else
would be more efficiently dealt with by some other policy.
Indeed, he concludes by asserting that if one takes into account
the effects of uncertainty in reducing U.S. capital outflows,
the best policy for efficiently allocating the world's
capital would be to subsidize such outflows!

While the result of static, global welfare arguments
seems to be indeterminate, Stern argues that such considerations are outweighed by the importance of capital outflows
from the U.S. for the system as a whole, as a supplier of
liquidity and a currency for transactions and reserves.

Kindleberger has supplied a theoretical rationale for
this viewpoint in terms of supply versus demand determined

capital flows. The capital exports of a mature financial center
are, he believes, primarily demand determined, providing the
rest of the world with liquidity in a manner which is
counter-cyclical.[12] This was the case with Britain in the
nineteenth century: recessions pushed capital out to the
rest of the world, whose demand for British exports was thereby
stimulated, raising British national income. A relative
recession in the rest of the world produced the opposite
reaction.

In the case of an immature financial center, capital
flows are supply determined, resulting in pro-cyclical long-
term capital movements. Kindelberger believes this was the
case with the United States in the inter-war period:
during periods of rapid economic expansion, capital flowed
out from the United States, forcing the rest of the world to
inflate with it. However, in a previous work,[13] Kindleberger
makes it clear that he sees U.S. capital exports during the
1960's as essentially demand determined, and thus a stabilizing,
counter-cyclical way of performing the function of world
banker. In this view, the U.S. capital flows to Europe
simply reflected differences in liquidity preference: U.S.
investors, in the aggregate, lend long and borrow short vis-
à-vis European investors. To the extent that this analysis
is correct, it is a powerful a priori argument against the
imposition of restrictions on long-term capital outflows from

the United States, since they provide a world public good in
the form of counter-cyclical, international, financial
intermediation. In any case, the implication of this theory
of capital flows is that restrictions would be ineffective
because of the fungibility of money.[14]

Finally, there are several analyses of the international
monetary system which could be taken to imply that restrictions
on capital outflows from the United States would cause
dynamic instability in the international monetary system, as
distinct from simply preventing international financial intermediation. In its simplest form, this dynamic stability problem
refers back to Triffin's original "liquidity shortage" thesis
cited in the previous chapter: world liquidity requires a
U.S. capital account deficit (assuming a secular trend towards
balance in the current account), but this deficit in turn
aggravates the confidence problem, which leads to demands for
gold conversion and a spiralling contraction of mutual claims
similar to the inter-war period. The point here is that while
U.S. capital exports are necessary for liquidity, given an
insufficient supply of new monetary gold, they are a
cause of dynamic instability. Thus, the Triffin thesis could
be cited as an a priori argument in favour of capital controls,
assuming that the liquidity problem was solved in some
other manner.

However, analyses focusing on dynamic stability could

equally be used to argue against capital controls. The
models constructed by Makin[15] and Mundell[16] are examples
of analysis from which one could make this inference.

Makin's mathematical model shows that the dynamic
stability of the system actually requires (contra Triffin)
an increase in the ratio of U.S. dollar liabilities to its
gold stock. He finds this to be the case in both his "policy
model" (where the interest rate on dollars is manipulated
to offset excess demand for gold) and his "market model"
(with no discretionary changes in the variables, but assuming
a single market for dollar assets and a market reflecting an
expected return on gold).

Mundell's model of "the short-run confidence problem"
shows how if policies are assigned so that the United
States adjusts monetary policy to the goal of price stability,
leaving the rest of the world to choose the proper ratio of
gold reserves to dollars, the result is a stable system. This
is implicitly a case against capital export controls by the
United States, insofar as they are a substitute for using monetary policy to restrain domestic inflation.

In conclusion, it must be said that, aside from the
obvious observation that decision-makers are unlikely to
have considered some of the finer points of welfare economics,
even had they done so they would not have found any consensual
basis for making presumptions as to whether a rational, welfare

maximizing state should or should not restrict long-term
capital exports. While the national welfare arguments do tend
to support the general concept of such controls, the global
welfare arguments provide an equally strong pull in the
opposite direction. It may be true that the national
welfare viewpoint is more relevant to an explanation of state
policy; yet this is not self-evident, especially considering
the great emphasis which both policy makers and economists
have placed on the role of the United States in providing
(regardless of longer-term motives) the services of a public
international banker.

Balance of Payments Theory

The second major body of writing which considers the
appropriateness of capital outflow restrictions is the theory
of balance of payments adjustment. The goal here is simply
to choose the most efficient means of achieving external
balance, the assumption being that this is for the benefit
of national, or possibly global, welfare. If economic
theory can provide a satisfactory explanation of the U.S.
capital controls, one is more likely to find it here, since
balance of payments equilibrium was the stated goal of all
of the capital control measures.

Both the classical, or monetary adjustment theory
associated with David Hume, and Keynesian demand theory postulate

an automatic adjustment mechanism for correcting a payments
imbalance; in this case, a deficit. According to classical
theory, a deficit reduces the money supply via gold losses
by an amount dependent on the domestic gold reserve ratio,
which reduces expenditure as people restore their cash
balances, causing a fall in the general price level and, finally,
a rise in exports and a fall in imports. Keynesian theory
finds the key to adjustment in income rather than price
changes: the shortfall in export incomes has a multiplier
effect on national income, and the decline in the latter
reduces imports via the marginal propensity to import. The
decision to impose controls on capital exports must, in
both models, therefore be based on the assumption that these
automatic processes either do not work fast enough or else
are impeded by other elements of the situation.[17]

The theoretical implications of restrictions on capital
outflows will be dealt with below, firstly as an aspect of
the "transfer problem," and secondly insofar as prescriptions
regarding capital export policy might be derived from more
general models of macroeconomic policy.

The Transfer Problem

The transfer problem is essentially this: when a
nation makes an unrequited financial or real transfer to
another nation, will the balance of payments loss be fully

offset by repercussion effects <u>before</u> either classical price (i.e., terms of trade) or Keynesian income adjustment mechanisms begin to operate? If the immediate result of the transfer is a net gain in the balance of payments, the transfer is said to be "overeffected"; and either the terms of trade will improve, or a Keynesian income-expenditure adjustment process will ensue (or some combination of the two). If there is a net loss before terms of trade or income adjustments begin, the transfer is "undereffected." Therefore, if one is to restrict the outflow of either real or financial capital, one is at least implicitly making the assumption that transfers are undereffected. The question is, then: can one make any a priori presumption about the direction of transfer effects which would enable one to suppose that transfer theory could explain the U.S. capital controls policy?

In a simplified two-country endowment model, each country has a given supply of a single good, which it consumes and exports to the other country.[18] The balance of payments effect is then determined by the marginal propensity to import the other country's export. When a transfer of purchasing power (T) is made, the exports of the country making the transfer rise by amount $\Delta X = m^*.T$, where m^* is the marginal propensity to import of the transfer receiving country. The imports of the transferring country fall by amount $\Delta M = m.T$, where m is the transferor's marginal propensity to import.

If $\Delta X + \Delta M = T$, the balance of payments loss of the transfer
is exactly offset. The rationale for restricting transfer
outflows would therefore exist if $\Delta X + \Delta M < T$, or $m + m^* < 1$.
An a priori argument for restricting transfers would thus
depend on having some basis for presuming that the sum
of the marginal propensities to import is less than unity.

Caves and Jones are of the opinion that this is not
the case, on the grounds of a general demand bias toward
imported goods. Countries tend to import commodities for which
they have a taste bias. Furthermore, if a real transfer is
also involved, the presumption is on an even stronger basis.[19]

Macroeconomic Models

One of the most widely cited models of internal and
external balance is that devised by Mundell[20] to combine
the classical Humean price analysis with Keynesian income
analysis. The model consists of three equations, measuring
equilibrium in the markets for goods and services (the IS
curve, which is the locus of combination of interest rates (r)
and money income (y) such that income equals expenditure, or
planned savings equals planned investment); equilibrium in
the money markets (the LM curve, which shows the combinations
of interest rates and income such that the demand for money
is equal to the supply); and equilibrium in the balance of payments (the BB curve, which shows combinations of interest rates

and income such that net trade and capital flows sum to
zero). Exports are assumed to be exogenously determined,
imports a function of income and capital flows determined by
the rate of interest. Figure 3.2 shows how this model may
be presented diagrammatically.

Figure 3.2. Capital Outflow Restrictions
Under Conditions of General Equilibrium

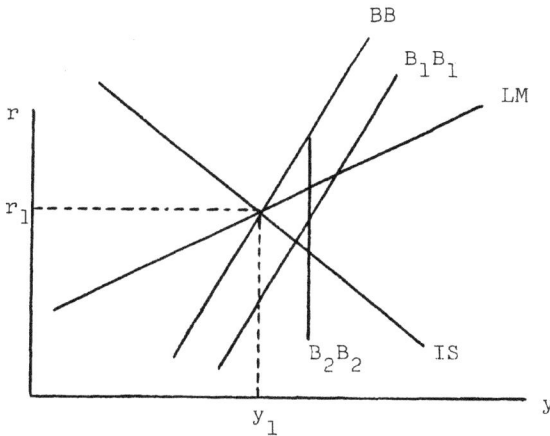

The combination r_1 and y_1 represents a simultaneous
equilibrium in all three sectors. The effect of capital
outflow restrictions is easily demonstrated. A tax, such
as the IET, on outflows would shift the BB curve downwards
to a position B_1B_1. For any given level of income, external
balance can be maintained with a lower actual rate of

interest. A quantitative limit on capital outflows (such as those imposed as under the VFCR, voluntary direct investment program and the FDIP) will shift the external balance curve to a vertical position B_2B_2, over some of its length.

Taking a situation where there is an initial balance of payments deficit, it is easily shown that both the tax and the quota are quite feasible solutions to the problem. In Figure 3.3 the equilibrium situation at point A results in a balance of payments deficit, which may be remedied by either a tax (B_1B_1) or a quota (B_2B_2) on capital exports.

Figure 3.3. Capital Outflow Restrictions
to Correct a Payments Deficit

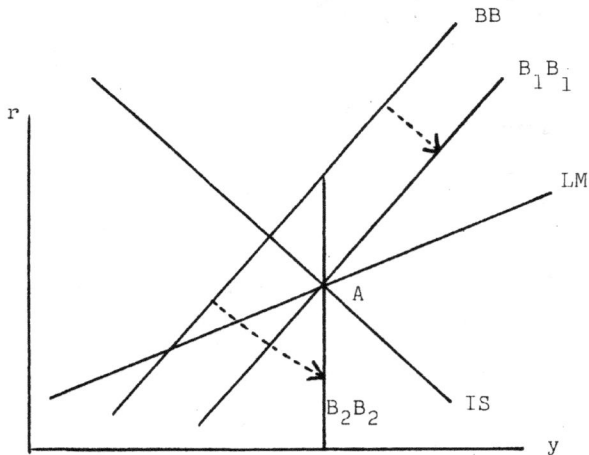

Thus, a general equilibrium model such as the one described above would suggest that a deficit may easily be cured by way of capital outflow restrictions, and hence might explain the policy decision to impose controls. However, the model says nothing about the optimality of controls, that is, whether or not they are the most efficient way of dealing with a deficit. Furthermore, the model essentially ignores the transfer problem.

Conclusion

The answer to the question posed at the beginning of this chapter is now obvious. A priori economic theory does not produce any consensus in predicting the effects of capital controls. Theory based on the maximization of national welfare suggests an "optimal" level of foreign investment, while global welfare theory mostly asserts that any controls are undesirable. Balance of payments theory is similarly divided. Partial equilibrium transfer theory does not by itself make any predictions about the effects of a transfer, beyond specifying the conditions for net positive or negative balance of payments effect. One can extract predictions from the theory only by making assumptions about demand patterns. A general equilibrium, Keynesian model with money and flexible prices, suggests that controls certainly work, but says nothing about their appropriateness relative to other instruments.

Thus, a rational state actor wishing to maximize welfare or choose the best means of correcting a deficit could find as many theoretical rationales for choosing one or the other courses of action. As Vernon puts it, "In the end, the decision whether to support or retard this kind of development on the part of U.S. enterprise must be made by what amounts to an intuitive leap";[21] and, one might add, Vernon's point is directed to the empirical evidence, not simply a priori theory. Economic theory cannot, therefore, provide a convincing explanation of this particular aspect of U.S. balance of payments policy. This does not necessarily mean that any rational state actor explanation is inappropriate, as the next chapter will suggest; what it does mean is that the policy explication must be basically political rather than economic.

CHAPTER IV

THE INDICES OF POWER AND THE LIMITS OF CHOICE:

PRESIDENTIAL POLITICS AND THE BALANCE

OF PAYMENTS, 1963-1968

> Late in 1964, President Johnson sat by at a meeting
> in the White House and listened to an exchange between
> McGeorge Bundy, his National Security adviser, and
> William McChesney Martin, then chairman of the Federal
> Reserve Board. Bundy suggested that the United States
> ought to be able to afford guns and butter, but if it
> found it could not and if in order to carry on the
> war in Vietnam, devaluation of the dollar proved
> necessary, it would have to be given serious con-
> sideration. To Martin such a course was inconceivable;
> if he had to choose, he said, between the war and
> devaluation he would rather get out of the war. No
> American President, he declared, could politically
> survive such an admission of financial defeat. President
> Johnson listened intently but did not comment.
>
> Henry Brandon, The Retreat of American Power
> (New York: Delta, 1972), p. 218.

The previous chapter has shown the inappropriateness,

or at least the indeterminate nature, of a rational choice

explanation of the policy in question, where one assumes the

decision-making unit is maximizing some explicit utility

function whose main variables are economic goals. However,

this does not exhaust the possibilities for explanations

resting on the idea of a rational actor, particularly when

allowances are made for two major barriers to rational decision-

making: lack of information and social norms and values.

Most governmental policies are, as Herbert Simon
suggests, "bounded" by informational constraints.[1] This
is particularly true of balance of payments policy, which
was the subject of widespread disagreement over the results
of various policy options. Lack of agreement encourages
decision-makers to focus on other criteria, notably norms
and values.[2] Max Weber considered this problem by distinguishing between "formal" rationality (choosing the most efficient means to achieve a given goal) and "substantive" or
normative rationality (to act according to a given set of
values).[3] This distinction is vital to the explanation offered
in this chapter: that the formal rationality aspects of the
problem (i.e., considering the most efficient way to solve a
balance of payments deficit) were so circumscribed by substantive rationality elements which eliminated the basic
alternative choices, that the resulting policy was determined
more by the latter than the former.

The explanation to be offered here suggests a link
between balance of payments policy and international
political goals in terms of what Jervis refers to as "the
logic of images,"[4] or more specifically, the way in which the
structure of the Bretton Woods system coupled the balance
of payments to the indices of American power and status. The
subsequent linkage between the balance of payments goal and
policies toward capital flows is provided by an interpretation

of policy in terms of what one historian calls "the limits of choice," or the reduction of a problem to a painful choice between an undesirable policy and one or several unacceptable alternatives.[5]

The Logic of Images

The purpose of this important work[6] in international relations theory is to show how states affect and manipulate the images which other states have of them. The central concepts of this analysis are the categories of signals and indices, and the notions of coupling and decoupling. Signals are "statements or actions the meanings of which are established by tacit or explicit understandings among the actors,"[7] such as diplomatic notes or military manoeuvres. The problem with signals is that both the sender and receiver must make inferences about the other's interpretation of a signal and also whether or not this interpretation may be used to predict future behavior.

Owing to the ambiguous nature of signals, states often rely more on indices, which are "statements or actions that carry some inherent evidence that the image projected is correct because they are believed to be inextricably linked to the actor's capabilities or intentions."[8] One example was noted by Cosmas, an early Alexandrian Christian, who observed that "the true sign of the power of the Romans was that their money was accepted everywhere in the civilized world."[9] Indices in general include actions which are too important to be used for deception, domestic events which influence foreign policy and statements or actions to alter the distribution of power.[10]

As Jervis notes, signals and indices may be difficult to distinguish. The key feature of an index is that it is "believed by the perceiver to tap dimensions and characteristics that will influence or predict an actor's later behavior and to be beyond the ability of the actor to control for the purpose of projecting a misleading image."[11] For both these reasons, the balance of payments situation of the United States should be considered as an index rather than a signal during most of the 1960's, since it was judged to be an influence on and a predictor of U.S. foreign economic policy, and also to be largely beyond the ability of the United States to control at an acceptable cost (i.e., the cost of manipulating the balance of payments as a signal would have been greater than the gains of achieving the desired impression).

In an international financial structure different from that which existed from 1960 to 1968, the balance of payments might well be used as a signal. This was the case during the period of "benign neglect," from 1969 to 1971, when the United States deliberately allowed its balance of payments position to deteriorate in order to force the Europeans and the Japanese to accept exchange rate changes. Here the costs of allowing such a deterioration were evidently judged to be less than the long-term gains from creating the desired international image.[12] The United States is one of the few countries which could afford to use balance of payments policy as a signal, both because of the small size of external activities relative to the domestic economy and because of its position as the reserve banker in the international monetary system.

Both signals and indices can be the subject of what Jervis calls coupling and decoupling. The attempt to influence whether others regard the things that you do as a signal and what the meanings of the signals are, so as to create new signals or destroy existing ones, constitutes the coupling or decoupling of signals.[13] Similarly, the coupling and decoupling of indices by an actor involves an attempt to affect the inferences which others draw from indices, "to convince his adversary to accept a given explanation of his behavior or to convince him that he (the actor) holds a given interpretation of the adversary's behavior."[14] Coupling adds meanings to a signal or index; decoupling takes them away.

The idea of coupling is interesting in this context since the public statements of the United States' policy representatives give ample evidence that, during the period

from 1960 to 1968, the balance of payments was being deliberately coupled to the image of American global power and
status. Conversely, the subsequent period of "benign
neglect" was an exercise in the decoupling of an index,
and the coupling of a signal.

The Limits of Choice

The notions of signals, indices, coupling and decoupling suggest some of the normative constraints which may
be imposed on rational decision-making. The result may be
the elimination of almost all available solutions to a
problem, so that the final choice bears little resemblance
to a typical rational choice model. Rather, one ends up with
a choice between two costly, though hopefully not equally costly,
alternatives.

One of the few policy analyses which actually follows
this approach is Farrar's explication of the events which
precipitated the outbreak of war in 1914.[15] Rather than seeing
the declarations of war as a result of a particular crisis
situation, organizational processes, personalities or innate
aggressiveness on the part of one or more powers, he finds
the decisions to go to war to have been the result of
perfectly rational judgments of costs, benefits and proba-
bilities in a competitive international system. Each of the
great powers' leading statesmen saw it as their duty to

protect or expand the power of their states. All would have
preferred a diplomatic victory, but also preferred the cost
of war, rather than accept diplomatic defeat. The analogy which
will be explored here is that U.S. balance of payments policy
was the result of a similar situation: the costs of alternative policies forced a choice which would not necessarily
be chosen if only purely economic arguments were to be considered.

A Synthesis: Economic Policy as

Political Choice

The application of the theories outlined above assumed
that the dominating goal in American international monetary
policy was to maintain a position of global power and influence.
The term power is here used in the general sense stated by
Knorr; that is, power is the means by which an actor induces
others to act in accordance with the actor's demands, wishes
or proposals.[16] More specifically, the kind of power to be
discussed here is that which Perroux calls "the domination
effect," where "unit A exercises on unit B an irreversible
or partially irreversible influence" by virtue of its relative
magnitude, bargaining power in fixing conditions of exchange
and its place in the system.[17]

This is not to say that international power was the
only or even the primary goal of policy-makers, but rather

that it was the way in which the balance of payments situation
was linked to the power aspects of foreign policy which can
explain or predict why capital controls were adopted as the
main strategy during the 1960's. The environment of the Bretton
Woods structure encouraged a coupling of the balance of
payments index to international power, resulting in a
situation where the United States had no acceptable alternative to controlling capital outflows.

The construction of this connection did not, as
Aubrey pointed out in 1964, come easily. The United States
was unwilling to recognize in the early 1960's that other
policy objectives could not be pursued without regard to the
balance of payments.[18] The coupling process occurred by way
of three mechanisms: the reserve currency role of the
dollar, the direct balance of payments effects of foreign
policy activities and the problem of domestic adjustment to
external equilibrium.

There is obviously room for disagreement as to whether
the reserve role of the dollar is an instrument of power or
simply reflects the distribution of power which inheres in a
gold exchange standard. In any case, even if the power of
the dollar were simply analogous to the universality of the
English language, as Kindleberger argues,[19] once the connection was established, the reserve role of the dollar could

not be prejudiced without reflecting on the political power dimension with which it had been associated.

The most direct process of index coupling occurred as governmental expenditures on foreign policy activities contributed to the deficit, resulting in an ironic dilemma: the world role of the United States was being maintained by means which damaged an index (i.e., balance of payments equilibrium) considered vital to the maintenance of this role. The Vietnam war and continuous differences with Western Europe over defense matters naturally sharpened this dilemma.

The third linkage between the balance of payments and global power occurred insofar as the payments deficit was perceived as a severe constraint on domestic economic expansion--a constant preoccupation of both Presidents Kennedy and Johnson.

These perceptual connections which, in the policy environment of the 1960's, dictated an inescapable link between the need to remove the payments deficit and the foreign policy of the United States are illustrated in Figure 4.1.

It should be emphasized that these connections were those which were in part deliberately drawn by policy-makers (perhaps to add urgency to policy proposals) and in part connections which were believed to exist independently of any deliberate coupling. The result, as Adler points out,[20]

was to compel the United States to seek a remedy for the
deficit without considering whether the situation was
actually one of fundamental disequilibrium and without
considering a full range of options.

Figure 4.1. Power and Economics under
a Gold Exchange Standard

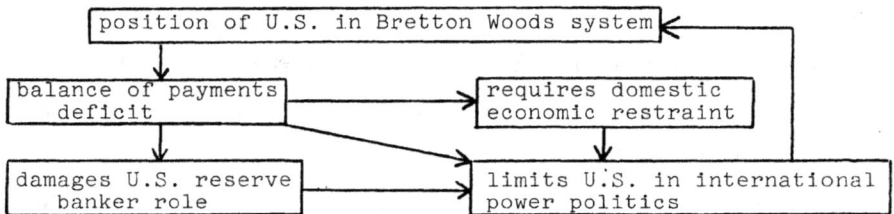

This non-logical (rather than illogical) coupling
prevented the situation from being considered simply as a
problem of rational economic choice. Had it been so considered,
the policy decision would have come to a choice between
financing the deficit (i.e., doing nothing) or acting on the
basis of one of the major models of internal and external
balance in the area of macroeconomics.

The first option was counseled by some mainly on the
grounds that the United States was simply performing the
useful global role of financial intermediation by way of its
payments deficit. Kindleberger, among others, was a tireless
proponent of this view.[21]

The two most well known policy models of internal and external balance are those associated with Professors Swan and Mundell.[22] The Swan model assumes that policy-makers have the use of both expenditure reducing (effective demand deflation) and expenditure switching (exchange rate changes in this case) alternatives. In Figure 4.2 below, the combinations of exchange rates and levels of effective demand which yield balance of payments equilibrium are denoted by the line EE, while the combinations yielding internal balance between unemployment and inflation are denoted by the line II.

Figure 4.2. Internal and External Balance with
a Flexible Exchange Rate

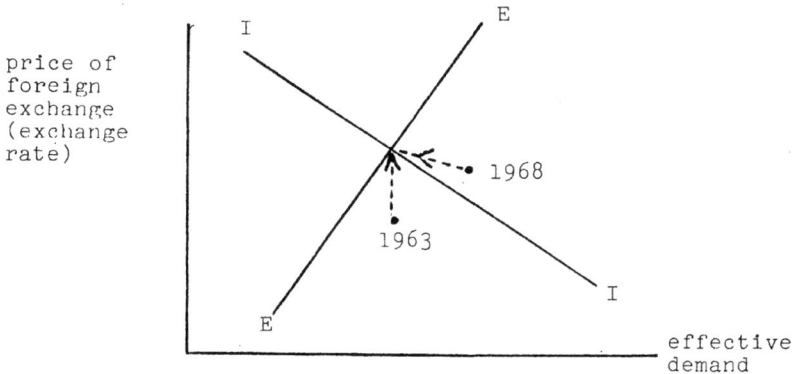

The situation facing the United States in 1963 may be simply characterized as one of a balance of payments deficit with unemployment, and in 1968 a payments deficit with inflation.

Devaluation is clearly required in both cases, combined with expenditure reduction in 1968.

If, however, the devaluation option is not to be considered, the best combination of expenditure reducing policies is suggested by the Mundell diagram illustrated in Figure 4.3 below. The policy alternatives are represented by the government budget expenditures (fiscal policy) and the interest rate (monetary policy), from which are derived internal (I_1I_1) and external (E_1E_1) balance lines analogous to the Swan diagram.

Figure 4.3. Internal and External Balance
with a Fixed Exchange Rate

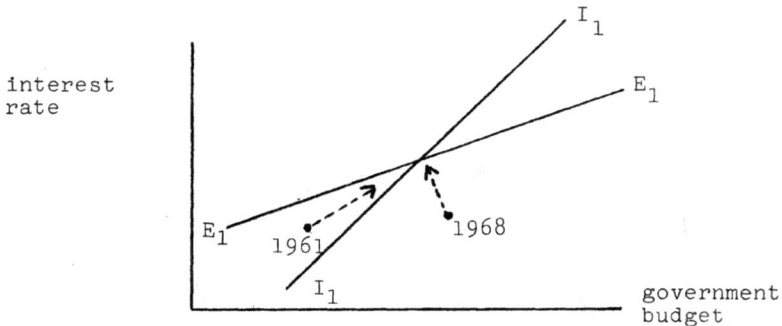

Here both situations again require the same policy: monetary deflation to raise interest rates, combined with fiscal stimulation in the early 1960's and fiscal restraint in the latter years of the decade.

Thus, considering the problem as an economist's
choice between policy instruments, the basic prescription
would have been either devaluation or monetary restraint.
The actual policy choice was determined more by the political
implications of the index coupling process, which resulted
in the major options of financing, devaluation, or deflation
being eliminated primarily on non-economic grounds. These
political influences may be found in all three basic options.

The unacceptability of a consistent expenditure reducing
policy in general is well documented in histories of domestic
economic policy and needs little further comment here.[23] To
the extent that the payments deficit of the 1960's was a
monetary phenomenon, the domestic counterpart of capital
controls was the inability or unwillingness to impose monetary
rather than fiscal deflation. That capital controls were
connected more with monetary rather than fiscal policy is
also suggested by the more direct linkage of monetary policy
to the balance of payments via interest rate effects on the
capital account. While monetary policy was restrained on several occasions during the decade it was not an effective
method of adjustment, either because of operational constraints, as in the case of the ill-fated Operation Twist,
or because it was not pursued for long enough to have any
lasting effect on the balance of payments. Internal expansion
via low interest rates, in the case of monetary policy, had

priority over external balance.

Fiscal deflation was even less feasible, since government expenditures and tax cutting were the major vehicles for the numerous programs which comprised the New Frontier and New Society. Theoretically, the political problems of deflation could have been circumscribed by assigning monetary policy (i.e., reducing the money supply) to the balance of payments, while allowing fiscal stimulation--a solution suggested by the Mundell model of policy assignment. However, even monetary restraint was not acceptable, largely because the two instruments cannot effectively be separated in practice, so that monetary restraint would have had unwanted fiscal effects.

Indeed, it may well have been that because of the peculiar situation of the United States, with its large non-traded goods sector in proportion to the balance of payments and the existence of large items not particularly responsive to deflation (e.g., foreign direct investment), that general deflation would have been the wrong course of action. Seymour Harris, in defending the piecemeal balance of payments tactics of the Kennedy Administration (to which he was an informal advisor) against deflation proposals, argued that "the cost of restrictive policies may become so great and the effectiveness of therapy so disappointing that a devaluation may be the only way out."[24]

An alternative form of expenditure deflation would
have been to reduce those governmental outlays which contributed directly to the payments deficit, such as foreign aid
and military expenditure. While some such measures were
taken,[25] they paled beside the effects of the Vietnam War on
the balance of payments. The policy implications of this
situation were not, however, clear to many commentators. Dudley
and Passell, for example, in testifying before the Joint
Economic Committee in 1969, reiterated their theme that

> the payments drain of external military commitments
> strikingly impinges upon the ability of the United
> States to maintain both high domestic absorption and the
> relatively free international movement of goods and capi-
> tal. It also reduces the capacity of the United States
> to promote lasting liberal reforms in the international
> payments system by maintaining the economy role of the
> United States as the world's primary payments debtor and
> chief benefactor of additional reserve creation. The
> modest involvement of the United States in the inter-
> national economy thus serves to define one dimension of
> the limits of American military and economic power.[26]
> (Italics mine.)

The historical record, however, would seem to imply
the opposite conclusion: the military power objectives of
the United States defined certain limits on its domestic
absorption, its involvement in the international economy
and its ability to promote structural reforms in the international monetary system. Without committing the fallacy of
causal imputation mentioned in chapter one, one can go a
considerable distance in agreeing with Cohen's suggestion that
the mandatory controls on foreign investments in 1968 were

direct result of the effects of Vietnam on the balance of payments in 1967.[27]

The major expenditure switching alternative was devaluation. While it is true that a logical tactical reason for not devaluing was the inability of the United States to prevent the rest of the world from also devaluing, a sufficient reason in the eyes of U.S. decision-makers was the reserve role of the dollar and the maintenance of the political position which this role entailed. It was probably for this' reason that the alternative of floating the dollar, thereby forcing the rest of the world to accept an effective devaluation of the dollar insofar as they were unwilling or unable to intervene in the foreign exchange markets to an extent sufficient to prevent the depreciation of the dollar, was not seriously considered, since the effect on the reserve status of the dollar would have been similar to a devaluation.

Commenting on the situation facing the United States in 1964, one economist wrote: "But this /the global optimality of floating exchange rates/ is an economic argument, whereas the more definitive consideration so far as policy-making is concerned is essentially noneconomic in character, embracing such questions as the effect of abandoning fixed exchange rates on the financial and economic (and perhaps political?) leadership of the United States in the Free World."[28]

The other large scale expenditure switching policy available was in the area of trade policy. However, any unilateral action to raise tariffs or quotas would not only have sabotaged the Kennedy Round of Trade negotiations, which it was hoped would raise exports more than imports, but would be most likely to have provoked retaliation by the United States' major trade partners. The same problem would have arisen with any large scale use of export subsidies.

The alternative to expenditure reduction or switching would have been to continue to finance the deficit. Many of the measures taken during the 1960's (e.g., the Gold Pool, Roosa Bonds) were intended to do this by maintaining confidence in the convertibility of the dollar at its existing gold parity. Even had it been true, as the Salant-Brookings study suggested, that the deficit was only temporary, it was unacceptable to Western European governments to think that they were financing the American deficit, particularly those deficit items which they found politically objectionable.

Thus the only major policy option left was some form of capital export control. The only major political argument, in addition to the various theoretical economic arguments against controls, was that they would damage the U.S. reserve banker role.[29] To some extent this was true--the various control measures did encourage the development of broader

capital markets outside of the United States. Yet this was
one aspect of being the system's banker which the United
States did want to share with others.

Adding to the "limits of choice" type of environment in which these balance of payments policy decisions took
place, was the manifest psychology of crisis which inspired
them. They were seen as short-term measures, designed to
buy time without too great a loss of reserves, avoiding devaluation until the underlying strength of the dollar recovered.[30] The purpose of each control program was, as
Wright and Molot point out, psychological: "They /U.S.
policy-makers/ had to be able to show an immediate statistical
improvement in the payments balance to restore international
confidence in the dollar."[31]

The control programs were frequently criticized
for being superficial, cosmetic treatments of the payments
problem which were implemented with some degree of cynicism
and little confidence in the results. They were, as Kindleberger suggests, a result of the "don't just stand there, do
something!" imperative.[32] This criticism ignores a crucial
element of the policy, namely that the controls were never
intended to be a long-term element in American foreign
economic policy. Officials concerned with the programs
emphatically assert they were believed to be workable and
effective for the short time period for which they were

intended to be applied.[33]

The result of this ad-hoc decision-making was something of a "sorceror's apprentice" effect: each measure had to be followed with new restrictions at regular intervals. However, this does not necessarily mean that the controls were merely ineffective cosmetics, since the objective situation was also changing rapidly, especially in the latter half of the decade with the Great Society domestic expansion, the Vietnam war and the foreign exchange market problems in Europe which helped push the Pound Sterling to the point of devaluation.

That the balance of payments policy of the Kennedy and Johnson Administrations can easily be seen to follow the kind of rational, political policy-making lines outlined above can be further illustrated by examining the evidence relating to the actual policy preferences of the two Presidents and their immediate advisors in the realm of balance of payments policy. It is obviously likely that one will find some disagreement on policy within the Presidential circle. What will be examined here are the views attributed to the President, or, in areas where the President does not seem to hold any particular preference, the dominant pattern of preferences among his closest advisors. One looks, then, at the "Presidential group" rather than any particular individuals. The available evidence suggests that both

Presidents Kennedy and Johnson perceived the index coupling
phenomenon, and reacted to the decisional problem in much
the same way as has been described above.

President Kennedy and the Balance of Payments

President Kennedy had had little experience with
balance of payments issues prior to 1960, save as an
advocate of protection for the New England textile industry.
As a candidate for the Presidency he was forced to confront
an issue with which he was not well acquainted. To make
matters worse, the incumbent Republican Administration, which
"seemed almost to welcome" the 1960 gold crisis as a
justification for monetary deflation, did not consult with
the Kennedy camp even after the election.[35] As the alarm of
European bankers over the prospect of Democratic fiscal
policies helped stimulate gold speculation, the balance of
payments became a campaign issue between Kennedy and
Nixon.[36] Even after his election victory Kennedy remained
concerned about the gold problem, commissioning several task
force reports on the subject and drawing attention to it in
his first State of the Union message, which emphatically rejected
devaluation because of the banker role of the United States.
Starting with his initial campaign speech on the gold crisis,
in October 1960, Kennedy gradually moved towards the kind of
piecemeal strategy which led to the Interest Equalization

Tax of 1963.[37]

As a "squeak-in" President, a former advisor recalls,
Kennedy was at first very timid in any area of economic
policy, even going so far as to promise Congressman Sam
Rayburn, the day after his election as President, that he
would balance the government's budget with no tax increases.[38]
While his domestic political situation was an important factor
inhibiting an early move to the expansionary policies
which became the major goals of the Kennedy Administration's economic policy, the balance of payments continued
to plague Kennedy, because of its linkage to both domestic
prosperity and international politics. Kennedy himself
said quite soon after his election that the two most important
problems facing him were nuclear weapons and the balance of
payments.

Close observers of Kennedy confirm this concern with
international finance. Tobin notes ". . . how vulnerable
the Kennedy Administration felt to potential charges that
through irresponsibility or inexpertise it mishandled the
balance of payments."[39] Sorensen comments that "few subjects
occupied more of Kennedy's time in the White House or were
the subject of more secret high-level meetings,"[40] although
he adds that most of Kennedy's advisors thought he became
rather too obsessed by the problem. Schlesinger, too, recalls
that "the balance of payments remained a constant worry to

Kennedy," and cites his reasons as being the belief that
a nation is only as strong as its currency and his contention
that "the great free nations of the world must take control
of our monetary problems before they take control of us."[41]
Both of the reasons correspond to the index coupling process
described above: the linkage of international politics to
the balance of payments via domestic economic policy and
the international role of the dollar.

In the area of monetary and fiscal policy Kennedy
gradually moved from an advocacy of fiscal restraint and
monetary expansion (during the election campaign), to a
belief in monetary restraint and fiscal expansion (in
1961-1962), and finally to the conclusion that neither
monetary nor fiscal policy should be dictated by balance of
payments considerations. Monetary policy, the domestic
instrument which most economists would choose to assign
to external balance, was particularly constrained because
of the political importance of keeping long-term interest
rates low. An empirical study of aggregate demand policies
and the balance of payments suggests that, for the period
1950-1967, both monetary and fiscal policy were applied to
the goals of employment and production, not to the
balance of payments,[42] which would suggest that Kennedy's
dilemma was hardly unique.

In his special message to Congress of July 1963,

Kennedy announced that he was "rejecting a choice between
two equally unpalatable alternatives--improved employment
at home at the cost of a weaker dollar or a stronger dollar
at the cost of a weaker economy. . ."[43] Hence one element
in a "limits of choice" situation: the unacceptability of
any consistently applied deflationary policy, both because
of its effect on prosperity and its perceived connection with
national power, since he believed that an active foreign policy
required "getting the /domestic7 economy moving" again.[44]

This conclusive rejection of deflation, according to
Harris, began in mid-1962 with Kennedy's observation that if
Europe could have faster growth without balance of payments
problems, then so could the U.S![45] The Administration was
thus forced to choose between three other basic options:
continued financing of the deficit, devaluation or capital
controls.

Devaluation was not a viable option. Kennedy believed
that "devaluation would call into doubt the good faith and
stability of this nation and the competence of its President."[46] The issue had come up during the 1960 campaign, when
Kennedy repudiated Nixon's suggestion that his domestic
policies would require a devaluation of the dollar. Indeed,
Kennedy seems to have believed that he could never devalue
the dollar and survive the next election.[47] The problem was
remarkably similar to Ellsberg's interpretation of the

Vietnam war escalation: no President felt that he could
pull out of Vietnam and still be re-elected.[48]

While Kennedy approved of the various minor financing
measures devised during his Administration, he did not
envisage any solution to the U.S. balance of payments problem
along the lines of a multilateralization of the functions of
a reserve currency. Doubtless influenced by Treasury
Secretary Dillon and his European colleagues, Kennedy saw
the elimination of the deficit as a prerequisite rather than
a result of the restructuring of the international monetary
system around a centrally created reserve.[49]

Thus, the way in which options and issue areas were
connected led almost inevitably to capital controls as the
solution. As Schlesinger puts it, "more and more, everyone
regarded control of long-term capital outflow as the key to
the situation."[50]

The chronology of the Administration's reluctant
move toward capital controls is well documented in other
places.[51] The issue had come up as early as 1960, when,
during a campaign speech at Philadelphia, Kennedy cited foreign
limitations on capital flows to the United States as one
reason for the gold crisis, a point which reappeared in almost
every message on balance of payments policy. Kennedy's
willingness to support the ideal of controlling outflows of
long-term portfolio capital was due to the numerical salience

of such flows, which rose rapidly in 1962 and 1963, and the
fact that it was the only major adjustment measure, possibly
capable of achieving dramatic results in a short time, which
did not have unacceptable political costs attached to it.
It was so attractive as an option that he was, in November
1963, considering a more far-reaching capital control program.[52]

The balance of payments choices made by Kennedy did
not, of course, occur in a vacuum. There were many advisors fighting for his ear on this subject, and their
opportunities were enhanced by Kennedy's own lack of sophistication in such matters. His opinions on balance of payments policy came from both conservatives, such as William
Martin (Chairman of the Federal Reserve Board), Douglas Dillon
(Treasury Secretary) and Robert Roosa (Dillon's Under-Secretary for Monetary Affairs), and also from liberal expan-
sionists, principally members of the Council
of Economic Advisors and informal consultants such as J. K.
Galbraith and S. E. Harris, both Harvard professors. The
importance of intra-mural politics will be discussed in a
following chapter; what will be done at this point is simply
to suggest where some of the influences on the choices Kennedy
made may have originated.

Since the keynote of the Kennedy style was "infor-
mality and a loose, highly personal style of operating,"[53]

and the President's own knowledge of international finance
was scanty, it is not surprising that the major influences on
him in this area came from those with both expertise and
authority. The choice of an Interest Equalization Tax
was consonant with the belief o Treasury Secretary Dillon
that ". . . the only other alternative that seemed available
would be to try to artificially and very drastically
restrict credit in this country. . .," and that the IET
was "not just a stopgap. . . .Rather it is an essential element
of a much broader program to restore lasting balance in our
international payments."[54] For reasons that will be outlined
in chapter six, the Treasury generally prevailed over the
Council of Economic Advisors in influencing Kennedy's
opinions. The CEA, Bureau of the Budget and private advisors (such as Galbraith, Harris and Samuelson) did not lack
an audience with the President, but when it came to final
choices, Dillon's influence seems to have been decisive.

The actual decision to impose the IET was probably
made in the late spring of 1963. The proposal was apparently
put into legal form by Treasury Under-Secretary Fowler, at
the instigation of Dillon.[55] According to Roosa, the
secrecy surrounding the preparation of the IET was the
greatest since the Cuban missile crisis.[56] For some months
pressure had been building on the Administration for some
direct action on the balance of payments from both the

European and American financial community, especially after
the poor second quarter balance of payments figures became
public.[57] Within the Administration there had long been
concern about, and interest in, taking measures against rising
outflows of long-term portfolio capital.[58] The concern
frequently took on an anti-European flavour, since it was
mainly European public and private securities and loan placements which were causing the large portfolio outflow.

The year 1963 began inauspiciously, with the Administration publicly admitting that it had given up hope of ending
the balance of payments deficit by the end of the year.[59]
During February and March gold losses increased, the United
States had to borrow foreign exchange through its "swap"
lines with other countries' central banks and the word
devaluation was heard even among the proceedings of an
American Bankers Association meeting. However, as late as
the second week of May, the Administration was still publicly
claiming that no major new balance of payments measures
were planned; although during his visit to Europe in June,
Kennedy emphasized monetary problems in conversations with
the West German government.[60]

The final choice of capital controls, the IET, as
the mainstay of Kennedy's balance of payments message of
July 1963 was, as the President testified, a reluctant
choice among disagreeable options:

In view of the continued existence of direct
controls and inadequate capital market mechanisms in
many foreign countries, and the wide differential between
the long-term rates of interest in the larger industrial
countries and the United States, there appear to be
only three possible solutions to this problem, two of
which are unacceptable under present circumstances:
--A substantial increase in our whole long-term
interest rate structure would throw our economy into
reverse, increase unemployment and substantially reduce
our import requirements, thereby damaging the economy
of every free nation;
--The initiation of direct capital controls,
which are in use in most countries, is inappropriate
to our circumstances. It is contrary to our basic precept
of free markets. We cannot take this route.
--A third alternative--the one which I would re-
commend--would stem the flood of foreign security sales
in our markets and still be fully consistent with both
economic growth and free capital movements. I urge
the enactment by the Congress of an "Interest Equalization Tax," which would, in effect, increase by approxi-
mately one percent the interest cost to foreigners of
obtaining capital in this country, and thus help equalize
interest rate patterns for longer term financing in the
United States and abroad.[61]

No doubt in response to critics who asserted that even if the

IET did help the balance of payments, it would do so by

severely damaging the reserve currency role of the dollar,

the President replied that the IET would be accompanied by

efforts to promote portfolio capital inflows into the United

States (i.e, maintaining the degree of international inte-

gration of capital markets necessary for the dollar to remain

as numéraire):

Investment by foreign savers in the securities of
United States private companies has fallen rapidly to
less than $150 million in 1962. The better climate for
investment that will flow from enactment of the program
for tax reduction and reform now before the Congress will

do much to improve this situation but a direct
action program is also needed to promote overseas
sales of securities of U.S. companies. Such a program
should also be designed to increase foreign participation in the financing of new or expanded operations
on the part of U.S. companies operating abroad.
. . . The increased freedom of capital movement and
increased participation by foreign citizens and financial
institutions in the ownership and financing of American
business, towards which these efforts are directed,
will serve to strengthen the economic and political
ties of the Free World as well as its monetary system.
Securities of U.S. private firms could be and should
be one of our best selling exports. An increasing
foreign investment in these securities will encourage
a more balanced two-way capital traffic between the
United States and other capital markets and minimize
the impact of net long-term capital outflows from the
United States on our balance of payments.[62]

Throughout Kennedy's balance of payments message,

his dilemma is clear: domestic deflation was precluded

both for domestic political reasons and for the effects

it might have on the U.S. international political position;

while all of the major external (or expenditure switching)

policies, save the IET, were precluded either because of

direct international political repercussions (e.g., tariff

policy) or because they would damage the status of the

dollar in the international monetary system and so in-

directly affect U.S. global power. Even the IET posed the

longer-term danger that insofar as it performed its function

of shifting long-term public and private financing out of

the United States, it could in time undermine the dollar as

the basis of the gold exchange standard, and the power of that

nation whose currency was coupled to the indices of power.

Kennedy had been assured that the IET would be
necessary only as a short-term measure until the external
balance improved--as, in its eternal optimism, the Administration was sure it would--and until foreign capital markets
built up the capacity to handle large securities placements.[63]
Again, however, the preeminence of the political dimension
of the problem was apparent. In his speech to the annual
meeting of the IMF in 1963, he stressed that while priority
was being given to the balance of payments, he pledged fiscal
aid to those non-communist countries whose access to reserves might be diminished by the diminution of the U.S.
deficit.[64] Kennedy (and later Presidents) never found a
satisfactory solution to this paradox: the indices of international power (mainly reserve currency status and government
transfers to other countries) required activities which
resulted in a balance of payments deficit prejudicial to that
very power he sought to uphold.

President Johnson and the Balance of Payments

Johnson assumed the Presidency at a time when a
number of factors were making the international financial
situation of the United States more difficult: in domestic
policy the expansionary policies of the Kennedy Administration
had to be pushed through; and in foreign policy the direct
expenditure drain of the Vietnam war, together with increasingly

ambivalent attitudes toward U.S. direct foreign investment
in Europe, made European-American relations difficult precisely a a time when the United States needed European support
to continue financing its deficit and to reach a mutually
agreeable solution to the Kennedy Round, the Special Drawing
Right negotiations, and problems within NATO. What follows
is an overview of President Johnson's views on balance of
payments, those of his closest advisors and a brief chronology
of events.[65]

President Johnson's pre-inaugural period in office
was, in the realm of foreign economic policy, simply a
continuation of the policies of Kennedy, under the advice
of Kennedy advisors--principally Dillon, who remained at
the Treasury until the spring of 1965. It has been said
that Johnson's interest in international affairs was less
than that of Kennedy, and that his foreign policy developed
"from his personality and his experience in office."[66] However, in the realm of balance of payments policy this
personality difference had little impact on the choice of
options, since Johnson faced much the same decisional para-
meters as did Kennedy.

As during the previous Administration, fiscal and
monetary restraint were not practical options. The
failure to enact a tax increase in 1966, together with a
failure to curb government expenditure, precluded fiscal

restraint as a method of balance of payments adjustment.
Indeed, a recent analysis of that period attributes the
eventual collapse of the Bretton Woods system to the inflation
induced by the "no-tax" decision of 1966.[67] Whether or not
the decision not to raise taxes was a major inflationary
move,[68] it was believed at the time to have a major effect
on the balance of payments.

Monetary policy was similarly unconstrained. While
Federal Reserve Chairman Martin did, on occasion, go
against Johnson's populist predilection for low interest
rates and an expansionary monetary policy, the Federal
Reserve did not consistently pursue a tight money
policy. During the few times when it did, as in December
1965 when the discount rate was raised, Presidential wrath
was sufficient to prevent the policy being consistently followed.[69] However, the Fed's preference for monetary
restraint probably helped Johnson justify the lack of fiscal
restraint in the expenditures of his own branch of government.

Undoubtedly one of the most important influences on
the balance of payments at this time was the Vietnam war,
which had both direct (i.e., foreign expenditures incurred
in maintaining the war effort) and indirect (i.e., inflation)
effects tending to cause a deterioration in the balance of
payments. President Johnson could no more accept a "guns

or butter" constraint than could Kennedy.

Neither could he accept devaluation, and so capital controls again became the major attempt at balance of payments adjustment until 1969. Vietnam became the standard excuse for lack of action--the deficits of 1966-1967 were described by the White House as an "unpleasant and unavoidable" result of Vietnam, the spokesman adding that "we are trying to keep the deficit as low as possible, but we are not embarking on any new programs just to reach equilibrium while the war is going on."[70]

The Administration did see the other side of the index coupling problem, that continued payments deficits undermined the global position of the dollar and therefore its ability to continue its international military policies. Its response, however, was to rely on an even tighter system of capital controls and public declarations of faith. As early as July 1964, Johnson announced that the balance of payments had "turned the corner,"[71] and his special message of February 1965 concluded on a highly optimistic note: "Let no one doubt it--we will eliminate our international deficit. We will maintain the dollar at full value."[72]

Thus the use of capital controls can be seen, as it was during the Kennedy period, as a "limits of choice" situation produced by direct and indirect coupling of the balance of payments to international politics. Both Johnson and his

advisors have emphasized their sense of not really having
a choice at all: "The contribution of American capital to
the world's growth and prosperity has been immense. But
our balance of payments deficit leaves me no choice."[73]

While Johnson did not particularly favour the idea
of capital controls, he did not have any fervent ideological
objection to them; on the contrary, he had much of the
populist's dislike for the big businesses and banks which
bore the effects of the control programs. Thus, once the
February 1965 program of voluntary controls became clearly
inadequate for its task, Johnson did not object to the
gradual tightening of these controls, culminating in the
1968 mandatory controls on direct foreign investment.

Although he did not directly take part in the debate
which preceded the 1968 program, he could hardly have been
unaware that it could have two major benefits: it would
help assuage critics who charged that the Administration
was doing nothing about the direct balance of payments impact
of the Vietnam war, and it would make it easier for Congress
to accept his proposed tax surcharge. The program would,
predicted Business Week, "raise substantially" his reputation
with the 90th Congress, which was "fed up with the implications
/sic/ from abroad that the U.S. would not satisfy its
international creditors."[74] By impressing his domestic
critics with both the gravity of the situation and the

severity of the remedial proposals, Johnson was attempting
to work out a viable tradeoff between objectives: the
controls not only made it easier to propose continuing
the war, but also did so in a way which would help prevent
too much damage to the reserve currency position of the
dollar (even if only because of the psychological effects of
the controls), and make it easier for Congress to accept a
deflationary tax surcharge. Tighter capital controls
enabled Johnson to make a slight tradeoff on the domestic
side which justified continuing the war and maintaining
the preeminent position of the dollar.

Several months later the decision was made to reduce
America's presence in Vietnam, partly eliminating one strand
of the policy dilemma. From the domestic angle, the capital
controls program drew attention to the financial situation
in such a way that ". . . the international gold market crisis
made clear the vital connections between passing the
tax bill and avoiding an international monetary catastrophe."[75]

As has been suggested, the balance of payments policy
of the Johnson Administration was not solely the result of
the President's own thoughts. The Treasury maintained a
strong voice in payments policy. However, the locus of
decision-making shifted back to the White House, notably to
Francis Bator, Johnson's Deputy Assistant for National Security. The power shift resulted from a variety of causes,

principally the relative strengths of personalities and the fact that insofar as he was interested in international monetary affairs, the new Secretary of the Treasury, Henry Fowler, concerned himself more with the expanding European-American dialogue on centrally created reserves (i.e, liquidity rather than adjustment).

Bator's central position in U.S. international monetary policy from 1965 to 1968 is attested to by several sources.[76] His views on the subject were expressed in an article in Foreign Affairs in 1968.[77] In Bator's view, the strategy which he successfully urged on President Johnson was to avoid any "radical surgery" (such as devaluation or deflation), use capital controls as a temporary holding operation, and at the same time work for a change in the rules of the system--"an orderly transition to an internationally managed SDR system, with improved procedures for adjustment."[78]

Bator supplied more sophisticated rationales for not doing things which the President did not want to do anyway: monetary and fiscal policy, according to Bator, are barely adequate to meet domestic objectives, and should not be used for external balance goals; and devaluation was precluded because other governments would not accept it. He favoured capital controls as the basis of this holding operation because capital flows were politically more vulnerable than any other item in the balance of payments accounts. His only criticism of the program was that the original 1965 voluntary controls should have had more "bite."[79] The controls were a "necessary evil" with many shortcomings: they "are apt to have a relatively short half-life in terms of effectiveness; they tend to get leakier with use; and they are wasteful."[80] However, he also rejected what he called "golden egg" arguments against controls (viz., that the balance of payments effects are rapidly recouped through induced exports and profit remittances). Yet his valedictory message to his successors in the Nixon Administration was that ". . . we have been right to do what we have done. . . . if anything additional has to be done about the balance of payments, I would tighten up even further on direct investment in industrial countries outside the dollar area."[81] As it turned out, his successors did precisely the opposite, but for much the same reason: to encourage structural reform of the international monetary system.

This policy probably took some time to develop. During its first year, the Johnson Administration simply continued Kennedy's policies, encouraging Congress to pass the IET. Toward the end of 1964, optimism about the balance of payments waned as it became clear that overseas bank lending (both short-and long-term) was rising rapidly, offsetting the effects of the IET.[82] The new program for 1965 was precipitated by a very large deficit in the fourth quarter of 1964, partly due to large new issues of Canadian securities in the United States.[83] While some thought was given to direct screening of capital flows or a penalty tax on direct investments, the predominant trend of thinking in the Administration was that "moral suasion would suffice."[84]

The President's special message on the balance of payments delivered on February 10, 1965, claimed that the IET had in fact been very effective in both reducing portfolio outflows and had "encouraged the broadening and deepening of capital markets in Europe,"[85] but that further measures were necessary to prevent substitution within the capital account from offsetting these gains. Hence his request for the extension of the IET for two years, the broadening of its coverage to nonbank loans of one to three years and to bank loans of one year or more, voluntary limitations on other bank loans, and the voluntary program for direct investors abroad.

Yet it soon became clear that the program would not produce any dramatic results in 1965--not only because of the shortcomings of the program itself but because of other problems, mainly the rapid escalation in Vietnam and the Dominican Republic episode of that year. In addition, the British government made matters worse by selling its portfolio of U.S. securities to bolster sterling.[86] Even by

mid-1965, Treasury Secretary Fowler was pessimistic enough
to refer to the controls as "a one-shot affair, capable of
large impact but small sustained effect."[87] Hence the considerable tightening of the program for 1966, along with
suggestions from Administration officials that a mandatory
program might appear in 1967.[88]

The year 1966 brought little improvement, and so
for 1967 the program was again tightened for both banks
and direct investors. In announcing the new guidelines, the
President abandoned his usual optimism, suggesting only that
the United States would move toward "equilibrium as fast as
the continuing foreign exchange costs of Vietnam permit,"
and that the controls would remain in place at least until
"hostilities in Vietnam have ended."[89] Some respite was
provided by higher short-term interest rates in the United
States, although its beneficial effect on the capital
account tended to frustrate the domestic intent of the
Federal Reserve.

By the beginning of 1967, it appears that the only
thing holding the Administration back from mandatory controls
was the belief that the Vietnam war would end soon. Fowler
told the Joint Economic Committee that the Administration
was basing its hopes on a rise in world interest rates
(relative to the United States), some NATO offset agreement,
and the tightening of the capital controls.[90] In all

likelihood, mandatory controls would probably have come
sooner than January 1968, had the responsible officials not
been preoccupied with more immediate problems in the rapidly
deteriorating international financial environment after the
climax of the Kennedy Round in June 1967, and the Rio
Agreement on SDR's in the fall.[91]

The decision to impose mandatory controls was made
in the aftermath of the devaluation of sterling, when, as
one former Treasury Undersecretary has put it, "things
really fell to pieces." This was literally true: a C-141
transport carrying gold to Europe crashed shortly after
take-off, spilling gold bullion over the hillsides of eastern
Kentucky.[92] The decision must have been sudden, since as late
as November 16, the Administration had planned only to
make the voluntary program more stringent,[93] and on
December 23 the President accepted the recommendation of the
Cabinet Committee on the Balance of Payments, that the
voluntary controls be carried forward in substantially the
same form in 1968.[94]

The devaluation of the pound shifted a great deal of
speculative pressure onto the dollar; so much so, that
President Johnson had to issue a public statement pledging
not to devalue the dollar,[95] an affirmation he was forced to
repeat many times during the months of November and December
1967. It was against this background that the Foreign

Direct Investment Program (FDIP) was hurriedly put together:
the basic outline was set out by top Treasury officials over
a single weekend,[96] and the Assistant Secretary of Commerce
for Economic Affairs (W. H. Shaw) was then given only five
days to organize the new Office of Foreign Direct Investment (OFDI), within the Commerce Department, before the
President announced the new program on January 1, 1968.[97]

Fowler later acknowledged that the decision to shift
from more stringent voluntary controls to a mandatory program was a panicky reaction to the devaluation of the pound
and a sharp deterioration in the U.S. capital account.[98]
This was not entirely due to short-term factors. The
capital account deterioration in 1967 was due also to more
U.S. purchases of foreign securities exempt from the IET
(e.g., international organization bonds, bonds of the
government of Israel, and new Canadian issues), a reversal
of the trend to liquidate U.S. holdings of foreign securities
(due mainly to the good health of foreign stock markets)
and the easier reserve position of U.S. commercial banks
in 1967, allowing them to give more short-term credits
to foreigners (within their VFCR limits).[99] Hence the
reappraisal: balance of payments gains of the magnitude
required could not be obtained, with an equitable distribution
of the burden, without mandatory ceilings.[100]

The suddenness of the decision is also attested to by

the legal questions which later arose. The FDIP was imposed
by Executive order under the authority of the Bank Acts of
1917, which were part of the Trading with the Enemy Acts.
Unlike the IET, there was no consultation with Congress
or private interests. Even some relevant bureaucratic
interests seem to have been left out. When an industry
representative asked the Commerce Department about the
legal basis of the controls, he was referred to an
Assistant Attorney-General, who in turn consulted the
White House and was told that while there was a legal basis
for the FDIP, there was no need to seek any formal legal
opinion.[101]

Conclusions

It is a widely held opinion that national security
decisions are the most susceptible to what is usually
referred to as the "rational actor model." It has been
suggested in this chapter that foreign economic policy
decisions can also be so viewed, even if only because there
was a high perceived national security element in the
problem: the coupling of a balance of payments deficit to
international power in such a way as to preclude the most
obvious options (viz., deflation, devaluation, and direct
cuts in current account transfers) and force two successive
Administrations to rely on capital controls as an adjustment

measure. Almost all of those involved would echo the opinion
of one Treasury official: "We felt we had no choice."[102]

It will be suggested in chapter eight that the capital
controls, while successful in their immediate goal of
shifting long-term financing out of the United States,
were ultimately a self-defeating strategy owing to transfer
effects onto the current account and substitution within
the capital account. The fact that the controls were
widely seen as, at best, a short-term panacea is not necessarily
inconsistent with the choice of controls as an adjustment
policy by a rational decision-maker. On the contrary, much
of the literature on psychological "avoidance" tactics suggests that this will be the result. Rivera states it thus:

> When either a person or an organization is faced with
> unacceptable alternatives, then an unrealistic third
> course of action is attempted and thoughts that challenge
> this action are ignored. . . . Lewin has observed that
> when a person is in an avoidance-avoidance conflict,
> trapped between two negative alternatives /viz., devalu-
> ation or deflation, in this case7, he tries to leave the
> field of conflict and often does this by fantasizing.
> It would appear that when he is forced to remain he
> may seize on a third alternative that appears to avoid
> the unpleasantness but is actually unrealistic. Once
> he has committed himself to this panacea an extreme form
> of dissonance occurs--extreme because contradicting thoughts
> challenge not just any decision but a decision that
> appears to be the only one acceptable. This force
> prevents attention to set-breaking ideas that might
> provide a solution to the situation.[103]

Despite differences in both personnel and Presidential styles, an examination of the goals, priorities and
constraints perceived by both the Presidents and their

immediate advisors is quite consistent with the selection
of capital controls as a "rational choice" solution, in
the sense of being a predictable outcome given that part of
the decision-making framework which was shared by both
Administrations. This shared framework consisted of one
primary hypothesis, that a balance of payments deficit prejudiced the global status of the United States. The coupling
process ran through three channels: the world banker role
of the United States, the direct connection (e.g., Vietnam expenditures) and domestic aggregate demand policies.
Why did decision-makers perceive the situation in a way
that put them in a severe "limits of choice" situation?
Partly, of course, because they genuinely believed these
connections to be objectively true. The underlying structure of the system excluded certain options, in terms of con-
ceivability if not feasibility. However, the connections
may also have been presented for the sake of eliminating
options which various actors did not like for other reasons.

    This raises a further question: to the extent that
there was some dissension among policy-makers, how well
does a rational actor interpretation actually explain the outcome, rather than merely providing a good predictive hypothesis which fits the selected historical material? Is the
explanation causally as well as predictively adequate?

    Between the IET of 1963 and the FDIP of 1968 there

would appear to have been sharp changes in the sources
of U.S. international monetary policy, even if the outcomes
themselves are still consistent with a rational actor
explanation. Hence this may be a case of what Friedman calls
"as if" rationality: the outcome is that which a rational
actor would choose, but the choice itself was the result
of some other considerations.

The development of the IET proposal may be seen as a
compromise between the desire of Kennedy (supported by the
Council of Economic Advisors) for fiscal stimulation and
the Treasury's concern for the balance of payments effect
of such stimulation combined with its rejection of any "radical"
means of dealing with the balance of payments. The willingness of all parties to consider capital controls originated
in the failure of previous measures to deal effectively with
the balance of payments in conjunction with Kennedy's
increasing reluctance to limit domestic expansion. By
1963 he was, as Seymour Harris tells it, a "convert"
to Galbraith-style Keynesianism and strongly influenced
by the expansionist inclinations of the CEA. However, while
the CEA-led "fiscalists" had their victory in domestic
policy, the Treasury (as a major bastion of the so-called
"structuralist" school) was able to exert a restraining
influence on the desire of CEA to promote major reforms
of the international monetary system as a means of dealing

with the balance of payments consequences. The Treasury's
view, accepted by Kennedy, was that any radical reform measures must be preceded by an improvement in the balance
of payments. Kennedy's deference to Treasury views in
this regard may have been due to what Schlesinger calls
an exaggerated respect for the requisites of "confidence"
in international finance.[104]

Kennedy had expected (or been told) that the IET
could be abandoned in 1965. He had firmly rejected any
controls on direct investment. This would indicate a general
attitude of optimism: the IET was a regrettable short-term
measure made necessary by the absence of any other acceptable
alternatives in the existing situation. Direct investment
controls were, in Kennedy's words, "contrary to our basic
precept of free markets" and "inappropriate to our circumstances."

The mandatory direct investment controls originated
in a situation analogous to a political "crisis"--President
Johnson's reluctance to raise taxes in 1966 and 1967 to
compensate for domestic inflation, and the balance of payments
effects of Vietnam expenditures, which were particularly
alarming in the fourth quarter of 1967. The impression one
gets is that the FDIP was a measure taken in some haste
at the highest levels of the Johnson Administration, as an
attempt to ameliorate a serious consequence of domestic

and foreign policy priorities. While the IET was also in
part dictated by a Presidential policy priority, it was in
both its conception and implementation more subject to
bureaucratic policy preferences and less influenced by the
demands of other states. Aside from being more directly
the result of Presidential initiative, the 1968 controls
were also in part a response to the pressures of other
countries. Between 1963 and 1968 the locus of decision-making
on balance of payments policy shifted from a primarily
Treasury dominated policy to an action dictated by Presidential policy and relatively unconstrained by bureaucratic
interests.

This is the general theme which will be pursued in
chapters five and six: that a causal explanation of the
capital control policies requires an examination of the
reasons why capital controls may have been chosen for
reasons other than those suggested above, namely the preferences of domestic governmental and private interests.
Chapter five will test the proposition that a pattern of
domestic interest aggregation could predict that the United
States would adopt capital controls. Chapter six will
explain the role played by intra-governmental bargaining
between the policy imperatives of the White House and the
domestic political context.

CHAPTER V

DOMESTIC INTEREST GROUP POLITICS AND THE
UNITED STATES CAPITAL CONTROL PROGRAM

The classical pluralist model of politics suggests
that government policies are the result of the aggregation of
domestic interests, the government itself simply performing
the functions of a cash register--adding up the pluses and
minuses. One need not, of course, take such an extreme
view of the importance of interest groups; rather, one may
simply ask how important were domestic interest groups in determining the decisions or implementation of the capital
control programs. As a specific hypothesis, one would ask
whether or not an examination of the interests and
relative power of interested groups would lead one to predict
that capital controls would be adopted.

The answer to be offered here is that this is not
the case. The controls were concentrated in their effects,
penalizing specific groups: dealers in and purchasers of
foreign securities (the IET), commercial banks (the VFCR) and
foreign direct investors (the voluntary, and later mandatory,
FDIP). The benefits of the controls were, at best, highly
diffuse in their national effects. The question to be dealt

with in this chapter then becomes: why did these directly
affected groups not prevent the implementation of the controls? It will be shown that the lack of fervent opposition
to the controls was in large part a function of one feature
common to all three of these directly affected groups. This
feature was size. The dominating actors in each group were
able to find acceptable ways of going over, under, through
and around the controls; though not, it should be added,
necessarily defeating the purpose of the controls in the
process. Those who were unacceptably hurt by the controls
faced the problem of "the logic of collective action," which
they were unable to overcome.[1]

It should be emphasized that the period being dealt
with here is July 1963 to January 1968. Once the FDIP
program came into full effect during 1968, it was stringent
enough to hurt even the biggest corporations. At this
point, serious opposition to the controls did build up into
a coherent force which probably had a great deal of influence
on the declaration of Presidential candidate Nixon, that he
would remove the controls. However, this aspect of interest
group activity is more directly related to the gradual removal of the controls after 1968 than it is to the reasons
why interest groups did not prevent the implementation of
the policies in the first place, and will therefore be left
to chapter eight, on interest group reactions and assessments

of the FDIP, and the decisions to dismantle the controls.

General opposition to the controls was not confined
to the groups most directly affected. The postwar historical
trend in both public and business elite opinion had been
moving toward the identification of an open international system with the national interest of the United States. Thus,
by the 1960's, public and business opinion (as well as most
academic economists) were against the idea of capital controls in principle. The Committee on Economic Development
(a business-academic group) repeatedly condemned the controls.[2] The editors of Business Week saw controls as not only
mistaken (better to encourage exports, and capital inflows
via corporate tax cuts) but as a dangerous trend toward full
exchange controls.[3] The New York Times was never quite so
bitterly against controls, but was quick to pick up on the
alternatives being discussed at the time (e.g., capital
issues committees, tax reform).[4]

The Interest Equalization Tax

While the New York investment community voiced "deep
disappointment" over the IET, there was a general feeling of
confidence that the bill would either never get through the
Ways and Means Committee, or that if it did, it would be suit-
ably altered to make it acceptable.[5] The basic alternative
they offered was a capital issues committee made up of Wall

Street underwriters![6] Action on capital controls had been
delayed for some time by Kennedy's reluctance to alienate
the business community, and one of the reasons the Administration chose the IET was because they thought New York financial interests would find it the least objectionable measure.[7] And yet, the IET was eventually passed with only
minor amendments.

One of the reasons for this failure of private
interests to achieve their goal was their own political inepti-
tude. Most of the testimonies and depositions to the House
Ways and Means Committee were, perhaps because of initial
overconfidence, so obviously self-serving that even the
most cynical legislator could not but react adversely. Most
of those who testified were either representatives of smaller
firms with heavy interests in foreign securities (e.g., the
International Holdings Corporation, a closed-end mutual
fund with 25 percent of its portfolio in foreign securities)
or representatives of peak associations (e.g, the Investment
Bankers Association of America). They either requested that
the IET be rejected outright, or that amendments be made
so as to exempt their own company or group.[8]

A few individuals who testified before the Committee
did have the political acumen to present their objections
in terms of the national interest. A representative of the
New York Chamber of Commerce testified that the IET would

reduce confidence in the dollar, ultimately harm the balance
of payments (through lost interest remittances and transfer effects), ruin New York as the world's financial
center, provoke retaliatory measures by other governments
and delay "real" adjustment. The NYCC suggested that a
better policy would be to make investment in the United
States more attractive rather than making investment
in other countries less attractive, by reducing taxes
and government expenditures.[9] A few other witnesses used the
trade argument, likening the IET to the Hawley-Smoot tariff
of 1930, or as in the following statement, to the Chicken
War tariffs between the United States and the EEC: "given
the justifiable importance assigned to trade expansion as a
long-term solution to the balance of payments problem, it is
important to recognize that there is little difference between a tariff on frozen U.S. chickens and a tariff on the
shares of a foreign company."[10] One more imaginative witness
also suggested that the IET would ". . . give enormous
comfort and aid to the Communist foreign investment program. . . ."[11]

Thus, objections to the IET tended to be either
blatantly self-interested or to invoke the national interest
in a rather unconvincing fashion. Very few witnesses
actually focused on the most vulnerable aspect of the
IET: whether it would really work. It was not until the

IET was well on the way to being passed that such arguments were produced.[12]

The expectation of ability to illegally evade the IET cannot explain the weakness of the opposition to the IET. Illegal evasion certainly did occur; the IRS filed tax liens totaling $14 million in 1965, in its first major enforcement action.[13] Most of the reported cases were those of individuals (mainly ones who attempted to manufacture fake certificates of U.S. ownership by the seller of the foreign stock) or smaller companies attempting to use "dummy" corporations in exempted areas (especially Canada) to purchase foreign securities.

The reason for the lack of concerted opposition lies in both the benefits and penalties of size. The largest underwriters of foreign securities were Smith, Barney and Company ($203 million of foreign corporate issues in 1962) and Morgan Stanley ($84 million of foreign government issues in 1962). Other major underwriters were First Boston; Dillon, Read; Merrill Lynch, Pierce, Fenner and Smith; Kuhn, Loeb; and Goldman, Sachs.[14] Significantly, none of these houses testified to the Ways and Means Committee's hearings on the original IET. There were three major reasons for this: caution motivated by conspicuousness, the wealth of domestic alternatives relative to foreign securities dealing, and the ease with which large underwriters could continue their business from overseas offices.

Bauer, Pool and Dexter, examining the tariff politics
of the 1950's, found that ". . . Wall Street played a small
part because it was afraid to use the power that it had. . . .
Contrary to the myth that Wall Street runs America, we
found that the bankers there are even more reluctant to exercise their power in foreign economic policy than Dupont and
the Big Three of the automotive industry." They quote a
Wall Street consultant as saying: "The bigger the banks
are, the less influential they are. The only banks that
have any influence are the pipsqueak banks in the small
towns. Those are the bankers who know their congressmen."[15]
In the case of the IET, it was the "pipsqueak" foreign securities dealers who protested most loudly, but since they were
also, on the whole, situated in Manhattan, they did not
have the close rapport with a congressman that a small town
banker might have. Hence the lack of sympathy on the part
of the Ways and Means Committee for their largely self-serving
arguments against the IET. Furthermore, the larger investment banks had already been subjected to informal pressure
from the Treasury, which had "urged" them to make more
foreign securities placements public rather than private, since
private placements were bought mainly by U.S. institutional
investors, whereas public placements gave foreigners the
opportunity to buy the securities, thus reducing the balance

of payments effect.[16] A number of foreign issues had been abandoned or postponed because of pressure from the government.[17]

A second major reason why the larger dealers did not protest much was that there were so many domestic alternatives available. Even those of the larger underwriters who were heavily involved in foreign underwriting had large domestic operations in corporate and municipal financing, which could easily expand to make up for any lost foreign business. These were, after all, the "go-go years: when prices went topless."[18]

However, the third and most important element in the situation was that these large firms did not have to lose their foreign business. The underwriting documentation could still be done in New York, and it was only the actual placement of the securities which had to be done outside of the United States. For the larger firms which already had established European offices, organizational expansion to take care of placement was a relatively simple matter--assuming the buyers were there, of course. Their foreign placement business was given an added boost by the direct investment restraints, which sent U.S. companies into the Eurobond markets. By early 1966, an increasing number of these placements were made by the European (especially London) offices of U.S. underwriters.[19]

Kuhn, Loeb, for example, cites itself as "a leader in the development of the Eurodollar bond market." Following the IET, the firm managed Euro-placements for a number of large international borrowers from countries which were shut out of the New York market by the IET. Notable among these were borrowers from Austria (e.g., the Republic of Austria); Denmark (e.g., the Kingdom of Denmark); Italy (e.g., Alfa Romeo, Ente Nazionale Idrocarburi); Norway (e.g., City of Oslo); Spain (e.g., Instituto Nacional de Industria) and Sweden (e.g., the Swedish Investment Bank).[20] Dillon, Read notes that it, too, was active in managing placements of securities from countries subject to the IET, particularly from France, Italy, Germany, Japan, Norway, South Africa and Spain.[21] Both of these banks were also extensively involved in foreign underwriting for U.S. corporations, following the direct investment controls.

Most of the reasons which apply to the supply side of the foreign securities market also can explain the lack of any great opposition on the demand side. In addition, the large-scale buyer of a foreign security was exempt from the IET if more than 10 percent of the voting stock in the corporation was purchased (i.e., the purchase constituted a direct investment).

In 1965, the Gore Amendment brought commercial banks under the Act with a provision applying the IET to long-term bank loans. Again, the advantages and disadvantages of size served to mute opposition. The official position of the American Bankers Association was that ". . . we have opposed the Gore Amendment all along; if it is in the public interest and necessary, the banking system will abide by it."[22] Since the amendment did not apply to loans made from foreign branches and subsidiaries, it did not unduly hurt those banks which could expand their branch deposits or subsidiary capitalization from non-U.S. sources. Bankers Trust was the first to tap the Eurobond market for a subsidiary, raising $20 million in convertible debentures for Bankers International (Luxembourg) S.A. in 1966. The issue was managed by Dillon, Read.

The Voluntary Foreign Credit Restraints

The reasons why investment banks and securities dealers did not effectively oppose the IET may be applied in their generality to commercial banks and the VFCR program; indeed, the advantages and disadvantages of size were perhaps even more salient in the case of commercial banks. In addition, commercial banks operated in an environment which reduced the incentive to resist the controls, regardless of the size of the bank.

Bankers did not, of course, welcome the VFCR program. Their preferred balance of payments instrument would

have been monetary restraint, and they frequently voiced their
resentment at the lack of government action to reduce the balance of payments effects of aid and military expenditure.
While the New York Times described their reactions as "cautious but favorable,"[23] they were also asking the question:
why pick on us?

Yet commercial banks in general were reluctant to oppose the VFCR because of historical weakness, norms of
reciprocity with the Fed, and their fear of alternative
measures. Commercial banks have traditionally been weak
lobbyists compared with other business groups. This is partly
a question of broad social norms and values: banks have
a very "special" role to play in the economy, a role laden
with moral connotations which make it rather unseemly for
the banker to lobby legislators or regulators (or at least
to be seen lobbying). For a variety of reasons, legislators
tend to react adversely to bank lobbyists: they see bankers
as advocates of high interest rates (which the legislator's
constituents do not like), they consider it improper for
banks to lobby and, not least of all, banks are unwilling
or unable to give the kind of benefits to a legislator that
many industrial corporations eagerly offer.

Furthermore, bankers had some reason to fear what
might be the alternatives to capital controls. The American
Bankers Association, in aggregate, was much against devaluation

or any change in the status of gold.[24] The few bankers who advocated such alternatives (namely Chase's Rockefeller and Bank of America's Peterson) were publicly denounced by both peers and subordinates within their own banks.[25]

In the case of the Fed, there are strongly established norms of reciprocity which inhibit bank resistance. The Fed offers benefits to banks--it is a lender of the last resort and will frequently alter regulations to avoid hurting growth areas in banking (e.g., Regulation Q, limiting interest rates, was frequently raised during the 1960's so as not to kill the growing market for Certificates of Deposit).[26] Yet the Fed can also withdraw benefits and refuse certain privileges, such as those relating to the establishing of foreign branches or subsidiaries. The Fed also had a great deal of freedom in administering and granting exemptions from the VFCR program; in 1968 it chose not to make the program mandatory. Business Week noted how this established relationship made regulation easier:

> The bank program is an administrator's dream, compared to the nightmare that Connor faces. Relatively few banks control the bulk of dollar outflow and inflows: Connor must ride herd on several hundred corporations. The banks are accustomed to being regulated, and a first-class reporting system long has been in existence. Each bank has a precise target, and its performance can be measured easily against the goal--which is to keep foreign loans from rising above 105% of the amount outstanding on Dec. 31, 1964.[27]

The other side of this relationship was, naturally,

a certain amount of leniency, reinforced by socialization
and cross-fertilization (particularly between the New York
banks and the New York Fed). Bankers were reported to be
". . . pleasantly surprised by the /V̄FC R̲7 guidelines."[28]
Discussions with the banks began in late 1964 with talks
involving Hayes (of the New York Fed), Dillon and (among
others) Walter Wriston of Citibank. The discussions were mainly
technical, concerning certain omissions desired by the banks
(e.g., foreign branch loans). Early in February, Martin
told the twelve largest banks the gist of the coming
program.[29] Since the Fed itself was not happy about the
controls, it had little incentive to be harsh.

This may be reflected in the ample leeway for further
expansion under the guidelines during the first three years
of the VFCR: $321 million in 1965, $911 million in 1966 and
$1204 million in 1967.[30] This does not necessarily mean
that banks were not reducing foreign credits below the level
they would have desired, or that potential borrowers were
not being turned away because of the program, but it does
suggest that, in the aggregate, banks were finding alternative methods of making foreign loans.[31]

Several of the reasons offered above for the general
lack of opposition to the VFCR obviously apply in particular
to the large banks (e.g., preliminary consultation on the
guidelines). The large banks had two major additional

incentives to comply with the VFCR: they were politically
vulnerable and they could circumvent the immediate effects
of the controls. Populist dislike of bankers can be
traced back to the Revolutionary War.[32] Franklin Roosevelt's
inaugural address blamed bankers for the speculative over-
production which he saw as responsible for the Depression:
". . . the money changers have fled from their high seats in
the temple. . . . We may now restore that temple to the
ancient truths."[33] Kennedy is widely cited as having
disliked bankers; he believed that bankers had started the
gold crisis of 1960 to prevent his election.[34] President
Johnson also had a populist's dislike of bankers (and big
enterprise in general). In response to the January 1968
program (which gave the Fed the option to make the VFCR mandatory), the American Bankers Association sent a telegram to
the President voicing their "deep misgivings," but tactfully
adding that they would "cooperate fully."[35]

The major reason for the lack of bank opposition to
the VFCR remains to be examined: the ability to shift lending
activities to branches and subsidiaries outside of the United
States. Again, this was a movement largely dependent on
size. There were two primary vehicles for avoiding the VFCR:
establishing subsidiaries or branches. A large bank holding
company has an organizational structure much like the one in
Figure 5.1.[36]

Figure 5.1. International Holding Company

Organization

```
                    ┌─────────────────────┐
                    │U.S. holding company ├───────────┐
                    └─────────────────────┘           │
┌─────────────────────────┐                           │
│Domestic & foreign nonbank│          ┌────────────────┴─┐
│subsidiaries (leasing,    │          │U.S. parent bank  │
│factoring, REIT's, etc.)  │          └──────────────────┘
└─────────────────────────┘            │              │
        ┌──────────────────────────┐   │              │
        │U.S. Edge Act subsidiary  │   │     ┌────────────────┐
        └──────────────────────────┘          │Foreign branches│
┌──────────────────┐        ┌──────────────────┐
│Foreign Investment│        │International      │
│Bank subsidiary   │        │Consortia Banks   │
└──────────────────┘        └──────────────────┘
```

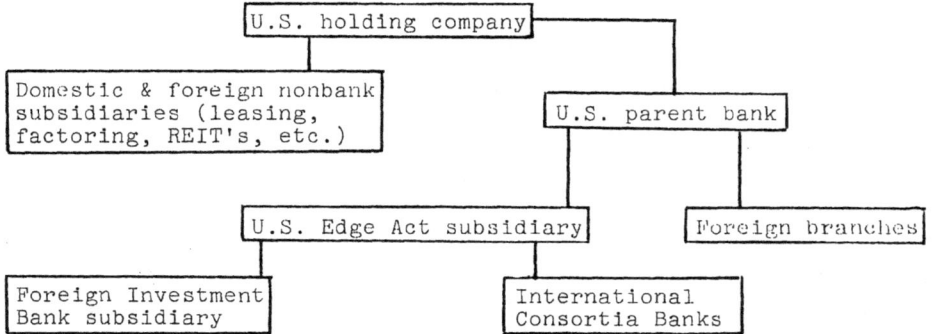

Under the original VFCR, banks' foreign loans were limited to a 1964 lending base, which itself discriminated against banks which were small and/or new. However, the VFCR guidelines specifically excluded foreign branch loans, which grew rapidly after 1964. Theoretically, this path was open to any U.S. bank, but in practice it discriminated in favour of the larger banks--they found it easier to get deposits (a depositor would naturally rather have a Euro-dollar deposit at Citibank than at a small Texas bank he had never heard of before then), and they did not have to rely entirely on the interest spread between lending and borrowing rates to remain profitable. Since the Eurodollar spread was, during most of the 1960's, less than the domestic interest spread in the United States, foreign branches which had to make profits solely on the spread found it rather tough going, and many were forced into being merely money brokers (i.e., taking less risk) rather than real borrowers and lenders. This was a problem which especially afflicted the small banks, since the larger (and older) foreign branches could not only buy liabilities at a lower rate, but had developed other local business to help raise earnings (e.g., financial management, merchant banking, etc.). Smaller banks which lacked either this deposit base or local business found themselves borrowing at higher inter-bank rates and lending in syndicates, both of which reduced their profits. Larger branches could earn money on a wider range of banking activities and could pick up more low-interest deposit liabilities and lend on their own, producing higher yielding assets and bigger profit margins.[38]

The effect which the VFCR was having on bank competition was not lost on the Fed:

> We have recognized all along that this program, as well as other programs, has involved some problems. The Board has been increasingly concerned about the incidental impact of this program upon the competitive position of the banks. Basing the program upon a situation prevailing at a particular date tended to "freeze" the competitive situation. While this was not desirable, it was not easily avoidable and was acceptable for a temporary program. However, as the program has been carried forward, possible distortions in competitive positions and, more basically, in the allocation of resources become more and more important.[39]

The other way in which banks could expand their
foreign operations in spite of the VFCR was to use their
Edge Act subsidiaries (through which they could engage in
overseas commercial <u>and</u> merchant banking in wholly or
partially owned foreign subsidiaries).[40] These subsidiaries
enabled the banks to perform investment banking functions
from which they were excluded in the United States by the
Glass-Steagall Act of 1933. This kind of activity is relevant to bank responses to the VFCR because the placement of
long-term debt securities was a partial substitute for re-
newable short-term bank loans (these so-called "roll-over
credits" became a common method of Euro-financing during the
1960's).[41]

The only major obstacle to using merchant or investment banking subsidiaries, rather than branches, to escape the
VFCR, was that subsidiaries require capitalization. This
must come either from the parent corporation, internal genera-
tion (assuming the subsidiary already exists) or from borrowings on the international capital markets. All of these
sources provided obstacles to small and/or new banks: direct
capitalization from the parent was limited by the voluntary
direct investment controls (see the following section), their
retained earnings and depreciation would have been low (if
they existed at all), and their ability to borrow long-term
in the international capital markets was limited by the

selectivity of demand in the Eurobond markets.

Foreign Direct Investment Controls

The response of companies to the voluntary direct investment controls of 1965 was one of cautious disapproval. Shortly after its inception, the New York Times polled a sample of chief executives from the 600 affected companies. Their responses (aside from pointing out that their particular company was actually helping the balance of payments) were fairly uniform, focusing on three points: firstly, the balance of payments is benefited, in the long term, by foreign investment; secondly, why pick on capital flows rather than the "real" cause of the problem (viz., government expenditure)?; and thirdly, their competitive position vis-à-vis foreign companies would be hurt.[42] Their criticisms were given suitable support from studies by the National Industrial Conference Board and the U.S. Council of the International Chamber of Commerce, both of which emphasized the complementarity of foreign investment and U.S. exports, and the need to maintain a competitive position in foreign markets (i.e., reduction in foreign investment would mean lost markets, not more exports).[43] The Machinery and Allied Products Institute and the National Association of Manufacturers also rushed to the breach with studies supporting the arguments noted above.[44] Business did not, however, attempt any kind of massive lobbying against the controls.

As in the case of the banks, fear of alternatives and more strict measures was one reason for this timidity. Foreign direct investors had already suffered from tax reforms in 1962, which repealed tax deferrals on the undistrib- uted earnings of foreign subsidiaries (i.e., removing an incentive not to repatriate profits),[45] and a failure to cooperate "voluntarily" could bring mandatory controls--a measure which Administration officials pointedly refused to rule out.[46] There was also the implicit threat of with- drawal of government purchasing orders.[47] The President of Pfizer was the only industrial executive to testify against the controls to the Senate Banking and Currency Committee in its mid-1965 hearings on the balance of pay- ments, and was congratulated by Senator Muskie, who commented that ". . . there has been some reluctance on the part of the business community to do that for reasons which I suppose are understandable."[48]

Larger companies were particularly vulnerable to pressure. In 1960, when Ford bought a controlling interest in Ford U.K. and Treasury Secretary Anderson telephoned McNamara in a vain attempt to prevent the purchase, McNamara could cheerfully ignore the request.[49] This situation rapidly changed. Chrysler's purchase of Simca in 1963 attracted adverse publicity.[50] When General Motors

announced that it was going ahead with a vehicle plant in
Belgium, after the announcement of the voluntary program,
it received a great deal of criticism, notably from Congress.
It was left to Secretary Dillon to point out that GM was
really a "victim of its own poor public relations," since
most of the financing was from non-U.S. sources.[51]

Oil companies were especially nervous. Standard Oil
(New Jersey) sent to Administration officials and produced
for Congressional committees a set of figures showing how
Standard Oil's international transactions were a net benefit to the balance of payments: for 1963, total receipts
(60 percent of which were profit remittances) exceeded total
outflow payments (55 percent of which were net oil imports)
by $360 million.[52]

Political vulnerability was only one of the incentives for compliance where size was of importance. Size
also provided advantages which reduced the incentive to
resist the controls: a say in the administration of the
program, including rules which favoured large and established foreign investors, and a wider array of financing
alternatives. The first, a certain degree of interest
osmosis between the Commerce Department and its Advisory
Committtee of business executives, will be discussed in
chapter six. Smaller firms lacked the influence channels to
change policy and the organizational capacity to find ways

around it.

Once the guidelines were established the major advantage for larger firms was in financing alternatives. The
relevant aspects of the financial situation of a typical subsidiary is illustrated in Figure 5.2.

Figure 5.2. The Financial Structure of
Foreign Direct Investment

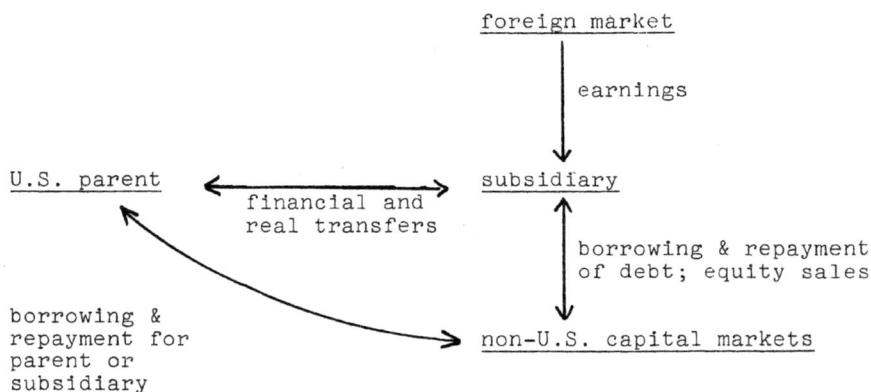

In terms of Figure 5.2, the voluntary controls, throughout their annual revisions, asked companies to:

(1) reduce net financial transfers to the subsidiary
(i.e., reduce direct investment outflows to and increase
remittances from the subsidiary);

(2) increase net real transfers to the subsidiary

(i.e., export to it but don't import from it) and to foreign markets generally;

(3) raise subsidiary earnings by developing new markets (i.e., internal financing of subsidiary expansion);

(4) borrow in non-U.S. capital markets, or, if possible, sell equities in foreign subsidiaries. Despite possible contradictions in these guidelines (e.g., the request to finance subsidiary expansion from retained earnings, but to also repatriate these earnings), large firms had a distinctive advantage: the base point allowance for financial transfers to subsidiaries and access to non-U.S. financial markets.

The base period adopted (1962-64) obviously favoured established foreign investors, and especially those that either had had the insight to anticipate controls or who had previously "overinvested." As early as September 1963, "business circles" reported that they were accelerating direct foreign investment in anticipation of contorls. The Commerce Department was "flashing a warning light" to them, though it is not clear, in the light of Commerce's position, whether the warning was to encourage them to do it quickly or not to do it at all.[53] Surveying foreign investment plans in mid-1964, Business Week found that even industries not expecting rapid foreign market growth were planning substantial increases in direct investment.[54] During the spring of 1965, companies

were again reportedly "rushing" capital out before the
Commerce Department could give them any explicit guidelines.[55]

The overinvestors were those who, for whatever
reasons (e.g., short-term tax advantages, market defense,
overestimation of market potential), had invested more than
they now desired and wished to slow down foreign investment.
Heller and Willatt, citing a Commerce Department study,
note that new American investments in Europe made since
1960 lost $80 million in aggregate in 1966.[56] Houthakker
was probably alluding to the same report when he told the
Williams Commission that the rush of U.S. capital to Europe
was "excessive from the point of view of profit considerations."[57] A recent empirical study of the decreasing rate
of return on U.S. investments appears to confirm this, concluding that the phenomenon was "real" in the sense of not
merely reflecting the immaturity of the investments (i.e.,
the lower aggregate rate of return one would expect with
newer investments.)[58] Insofar as taxation was a motive for
overinvestment, this incentive had been partly removed by
tax changes in 1962; and furthermore, corporations may
have begun to realize that tax avoidance may not be a profitable criterion for foreign investment beyond the short term.[59]

A major effect of the controls was to push U.S.
companies into the Eurodollar, Eurobond and, to a lesser
extent, national securities markets for debt and equity

issues. However, U.S. companies not only had to have
established reputations to tap these sources, but they had
to be able to absorb the frequently higher debt servicing
costs. The largest companies could float Eurobond issues at
not much more than domestic U.S. rates.[60] Others had to
utilize revolving short-term credits in the Eurodollar
market, at a higher borrowing cost.[61] The high debt/equity
ratios this produced did not hurt the parent corporation's
balance sheet, as long as the parent did not guarantee
the debt. By 1968, U.S. corporate international issues
constituted 58 percent of the Eurobond market, compared with
34 percent in 1965.[62]

The large U.S. Eurobond borrowers could make their
issues even more attractive by establishing financial subsidiaries in tax haven countries, so that foreign purchasers
could avoid U.S. withholding tax or interest income paid to
foreigners. Among the first to do this in 1965 were Monsanto,
Standard Oil (Indiana), American Cyanamid, U.S. Rubber, Gulf
Oil and Socony Mobil.[63]

As the Euromarkets began to get "crowded" in 1966-67,
these large companies were able to increase their dominance
by offering debt securities convertible into the common stock
of the parent corporation. Convertible issues rose from
43 percent of U.S. corporate international issues in 1965
to 60 percent in 1967. In 1968 convertibles totaled

$1642 million as compared with $593 of straight debt,[64]
largely in response to the more stringent mandatory capital
controls.

Foreign equity issues did not prove to be a feasible
way of raising capital since, until 1969, the were counted
as part of capital transfers (since the foreign buyer could
sell the equity in the United States), and because they had
to be sold at a discount to induce buyers to purchase
shares which could be more easily purchased in New York.[65]
This lack of an equity alternative also discriminated against
small companies. In the domestic securities markets, a small
company can at least have shares listed on, say, the American
Stock Exchange, if it is not large enough to issue debt
securities. In the case of off-shore financing, debt issues
were the only major vehicle available beyond internal sources.
Nor were local, or national, equity markets a suitable financing
alternative: governmental controls on dividend and equity
payments are common outside the United States (especially in
weak currency countries), it is easy to convert a loan into
equity if necessary (but not vice versa) and also because
equity financing often produces tax penalties not incurred
with loans.[66]

Lack of opposition to the controls due to the avail-
ability of alternatives should be distinguished from elements
in the situation which might either produce an ambiguity of

interest such that the firm takes no stand at all, either for or against the controls, or which might make the firm actually favour controls.

In examining the tariff issue, Bauer, Pool and Dexter noted that "Large firms have a more complex and wider range of interests" and are therefore less likely to take a firm stand on an issue of public policy which affects the firm.[67] Harms suggests that one result of the voluntary program was to increase the organizational power of the European subsidiary managers, who for the first time became aware of their important contribution to the company as a whole.[68] This would, of course, depend on the extent to which the subsidiary manager's incentives were structured: if his salary (or bonus) was tied to the subsidiary profit (a not uncommon phenomenon), he might be expected to oppose the capital controls insofar as off-shore or local financing was more expensive. However, this conflict of interest would have been more acute for the manager of the subsidiary of a non-major U.S. corporation, since certain types of large corporation could borrow more cheaply in the Eurobond markets than in the domestic U.S. market.[69]

On the other hand, there may have been forces working in the opposite direction. Where the organizational structure of the firm is more centralized, decision-making on methods of financing subsidiaries tends to get passed on to the head office. The more complex the financing situation, the more power that would pass to the head office. The President of Pfizer International told a Senate Committee that the controls were causing a power shift within corporations toward the management more concerned with domestic business, adding that ". . . I know from personal experience that there are very few U.S. companies where the international business is really regarded internally with the same interest and attention by the top management as the domestic business."[70]

In any case, the effect noted by Bauer, Pool and Dexter is apparent: size produced internal conflicts of interest which made it harder for a large, complex organization to be able to take an unambiguous stand either for or against the capital controls.

In cases where the firm was not stricken with internal divisions, it may even have seen controls as a positive benefit. Foreign direct investment tends to occur in industries which are both oligopolistic and innovative.[71] These firms would not only have had high base point allowances and easy access to international capital markets, but may have actually welcomed the controls insofar as they increased the firm's dominance in both domestic and international markets.

Horst has argued that foreign direct investment in many industries tends to increase the firm's oligopoly power within the U.S. market.[72] Where this is the case, the firm might

welcome controls on foreign investment as a means of maintaining
its domestic market power. For similar reasons, U.S. foreign
direct investment may reduce competition and increase
oligopoly power in foreign markets.[73] A firm whose only
major foreign market competitors (either actual or potential) were smaller domestic companies which had not yet
gone multinational, might welcome capital controls as a way
of maintaining both domestic and foreign market dominance.
An example of this type of industry could be the general area
of electronic microcircuitry and semiconductors. This is
a field where U.S. firms have had a technological lead (of
at least several years) over European and Japanese firms.
The largest U.S. firm is Texas Instruments, which has annual
sales of about three times its nearest competitor, National
Semiconductors. These companies, to the extent that they were
already established in foreign markets, may have welcomed
capital controls as a means of keeping out their immediate
competitors, which would have been smaller U.S. electronics
firms. Computers might be another example--the capital controls
would have had the effect of hampering the efforts of smaller
U.S. domestic competitors of IBM from challenging this
market leader in other countries, since IBM was an established
foreign investor long before even the voluntary controls came
into effect. A great deal of U.S. direct investment in
Europe has been in the high technology area, where the

major U.S. firms found European competiton weak and divided.[74]

Therefore any kind of control in capital exports from the United States could only have the effect of consolidating the market dominance of these giants.

It would appear then, that a major effect of controls on foreign direct investment (especially one where allowances are based on a previous level of investment) discriminates against small and/or new firms. The controls certainly did not result in disinvestment by any major corporation: among a sample of Fortune 500 companies which disinvested between 1967 and 1971, only 7.9 percent of them listed U.S. governmental controls as the reason for liquidating a foreign investment.[75] Major opposition to the direct investment controls did not emerge until 1968, but even then a good part of the clamour was from smaller companies in less innovative areas such as chemicals, food production, construction and paper.[76]

Having suggested why those groups which were directly affected by the controls did not act more vigorously to oppose the policy, attention will briefly be directed to two groups of marginal relevance: labor and academics.

<u>Labor</u>

It need hardly be emphasized that today, in the mid-1970's, organized labor is in favour of restricting U.S.

direct foreign investment, primarily on the grounds of its
effect on income distribution.[77] This awareness has been reflected in the minority statements appended to the Williams
Commission Report in 1971[78] and in the Burke-Hartke bill of
1972-73. The debate has focused on three related issues:
income distribution, trade union bargaining power and employment.

The income distribution argument has been presented
in its most sophisticated form by P. B. Musgrave, who uses
1968 data to demonstrate that, regardless of assumptions
about capital displacement (i.e., the extent to which the
foreign investment comes out of the U.S. capital stock and
is not replaced), labor's share of national income would
have been slightly over 2 percent higher than it actually
was in 1968 (77.2 percent) had there been no foreign investment.[79] The argument is, however, flawed insofar as it
presents a zero-sum game perspective. In addition to the
rather obvious point that what matters to labor is absolute,
not relative income, there are a number of reasons why labor
might not benefit from the constriction of foreign investment. Firstly, the rate of return on domestic capital would
be reduced, causing a reduction in savings, investment and
capital accumulation, thereby reducing both employment and
tax revenues in the future. Secondly, the attractiveness of
research and development would be reduced for "product cycle"

type foreign investors, having both direct and indirect effects on labor. Thirdly, the desirability of foreign investment from labor's point of view should depend partly on the extent to which the industry is capital or labor intensive. What is needed for more conclusive policy recommendations is a general equilibrium approach.

The question of bargaining power is also difficult to ascertain. Empirical studies which might show a meaningful correlation between wage settlements and size of foreign investments have yet to be published. The employment argument has also been inconclusive. A Senate report on the multinationals in 1973 lamely concluded that it could make no general conclusions on the effect of foreign direct investment on U.S. labor.[80]

These arguments are, however, largely irrelevant to the policy-making period of 1963-68. U.S. labor did not begin to criticize foreign investment on the grounds discussed above until the 1970's. During the period in question labor was in favour of the capital controls, but for different reasons: labor leaders saw capital controls as a way of forestalling domestic deflation as a means of balance of payments adjustment. The AFL-CIO supported the IET, but also added that it would not like to see direct controls on foreign investment[81] (perhaps because this could lead to direct controls on wages?). Testifying to the Joint

Economic Committee in 1962, AFL-CIO Research Director

Ruttenberg emphasized the long-term balance of payments

benefits of foreign investment. Glimmerings of labor's stand

in the 1970's may be found at this early stage: "While I would

not advocate strong restrictions on capital outflows . . .

capital investments to other nations do not necessarily benefit

this economy."[82] This was a rare and isolated comment on

the welfare effects of capital outflows. During the 1960's

the AFL-CIO position was that ". . . supervision of private

capital outflows is an essential mechanism to curb balance

of payments pressures without inflicting dangerous defla-

tionary pressures on the domestic economy."[83] Early in

1968, Walter Reuter pointed to the "unfairness" of asking

workers to moderate wage claims while corporations were

hastily exporting capital in anticipation of tighter

controls.[84] The initial reaction of the AFL-CIO to the

FDIP was one of approval.[85]

Thus, while organized labor now focuses on the direct

(primarily microeconomic) welfare effects of capital flows,

during the 1960's it approved of controls for indirect

macroeconomic reasons (viz., controls are better than unem-

ployment as a balance of payments policy). For this reason

it was in favour of the controls but not at all vigorously

active in promoting these measures. This lack of attention

helps to explain why, as the following chapter suggests,

the Congress played no active role in balance of payments

policy during the period 1963-1968. Whatever influence labor

had on the capital controls policy was indirect, insofar as

labor could obstruct the use of other policies--most obviously,

deflation.

Academic Economists

> This was the State's Craft, that maintain'd
> The Whole, of which each Part complain'd:
> This, as in Musick Harmony,
> Made Jarrings in the Main agree,
> Parties directly opposite
> Assist each oth'r, as 'twere for Spight;
> And Temp'rance with Sobriety
> Serve Drunkenness and Gluttony.
> Bernard Mandeville, The Fable of the Bees, 1705

Academic economists of the present day still, with

some notable exceptions, reflect the philosophical debates

which gave birth to their discipline. Modern economic theory

is still largely based on the philosophical premise of

Mandeville's poetic allegory: the only purpose of govern-

ment is to preserve the structure of society, within which

free market forces (". . . Parties directly opposite") should

be unrestrained so that they will ultimately produce a wel-

fare situation of Pareto optimality (". . . Musick Harmony").

The general consensus was, therefore, that capital controls

were undesirable both for ideological reasons and because

most market economists doubted their efficacy. There were,

however, distinct groups of economists as well as some notable exceptions to the consensus. Three major groups will be examined: governmental academics (those with formal or informal positions, either in office or in an advisory capacity), non-government organization academics (e.g., Brookings Institution), and pure academics (those with no apparent affiliation other than their university).

In reviewing academic opinions of the controls, two caveats should be noted. Firstly, the comments below are limited to the period 1963-1968. There has since been a movement of academic opinion in favour of controls, although not necessarily for balance of payments reasons alone.[86] Secondly, the reader might keep in mind that much of the academic criticism of the controls was misplaced insofar as it assumed that the purpose of the controls was to actually reduce foreign investment rather than simply shift the financing of it to non-U.S. sources.

The first group, the policy academics, were more important during the Kennedy years, when a number of academics fought for the President's ear. Most notable among these were Samuelson, Harris, Galbraith and Triffin. The Johnson Administration does not appear to have been at all receptive to this kind of informal academic influence, except with regard to SDR's.

Paul Samuelson of M.I.T. authored a pre-inaugural Task Force Report which advised Kennedy that the choice of policy tools would be limited by the balance of payments, and obliquely pointed to the need for more activity on the capital account, particularly in directing the application of monetary policy toward external balance. However, he also added that it would be "unthinkable" to allow domestic policy to be dictated by the balance of payments.[87] Privately, Kennedy's Economic Advisory Group advised Kennedy to devalue immediately upon taking office. During the following years Samuelson expressed his preference for devaluation several times. At a Washington symposium in the spring of 1963, with Kennedy in the audience, he argued that if the dollar were overvalued, "adjusting to that situation by running a slow-growth economy is a remedy worse than the disease."[88] Samuelson was against the IET not only because he saw it as a poor solution but because he also believed the cost of losing a great deal of the financial intermediary role of the United States would be great.[89]

Samuelson's preference for devaluation was shared by Tobin in the CEA, but no others of note. Seymour Harris, Kennedy confidante and senior economic consultant to the Treasury, rejected devaluation as unfeasible (since other countries would follow), believed that ultimately some kind of capital controls would have to be adopted, and favoured a tax penalty rather than direct controls.[90] While this was the policy which Treasury adopted, it is unlikely that Harris'

opinion provided much more than a convenient academic
rationale for decisions already taken.

J. K. Galbraith was the most fervent advocate of controls on direct as well as portfolio investment, at a time
when even the latter were barely palatable to most of the
President's advisors. He rejected the other major solutions
as inappropriate: the United States could not devalue because others would follow, liquidity creation would have to
be premised on the assumption that the deficit was a very
short-term phenomenon (which he believed was not the case),
and Galbraith rejected the belief (popularized in Salant's
Brookings Report of 1963) that European inflation would
correct the U.S. deficit. Galbraith's view, that capital
controls were an unavoidable measure whilst longer term
improvements were encouraged on the current account,
came to be widely accepted among advisors around Kennedy.[91]
However, since Galbraith had been in India until the fall of
1963, he could not have been directly involved in the IET,
although his opinions may have encouraged those who did favour
the measure. In any case, his main concern upon his return
from India was to oppose the proposed tax cut.[92]

Aside from academics who had direct contact with
Kennedy, there were others who had contact with top Admini-
stration officials, Most notable among these was Robert
Triffin, a consultant to the CEA (and Yale colleague of CEA

member Tobin). Triffin was not in favour of controls on
capital movements, which he referred to as "undesirable
palliatives and stopgaps."[93] However, as was noted in the
previous chapter, pressure on the Administration to take
action on the liquidity question was building up from many
sources, quite independently of Triffin's own ideas and his
advice to the CEA.

In summary, the influence of policy academics on
balance of payments policy during the Kennedy Administration
was marginal. This area of policy was closely guarded by the
Treasury, and insofar as policy academics were important,
it was more in the role of providing rationales for what policy-
makers wanted to do, rather than actually influencing the
decision-making process itself. Under the Johnson Administration, policy academics were virtually non-existent in this
issue area.

Of the group referred to as non-governmental organization academics, one of the most influential was Walter
Salant, director of the Brookings Institution study referred
to in chapter two. Given the study's assumptions (full
employment with price stability), the study optimistically
rejected the need for capital controls:

> From these estimates, it appears that long-term
> capital transactions of the United States will con-
> tribute strength to the basic balance. While it is
> true that the balance of payments could be improved
> even further for any single year by a cessation of

long-term capital outflows during that year, this
improvement would be more than offset by subsequent
losses. The U.S. balance of payments has already felt
the strain of adjusting to an increased level of
capital outflows, and now it is moving into a position
where it will reap benefits from these outflows. Only
in the very unlikely event of an accelerated growth
of outflow of new funds would long-term capital
transactions be a negative force.[94]

The Salant report was published at the end of July
1963, and while it reflected the general climate of optimism
which led to a piecemeal measure like the IET, it came too
late to have been a significant influence on the policy.
By the time that the decision had been made whether or not
to control direct investments, the assumptions of the
study were manifestly dated.

The consensus among pure academic opinion during this
period was against capital controls, arguing that controls
were either a bad policy or that they would not work, or
both. Preeminent among the "bad policy" arguments was that
which emphasized what damage controls might do to the
reserve currency role of the dollar. Kindleberger, Salant,
Depres, Kenen and Aubrey all maintained some variant of this
argument.[95] The reserve currency argument was often combined
with the assertion that the controls would not work because
of the fungibility of money. Halm has pointed out that
the two arguments may not sit well together: if money is so
fungible that controls will not work, then this same
fungibility should produce domestic capital markets sufficiently

integrated to make international financial intermediation
unnecessary.[96] One could, of course, maintain that money is
fungible enough to leak around controls but not fungible
enough to produce integrated domestic or regional capital
markets--since substitution between portfolio assets is
naturally easier than substitution between portfolio and
real assets, and since the social-institutional constraints
may differ in each case. However, one is then debating a
question of degree, and the argument loses its clarity.

Aside from the financial intermediation thesis,
many economists rejected controls simply on the grounds that
". . . the balance of payments is determined by macroeconomic relationships and should be controlled by macroeconomic policy instruments (specifically the exchange
rate and monetary and fiscal policy) rather than by microeconomic policies. . . ."[97] The trend in macroeconomic
theory--away from Keynesianism toward monetarism--also
tended to produce a rejection of controls on the grounds that
they would not work. Capital flows, the monetarist argues,
are the result of stock adjustments of assets between
countries, and changes at the micro-level can therefore
have no lasting flow effect on the balance of payments.[98]
Of the three major reasons for rejecting controls (transfer
effects, substitution effects and interest rate elasticity),
the first two are closely connected with the emergence of the

monetariest emphasis on stock adjustment rather than flows
in international finance.

The most widely known opponent of capital controls on
the grounds of transfer theory was Fritz Machlup,[99] who argued
that the U.S. deficit was a "transfer gap" of unrequited
financial transfers, and an artificial reduction in financial
transfers would not cure the deficit since exports would
fall and imports would rise (see chapter three above).
The only way to achieve fully effected financial transfers,
according to Machlup, would be to devalue the dollar. Even
if one could impose a sufficient number of controls on external transactions so as to inhibit transfer offsets, this would
not be restoring balance, but only suppressing the manifesta-
tions of imbalance.[100] One might note here the similarity
to monetarist arguments against wage and price controls.

The substitution argument likewise bears some similarity
to the monetarist position: capital controls will merely
produce s substitution of an uncontrolled capital flow for
a controlled flow. This result is implied in Cooper's
notion of interdependence.[101] The assumption here is that
there has been a secular increase in the interest elasticity
of capital flows. Yet capital controls could equally well
be rejected on the grounds that the interest elasticity of
capital flows is too low. Bell, Cohen and Aubrey did not
believe the IET would work because long-term portfolio

capital flows were determined more by institutional   factors.[102]

Those academics who were not unalterably opposed to
controls of any kind tended to suggest alternatives which would
interfere as little as possible with the price mechanism.
Cohen, for example, suggested that a better alternative to
quantitative controls on direct foreign investment would be
a scheme whereby the foreign investor would have to pay a
deposit with the Federal Reserve, for an amount of time to
be determined by the speed of the transfer equilibrating process.[103]

Thus, since academic opinion was generally against
controls on both ideological and analytic grounds, it would
be difficult to argue that they had any influence on the
evolving policies, with the possible exceptions of Treasury
consultant Harris and Presidential confidante Galbraith.
What academics did do was to begin setting a climate of
opinion which helped determine the policy which led to the
removal of controls after 1968, namely the policy of "benign neglect" (itself a product of the academic Gottfried
Haberler), the purpose of which was to achieve exchange rate
adjustments.

Digression: A Marxist Interpretation

It would be difficult to maintain that Marxist or
quasi-Marxist thought has actually influenced American policy,

yet the case of capital controls is interesting in this
context because it appears to contradict a basic tenet of
Marxist explanations, that the foreign economic policy of an
advanced capitalist state is dominated by the need to maintain an open world market in real and financial goods and
services. This is true both of those who see the policy as
a conscious choice and those who see it as a historical
necessity.

There are two major alternatives in making Marxist
theory consistent with history. Firstly, one can assert
that this was a case where "state" interests (the existence
of which Marx himself suggested in the Eighteenth Brumaire)
dominated the interests of individual capitalists, the
former acting in the real long-term interests of the system,
which the individual capitalist is too short-sighted to
perceive. Magdoff, for example, suggests that the overall
and long-term interests of the system may require resisting
the immediate interests of the capitalist class.[104] A
recent Soviet history of the international monetary system
also suggests that the capital export controls can be
explained in this manner: ". . . these private group
interests stood in opposition to the general class interests
of U.S. finance capital, to preserve the dominant position
of the dollar in the world monetary system. . ."[105]

Secondly, one might explain the apparent discrepancy

by distinguishing between big and little capitalists. It
has been shown that large foreign investors were not
necessarily injured by the controls (and may even have
welcomed them). A Marxist might claim that the possible benefits to large firms explains the controls, since, as Marx
himself noted in the Manifesto, strong capitalists dominate
weak capitalists, resulting in an ever increasing concen-
tration of the ownership of the means of production.

These two approaches could be synthesized: the
"state" imposed capital controls for the long-term interests
of the monopolistic elements in the system. This is probably
the explanation which would be offered by Mandel, who draws
together a theory of both state interests (viz., foreign
investment has eroded American power) and monopoly interests
(viz., the state must guarantee the profits of the mono-
polists).[106] While such theories are consistent with the
actual outcome, the means of explanation is rather strained.
A body of theory which can equally well explain a "closed"
and an "open" system by shifting between state, private and
systemic interests is so elastic that its explanatory power
is of dubious usefulness.

Conclusions

The major portion of this chapter was directed to the
question of why those groups directly affected by the capital

controls did not resist more vigorously than seems to have been the case. The critical variable here was size: large securities dealers, banks and direct investors were adversely affected by the controls, but not to a sufficient extent to make it worth the cost of a direct confrontation with government policy-makers. Therefore, a classical pluralist explanation of policy is inappropriate insofar as it suggests that policy would reflect a balanced aggregation of those affected interests which were articulate on the issue. The weight of those interests which were against controls would clearly have been greater than the weight of those interests who may have benefited--such as labor (which was not very articulate on the issue in any case), the academic community and perhaps the few direct investors for whom the costs of the controls were less than the positive benefits (e.g., helping to maintain their market power).

This is not to suggest that non-governmental interests had no influence. Rather, it is to suggest that their influence was indirect, or one of helping to "set the agenda."[107] The directly affected groups had the opportunity to influence the form and content of the controls. Others were able to help preclude alternative balance of payments policies (e.g., organized labor and deflation) or to influence the general climate of opinion which led to the removal of the controls (e.g., academics). The result

was a generally permissive environment for policy-makers on
the subject of capital controls. In the relative absence of
strong and vocal private interests, a great deal of scope was
left for intra-governmental disagreement in shaping policy.

CHAPTER VI

BUREAUCRATIC POLITICS AND CAPITAL CONTROLS

The previous chapter suggested that there was no
coherent domestic opposition to the capital control programs.
Therefore, if interest aggregation is to be an important
element in explaining the capital control policy, it must
be found within the interstices of the government itself.
The purpose of this chapter is to consider those groups which
fall into the general category of "bureaucratic politics"
as defined by Allison.[1] While this chapter does consider one
group of actors (viz., Congress) not normally included under
the rubric of the bureaucratic politics paradigm, the
term is still quite appropriate since, for various reasons,
Congress did not play a vital role in the evolution of the
capital control programs from 1963 to 1968.

Ideally, if the bureaucratic politics model were to
be a better explanation than a rational state actor model,
it, too, would have some predictive utility. This is,
however, difficult to establish, since the model itself
postulates a lack of predictability: "The decisions and
actions of governments are intra-national political resultants:
resultants in the sense that what happens is not chosen as

a solution to the problem but rather results from compromise,
conflict and confusion of officials with diverse interests
and unequal influence. . ."[2] At a lower level of analysis
there is a problem in even predicting the policy positions
of the individual actors, since although one can generally
apply the axiom that this is determined by institutional
position, Allison concedes that each individual brings to his
position his own "baggage" of norms and values.[3] Considering
also, as Allison admits, that the channels of influence ("action channels") can be altered by exogenous factors (such as
Presidential actions), the problem of devising a predictively adequate alternative to a rational state explanation is a formidable one. However, given this limitation,
the bureaucratic politics model can provide the basis for some
broad speculative predictions and, at the very least, can help
explain why a rational state explanation provides a good
predictive fit by breaking down the conceptual fiction of
the unitary actor to discover which groups' policies were
actually determining the national interest on a particular
issue at a particular time.

Most studies of bureaucratic politics have, to date,
been confined to issues relating directly to national defence,
and not until very recently have studies appeared which
apply the model to foreign economic policy.[4] Economic
policy is an especially fertile field for bureaucratic

politics theorists and their critics. Pierce, in his study
of fiscal policy formation, explores this theme, concluding
that "The President's role in the organizational process
is . . . less often one of making fiscal policy decisions
and more often one of managing the actual decision-makers or
deciding which of his advisors' decisions to accept."[5]

This situation is even more in evidence in the
area of balance of payments policy, probably because the
issues are in some ways more complex than domestic economic
problems and organizational "territories" are not so clear-
cut. The result, as former Federal Reserve Board Governor
Maisel puts it, was that "there was a failure to present the
President with a clear picture of the relevant costs of different options."[6] Hirsch (writing in the mid-1960's) quotes
an exasperated "balance of payments controller": "Businessmen convince me that private investment helps the balance of
payments, the State Department proves that aid is a positive
benefit, the Defense Department swears it is now operating
entirely in dollars and cents--funny we have a balance of
payments problem at all."[7] Representatives of private
enterprise found this situation equally irritating, as one
of them stated to a House Committee: ". . . it has long been
my conviction that the United States does not have an integrated commercial policy and is not properly organized govern-
mentally to develop and administer such an integrated policy."[8]

There were several formal arenas set up specifically for the discussion of balance of payments issues. Firstly, the Cabinet Committee on Balance of Payments Policy, which included representatives of the Treasury, State, Commerce, Defense, AID, Bureau of the Budget, CEA and the White House staff. The Federal Reserve was also a frequent participant. International monetary policy in particular was also discussed within a similar committee at the Under-Secretary level. While the form of this committee changed over time, it generally included representatives from the Treasury, State, Federal Reserve, CEA and the White House (usually from the NSC).

The various capital control policies directly involved three agencies: the Treasury (in charge of the IET), the Federal Reserve (for the VFCR) and the Commerce Department (for the voluntary and later mandatory direct investment controls). In an indirect way, the CEA was also involved in the debate over these programs. Most of the remarks below will be directed to these four groups. To the extent that other institutional actors become involved, their interest was generally a function of the effects of capital controls on their own interests and organization missions. In this connection, the Departments of State and Defense, and the Bureau of the Budget will be briefly considered. Finally, an assessment will be made of the role of the Congress in shaping the capital control programs.

The Treasury

The Treasury was by far the most important institutional actor in this case study, not only because of its direct responsibilities but also because, as Schlesinger notes, control over balance of payments policy "gave the Treasury its most potent leverage over general economic policy."[9] A major instrument of Treasury's power in the international monetary area was its chairmanship of the various committees involved, which were, as Roosa candidly admits, used to get other agencies behind the Treasury and so prevent them from going directly to the President. The influence of the Treasury was generally in a conservative direction--in both the Burkean and Keynesian senses of the word. Federal Reserve Board Chairman Martin usually joined this conservative bloc in opposing, under the Kennedy Administration, an amorphous "liberal" bloc consisting of most of the CEA (particularly Heller and Tobin) joined by the Labor Secretary Goldberg and David Bell from the Bureau of the Budget. While the Treasury was not always able to prevail in determining the direction of policy, especially after Fowler replaced Dillon as Secretary in 1965, Treasury's dominance over other bureaucratic actors prevailed insofar as both the VFCR program and FDIP received policy direction from the Treasury.[10]

From 1961 to 1964 the two most influential men in determining balance of payments policy were Douglas Dillon, a
former investment banker, and Robert Roosa, a former
economist at the New York Federal Reserve. It was Dillon's
conservative, Republican leanings which made him attractive
to the new Kennedy Administration. Dillon was, predictably,
against expansionary macroeconomic policies, horrified by
the idea of devaluation and highly sceptical of plans for the
"reform" of the international monetary system put forward by
the more persistent CEA "liberals." His general world-view
would suggest that Dillon would not have favoured interventions
in the private enterprise system, such as the IET. This is
probably true, since Dillon saw the IET as a temporary crisis
measure whose purpose was as much psychological as it was
economic: "We must demonstrate conclusively that we are
willing to meet the challenge before us."[11] Galbraith com-
plained of the reluctance of the Treasury to give priority
to the balance of payments over free market forces.[12]
President Kennedy himself is said to have remarked that he
wished the Treasury had suggested the IET earlier, since it
was "absurd" to be reducing essential governmental expenditures for the sake of private capital flows.[13] Dillon undoubtedly consistently adhered to the view he expressed to
the Joint Economic Committee in 1961: "It would clearly be

to our own long-run disadvantage, as well as contrary to our
principles, to impose general restraint on foreign investments."[14]

Dillon's Undersecretary for Monetary Affairs, Roosa,
was if anything more conservative than Dillon, and particularly contemptuous of "abstract" academic theorizers who
purported to have the perfect plan for reorganizing the
international financial system. He had, in Seymour Harris'
view, ". . . been exposed too long to the Central Bankers,
who had very narrow and classical views on monetary and
fiscal policy."[15]

"Practical men," as Keynes wryly noted, "who imagine
themselves to be devoid of intellectual influences, are usually
the slaves of some defunct economist."[16] In Roosa's case,
the defunct economist is hard to specify; however, his basic
plan was simple: to maintain "fixed and immutable parities,"
a fixed gold price and the role of the United States as the
world's banker.[17] In Roosa's view, fixed exchange rates and
the reserve currency status of the dollar were inseparable
issues, the latter precluding any deviation from the former.
"The special responsibilities of the United States as world
banker," Roosa told the Joint Economic Committee, "stem from
the fact that the dollar is the cornerstone of the world's
exchange rate and payments system. . . /providing/ the United
States with a greater flexibility in financing its balance
of payments deficits and, until recently, /giving/ the United

States greater freedom to follow the desired domestic and foreign economic policies than would otherwise have been the case."[18] Roosa's reserve currency argument against devaluation prevailed with such convinction that it carried him through periods when, for personal reasons, Kennedy would like to have seen him leave but was persuaded by others that this would cause a "run" on the dollar.[19]

Considering his views on the role of the dollar, it is not surprising that he was also against proposals for more liquidity in the system: the problem was "discipline" (i.e., adjustment) not liquidity. While he later acknowledged that the ending of the U.S. deficit might cause some liquidity problems, he abhorred the thought that it might come from a supra-national authority "bearing neither the responsibilities nor the disciplines of sovereignty."[20] Dillon agreed, and while both were at the Treasury the "liquidity shortage" proponents made little headway. At one point in 1962, Ball (State), Kaysen (Deputy Assistant for National Security Affairs) and Tobin (CEA) all tried to get "liquidity" out of the Treasury and into the State Department, without, needless to say, any success.[21]

Roosa's preferred strategy was, in his own words, "to begin a series of experiments" in cooperation with other central banks and finance ministries to "find ways in which the strength of other currencies could be mobilized to give peripheral support to the dollar," thereby "multilateralizing the reserve currency responsibilities"[22] (but not the benefits!). He did not believe that such informal cooperation could achieve any lasting structural adjustment, but saw it rather as the best holding operation in lieu of domestic demand policies.

Thus, Roosa's support of the IET proposal fits in with his general predilection for "tinkering," particularly since he saw this as only a temporary measure. Both Roosa and Dillon were quite adamant, in their Congressional testimonies, that the IET was not a "control":

> This country rejects direct controls on the flow of capital, not only because they would be inconsistent with our traditional and fundamental objectives of freeing trade and payments between countries, but for immediate dollars-and-cents reasons--they would cost us more than they could possible save. Our own money and capital markets are the most highly organized, most efficiently diversified, of any in the world. To try to impose controls over outward capital movements in any one sector of these markets, say, bank loans, would only invite capital flight through many others. And to try instead a comprehensive approach--clamping the cold hand of capital issues controls, or credit rationing, over the entire sweep of the markets--would literally congeal the bloodstream of American capitalism.

*   *   *

> To those who favor some administrative check on outflows of capital, or those who want some arbitrary forcing up of interest rates on bank loans and capital issues to thwart flows abroad, the answer must be essentially the same--neither the public nor the private sectors can be expected to take action which might handicap the functioning of a competitive, market economy, a capitalist economy. But there are many answers that can be sought short of that prescription. None will cut through the

problems with a single, decisive thrust; each will
seem minor in itself, but will gain decisive strength
by being an incremental part of a comprehensive total
effort.[23]

The above quotation, from a speech Roosa gave in 1962,

suggests that while controls in general were not to his liking,

he would not object to a measure which could be seen as part

of the price or market mechanism. The Treasury was pushed

in this direction in the first half of 1963 by several

factors: Kennedy's decision to opt for more fiscal expansion

(in the form of a tax cut), the increasing pressure on the

Administration to take a more positive attitude towards the

international liquidity question, and a rising outflow of

long-term portfolio capital.

The announcement of a comprehensive tax reduction

bill for 1963 gave the Treasury more cause to worry about

the balance of payments. In addition, Dillon was beginning

to worry about the effect of military expenditure and

foreign aid on the balance of payments.[24]

Treasury's reluctant move on the liquidity issue, which

was then being pushed heavily by the State Department and the

CEA, was in large part a hedging move against the failure of

the existing balance of payments policies. The import of this

for the genesis of the IET is that Dillon and Roosa probably

hoped that further action on the balance of payments might

slow down the demand for more liquidity. Dillon implied as

much in his speech to the annual meeting of the IMF in
October 1963: "The United States does not view possible
improvements in the methods of supplying international
liquidity as relieving it of the compelling and immediate
task of reducing its own payments deficit."[25] He also feared
that ". . . they /the Europeans/ are inclined to think
that we are just trying to find some way to avoid
bringing our own international payments into balance rather
than trying to really improve the world system."[26] In any
case, the rising salience of the liquidity issue marked the
beginning of a gradual decline in Treasury's power in the realm
of balance of payments policy.

Whether it was Dillon or Roosa (or perhaps one of
their aides) who first thought of the IET proposal does not
matter.[27] In early March 1963, Dillon and Commerce Secretary
Hodges reportedly discussed the possibility of controlling
foreign security issues in the United States.[28] Commerce
Department records confirm that the matter was extensively
discussed in a report of the Long Range International Payments Committee (LRIPC), chaired by Roosa, to the Cabinet
Committee on the Balance of Payments.[29] At LRIPC meetings
the State Department, Federal Reserve and the CEA had
been highly critical of Treasury's inaction,[30] and were re-
warded by being kept out of the framing of the IET proposal;
the CEA and State, at least, were not informed until two

days before the public announcement.[31]

A further factor in favour of the IET was the lack
of progress in Treasury's attempts to build a cooperative
spirit with its European colleagues on this question. As
Dillon told the Joint Economic Committee, he had been trying
to persuade the Europeans to take measures to improve their
own capital markets, but had made no progress. Whenever
Roosa visited Europe he was sent back with the rather un-
charitable suggestion that if the United States had a problem,
why didn't they just raise long as well as short-term interest
rates?[32]

The year 1964 did not bring encouraging results: bank
loans appeared to be substituting for foreign securities
issues, foreign direct investment rose from $1.98 billion
to $2.33 billion over the previous year, and the deficit on
government transfers continued upwards. The result was
the "voluntary" restraint program on foreign direct investment, announced in February 1965. Dillon himself obviously
had misgivings about restraining direct investment. In that
same year he told a Senate committee: ". . . whenever anyone
asks me what is the major reason you have long-term hope for
major improvements in your balance of payments, that /direct
foreign investment/ is the reason. It is this return from
this private investment which is abroad."[33] The decision
was apparently a result of "collective discussions" among the

Treasury, Federal Reserve and CEA, which overruled Dillon's preference for monetary restraint as an alternative.[34]

Dillon resigned shortly afterwards, to be replaced by Henry H. Fowler, who had previously been Dillon's deputy. Kermit Gordon, formerly of Kennedy's CEA and President Johnson's Bureau of the Budget, described Fowler as "direct controls oriented," suggesting that it was something of an in-house joke at the time, that one could always depend on Fowler to suggest controls as the solution to any problem.[35] Fowler's term at the Treasury was one of a slow decline in its power relative to Presidential advisors in the White House. Perhaps because of this Fowler devoted himself more to the negotations which led to the creation of Special Drawing Rights than to active adjustment measures.

Treasury lost control in two major areas. Firstly, Francis Bator began to take the initiative on balance of payments policy to, as Brittain, has noted, "nudge the locus of control for monetary discussions away from the Treasury."[36] The Cabinet Committee on the Balance of Payments changed from an instrument of Treasury dominance to being a body which made recommendations to Bator, who then presented options to the President. Secondly, the Treasury seemed to lose any idea of what the Department of Defense was doing with its own expenditures. By mid-1966 Fowler was giving a standard reply to questions as to the "temporary" nature of the voluntary controls: they will last as long as does the war in Vietnam.[37]

Despite its decline in influence relative to White House advisors, the Treasury became more and more in favour of capital controls from 1965 to the end of 1967, and for this reason was able to retain direction of the various programs. This is evidenced primarily in a Treasury study undertaken in 1965-67.[38] The study suggests that with regard to direct investment in Europe, the recoupment period (i.e., the number of years required for the transfer to produce a balance of payments surplus equal to the initial loss) varied from a minimum of 6.5 years to a maximum negative value (i.e., the loss would never be offset). In the case of Europe, the most obvious candidate for more stringent controls, the period varied between 6.5 and 10.8 years. Regardless of the validity of the study's assumptions, it undoubtedly provided a technical rationale for tightening the voluntary controls, on the presumption that it would be temporary and that a presumed improvement of the balance of payments (after the end of the Vietnam war) would compensate for the future period of lost recoupment earnings. Undersecretary Deming made this clear in a written reply to Congressman Curtis' enquiry about the effect of capital outflows on U.S. exports: Deming played down the export inducing effect of U.S. foreign investment, pointed to the

possibility of export displacement (on the grounds that the
export market would not, in many cases, have been lost to
foreign producers had the foreign investment
not been made), and mentioned the possible increase in U.S.
imports from U.S. foreign subsidiaries.[39]

Anti-foreign investment feeling among Treasury
economists seems to have been building up for some time
before the Hufbauer-Adler report. In defense of that portion
of the 1962 Revenue Act which reduced tax concessions to foreign
investors, the Treasury prepared a study which purported to
show that each dollar of U.S. foreign direct investment in
manufacturing industries yields only nineteen cents in annual
net exports to that subsidiary. In the case of Europe the net
export effect was calculated to be only four cents per dollar
of investment, and even this small recoupment would, the
report suggested, be offset by the extent to which U.S.
foreign subsidiaries are export displacing.[40]

Thus, with studies in hand, a control-oriented Treasury
could in 1967 present the following argument: the capital
restraints are not meant to actually reduce U.S. foreign investment, but only to shift its financing outside of the United
States; however, to the extent that investment is reduced,
one should not be alarmed because the beneficial trade effects
of foreign investment are small and the recoupment period
long. In terms of the transfer theory outlined in chapter

three, the Treasury position was that transfers are undereffected over a policy-relevant time period. Treasury's
enthusiasm for controls is well illustrated in a booklet it
published in January 1968, entitled "Maintaining the
Strength of the United States Dollar in a Strong Free World
Economy."[41]

While the actual decision to impose mandatory controls
(the FDIP) in December 1967 was probably made more in the
White House than in the Treasury (despite Bator's departure
in the fall of 1967), it was a decision with which Treasury
could happily go along. Prior to Bator's departure he had
initiated meetings with representatives of Treasury, State,
Commerce and the CEA. The principal figures in the actual
decision were Edward Fried (Bator's replacement), Fowler,
Deming, Knowlton (Assistant Secretary of the Treasury for
International Affairs) and Duesenberry of the CEA; and of
these the key ones were Fried, Deming and Knowlton.[42] The
administrative details were then worked out by John Petty,
Knowlton's deputy.[43]

The FDIP program was then given to the Commerce
Department for administration under a new Office of Foreign
Direct Investment (OFDI). There were two major reasons for
this. The framers of the policy did not want it to be too
harshly administered, and therefore preferred to have it
run by a department with a reputation for being pro-business

and anti-control rather than by a pro-control department.[44]
In addition, Treasury probably did not want the program
because it would be both unpopular and a drain on the Department's resources.

The Federal Reserve

The major role of the Federal Reserve was, of course,
in connection with the VFCR program introduced in 1965. The
Fed was for the most part opposed to controls for fairly
predictable reasons: it would have preferred a more judicious
monetary policy and it disliked unilateral measures, preferring cosy meetings in Basel where things could be worked
out in a more gentlemanly fashion. However, the Fed
acquiesced, mainly because of its lack of creative (as
distinct from delaying or veto) power, and partly because
of divisions within the Federal Reserve Board itself.

The Fed was particularly sensitive on the question
of monetary expansion during the period immediately after
the inception of the VFCR program, since it had been
subjected to heavy criticism by conservatives for being too
expansionist during the Kennedy period.[45] Federal Reserve
Board Chairman Martin claimed that the Fed had an obligation
to help the Treasury borrow, but added that ". . . there is
a reciprocal obligation on the part of the Treasury to conduct
its operations with recognition of the Federal Reserve's

responsibility for healthy credit and economic conditions, and for stability of the dollar."[46]

However, several factors may have made the Fed somewhat less inclined to oppose capital controls on these grounds. Firstly, Operation Twist--the best alternative the Fed could get--was a failure, and may even have worsened the long-term capital account insofar as lower long-term interest rates were an important factor in drawing foreign borrowers to the U.S. capital markets. The Fed had been intervening in the long-term securities markets since 1960. Secondly, capital controls can help to make monetary policy more effective under a fixed exchange-rate system, preventing capital flows which would normally offset the effects of monetary policy. In the long term, however, the controls may have contributed to a reduction in the effectiveness of U.S. domestic monetary policy, insofar as the Euromarkets (which, on several occasions, enabled U.S. banks to thwart the Fed's objectives) were stimulated by the controls.[47] Thirdly, the Fed had found interest rates to be a politically sensitive and dangerous issue with the Congress, which had a natural preference for an expansionary credit policy.

The second major reason for the Fed's reluctance to endorse capital controls was its general "internationalist" leanings. The main reasons for this bias are political socialization (e.g., participation in currency networks,

gold market management and routinized consultation with
foreign colleagues) and its perceived institutional mission:
to preserve "the integrity of the currency."[48] Both these
reasons would suggest a general antipathy to capital controls,
which were not only lacking in formal transgovernmental
cooperation but would fall into a category of actions thus
described by Martin: "We /the Fed/ would not favor
any action that might be interpreted by financial markets
as impairing the full convertibility of gold and dollars held
by foreign monetary authorities."[49] Capital controls would
not by themselves threaten this aspect of "the integrity of
the currency," but they could easily be taken as movement
in that direction--which, in fact, they were.

It should be noted that the internationalism of the
Fed did not extend to approval of the liquidity negotiations
of the 1960's, leading to the SDR. Liquidity was, in the
Fed's view, something to be controlled even more strictly than
the domestic money supply.

The Fed was not able to assert its policy preferences
for any extended period of time. While the Fed is technically
independent, it would be politically impossible for it to
consistently resist the executive branch of government.
What the Fed can do is to use its negative or delaying power
to play the role of Socratic gadfly. Former Board member
Maisel complains that this problem is especially acute in the

international sphere--while the Fed did take its domestic
responsibilities seriously, it allowed the President and the
Treasury to "misuse" policy instruments in international economics.[50]

This lack of political bargaining power enhanced the
importance of personality. Martin (chairman until 1970)
was known for his ability to stand up to Presidents, particularly for the famous incident in 1965 when Martin bluntly
confronted President Johnson with information that the Defense Department was being somewhat less than candid about
its expenditure figures, and told the President that either
monetary or fiscal correction was required. The President
demurred, and the Federal Open Market Committee voted to
raise the discount rate. Ultimately, however, Martin could
not resist monetary expansion.

Martin's situation with regard to capital controls was
much the same. His view was that "whatever temporary advantage might be gained for our balance of payments deficit by
controls over capital movements or other international transactions would be more than offset by the damage such controls
would do to the use of the dollar internationally."[51] With
regard to the IET, Martin was mollified by the fact that the
proposal came from the Treasury (a conservative ally at that
time) and happy that it was not a direct (i.e., quantitative)
control. His expressed opinion to Dillon was: if it has to

be done, do it quickly by Executive Order.[52] To the financial

press, his comment was that he would have preferred "other

means."[53] He had similar feelings about the VFCR program:

"It is no secret that some scepticism has been expressed both

here and abroad as to whether such a voluntary program can

succeed."[54]

What Martin wanted was, of course, monetary re-

straint. In the spring and summer of 1965 he delivered several

speeches in which he compared the economic expansion of the

1960's to that of the later 1920's, with the warning that

unless the political leadership acted responsibly with re-

gard to aggregate demand policies, there would be a

similar downfall. He specifically emphasized the importance

of a "stable dollar," warning that voluntary controls on capital

flows were insufficient to maintain such stability.[55] And

yet, if "responsibility" was absent in politics, Martin would

accept controls in lieu of an even greater evil:

> I would hope and pray that the time does not come that
> we will have to devalue the dollar. The devaluation of
> the U.S. dollar will not be the end of the world, but I
> think it will be a setback to our prestige and position
> in the world from which it is going to take us years to
> recover. I think it will also cause a slowing down in
> not only our trade but in world trade. And that is why
> I think that the Federal Reserve Board should do everything
> it can, along with the Administration, to see that this
> unhappy development does not occur.[56]

Other members of the Board, such as J. L. Robertson,

shared Martin's scepticism with regard to the efficacy of

controls, but not his preference for deflation as a balance of payments policy.[57] Another Board member, S. J. Maisel, also shared Martin's dislike of controls, but for a quite different reason: he saw them as inappropriate when used to maintain the exchange rate at an artificial level.[58]

The two principal dissidents from this view were Board members G. W. Mitchell and A. F. Brimmer. Of these, the most outspoken was Mitchell, Kennedy's first appointment to the Board, and one whose views more closely resembled those of the CEA "radicals" than those of his colleagues. Indeed, Mitchell may have been the first U.S. official to publicly suggest the idea of an IET.[59] In any case, he made his position clear to the Joint Economic Committee in February 1963:

> . . . the role of monetary policy can be. . . only of limited effectiveness in dealing with the basic balance of payments problem. . . In general, we need to explore the possibilities of various tax measures that might, consistent with our obligations as an international good neighbor, and with the status of the dollar as a world reserve currency, discourage capital markets that appear to flow 'uphill' to countries that are already capital rich.[60]

Another Board member who approved of the controls was Brimmer. A former Commerce Department official who had been in charge of the voluntary direct investment program, he came to the Board in 1967 and took charge of the VFCR. While Brimmer viewed controls as in principle undesirable, he was an eloquent defender of the program both to Congressional committees and within the Administration.[61] There may have been a certain "cognitive dissonance" effect at work here, since Brimmer had come from a department well known for its opposition to capital controls.

In addition to members of the Board, mention should also be made of the President of the Federal Reserve Bank of New York, Alfred Hayes, who not only sits on the Federal Open Market Committee but is in charge of the Fed's foreign exchange operations. In effective power, he probably ranks second to only the chairman of the Board himself. His views appear to have been similar to those of Martin. In a speech to the Economic Club of New York in April 1963, he said: "Any form of exchange control, whether by legal restriction or moral suasion, is dearly excluded if we adhere, as I am sure we will, to the sound principle of a free flow of trade and payments."[62] Two days before the IET was announced, he reiterated his views in a telephone conversation with Dillon.[63] In October of 1964 Hayes publicly "hinted" that he favoured letting the IET expire in the following year.[64] In his annual report for 1964 he suggested that the effects of the IET were being thwarted by substitution effects within the capital account (viz., bank lending, corporate placements of short-term funds abroad and increased foreign direct investment), and hence "for the period immediately ahead monetary policy might have to pay increased attention to international considerations."[65]

The predominant view within the upper levels of Fed hierarchy was, then, that controls were an undesirable policy measure. On several occasions the Board requested the President to order the removal of the VFCR,[66] and in 1968 the Fed declined to use the power given it to make the VFCR mandatory. However, the Fed did not have enough power to assert its aggregate preferences against either the Treasury or the White House.

The Department of Commerce

Of all the agencies involved in the control programs, Commerce was the most consistent and internally unified opponent of them. The Commerce Department, however, had no power. It has, as one industry critic said, ". . . been rather passive and let itself be pushed around by the Treasury for the past twenty years."[67]

Commerce was against capital controls in general because its organizational interests lay in other directions, particularly in the promotion of a favourable trade balance. In July 1963, probably in reaction to the IET, Commerce Secretary Hodges submitted to Kennedy his own three-point plan to improve the balance of payments: reduce U.S. anti-trust restrictions on overseas operations, promulgate regulations concerning the carrying of cargo on U.S. ships and try to increase agricultural exports.[68]

The new Secretary of Commerce in January 1965, John Connor, was equally anti-control. Business Week reported that he "plugged hard behind the scenes" for a voluntary approach to capital control rather than some of the more stringent measures which Treasury had proposed, such as a doubling of the IET.[69] He was, however, in a difficult position, since if he did not attempt to make a success of the voluntary controls, he would find even more repugnant measures forced on his department. This did occur, and once Connor had left the Administration he felt free to attack the control programs as a failure which should be scrapped by the next Administration.[70]

In attacking capital controls, Connor was at least in part responding to what Commerce Department studies had indicated was an important stimulant of U.S. exports. In a survey based on 1962-1963 data, the Commerce Department indicated that foreign direct investment and U.S. exports are complementary.[71] A former special assistant to the Secretary of Commerce repeated this argument to the House Foreign Affairs Committee in 1969.[72] Another former Commerce official, Jack Behrman, has repeated and elaborated the same argument in a number of journal articles.[73]

Secretary Connor tried, in vain, to persuade the Treasury to make the 1965 program a purely "informal" agreement with foreign investors, arguing that companies would

cooperate more if they were not tied up in "red tape."[74]
Commerce not only got a Treasury-devised formal program, but
had to administer it as well. While the Treasury well knew
that Commerce would not like its new mission, Treasury did not
want to divert its own resources to building the necessary
administrative structure, which already existed in Commerce.[75]
During the fall of 1965 The Economist's Washington corre-
spondent found a "fierce debate" going on about whether or
not to make the controls mandatory.[76] What had been happening
was that Commerce had been "dragging its feet," as Bator
phrased it, in putting the voluntary controls into effect,
and consideration was being given (presumably in the White
House) to not only removing the program from Commerce jurisdiction but tightening the controls to the point where they
would have been mandatory.[77] In the end, this did not
happen--the controls were simply tightened somewhat for
1966. The battle did not end here, since Connor frequently
made public statements to the effect that the controls would
end in 1967, despite denials of this by Fowler.[78]

The background to the Janury 1968 program was similar:
Commerce got a program Treasury devised but did not want to
administer. As a former OFDI official put it:

> The decision to introduce a mandatory program of re-
> straints on foreign direct investment flows came as
> a traumatic shock to virtually everyone affected by it,
> including the Department of Commerce. If ever an agency
> assumed responsibility reluctantly, this was the occasion.[79]

At this time, there was talk of abolishing Commerce altogether,[80] so the kind of "foot-dragging" indulged in during 1965 was clearly inadvisable.

In addition to its lack of bureaucratic power, Commerce was also probably weakened by its reputation as a business interest lobby. Connor himself defined his job in terms of "bringing business views to bear powerfully in the top policy-making levels of government."[81] The initial voluntary program (applicable to some 500 corporations) was to be guided by an advisory committee picked by Connor (himself just departed from the presidency of Merck & Co.), and consisting of representatives from Socony Mobil Oil, American Machine and Foundry, General Electric, Gillette, Whirlpool, B. F. Goodrich, First National City Bank, Pennsylvania Railroad and Goldman, Sachs.[82] On the advice of this committee Connor agreed to less stringent reporting requirements in October 1965,[83] which may have precipitated the suggestions that the program should be taken away from Commerce. Despite these threats, Connor again announced, in the fall of 1966, that he agreed with the advice of his business advisory committee, that the voluntary program would not be effective in 1967 owing to the inability of the participating firms to borrow long-term funds internationally at acceptable rates.[84]

The Council of Economic Advisors

The CEA, established under the Employment Act of
1946, has traditionally concerned itself with domestic rather
than international economics.[85] It was not until 1969 that
the CEA as a group began to play a major role in U.S. international monetary policy. During the Kennedy and Johnson
years individual members did express their own opinions on such
matters, but to the extent that there was a CEA "position"
on an international issue, it was the result of the domestic
implications of the question at hand. While the CEA tended
to be fairly cohesive on domestic issues--each President chooses
his own CEA--their opinions on international matters were usually more those of the individual.

Kennedy's CEA (W. Heller as chairman, J. Tobin and K.
Gordon) was concerned mainly with domestic expansion. As a
group, they did not like controls because, insofar as
domestic reflation did require balance of payments action,
they preferred other policies. As long as deflation was not
used to correct the balance of payments deficit, the CEA as
a group did not actively concern itself with the issue.
The CEA's only major foray into the international arena was
in commissioning a study from the Brookings Institutuion which
concluded that there was no need to deflate the U.S. economy
for balance of payments reasons because Europe was inflating
at a faster rate.[86] It was the tax cut proposal of 1963

occupied most of their time.

Heller's only comment on capital controls in his history of the period is that they are bad microeconomics--but better than deflation.[87] Gordon probably thought the same; in February 1965 he telephoned Dillon to express his concern over "gossip" that the Commerce Department was "not serious" about the voluntary program.[88] Of the three, Tobin was the one who was active, even somewhat conspiratorial, in the balance of payments area. First of all he found a rationale for not worrying too much about the external effects of growth: if domestic expansion is combined with increases in productivity the trade balance will not be a problem, and on the capital account side, reflation should stimulate capital inflows to offset any negative effect of lower interest rate policies.[89] As balance of payments measures did become necessary, Tobin turned to the idea of floating the dollar or, as a second best solution, more liquidity; controls were apparently not one of his preferred options. Tobin presented his argument for floating (viz., that it took care of the devaluation problem, of trying to prevent other countries also devaluing, by simply cutting the dollar loose from gold completely) to a White House meeting in September 1963, consisting of Kennedy, Galbraith, Dillon, Roosa, Gordon, Bundy, Ball and Sorensen. In Tobin's own account, Galbraith, Dillon and Roosa were too appalled to

think of an immediate rebuttal, since they were so used to
giving their usual argument--that devaluation was technically
impossible.[90]   It is not surprising that Tobin dismissed the
July 1963 measures (the major one being the IET) as "a few
new measures, none of deep import."[91]

Under President Johnson the CEA was again concerned
mainly with the domestic economy, especially with the need
for a tax increase, which both Heller and his successor,
Gardner Ackley, prodded the President to implement. The formal
CEA view of capital controls was that they are in principle
undesirable, but temporarily necessary since the United
States has been over-exporting capital and that such controls
are preferable to cutting "essential international commitments, interfering with international trade or restricting
the domestic economy."[92]   Privately, however, the CEA may
have opposed controls, particularly the mandatory program.
Ackley's opposition to the January 1968 program may have
prompted him to leave the Administration in February 1968.[93]
His replacement as chairman, A. M. Okun, does not even mention
the controls in his economic history of the period.[94]   Otto
Eckstein, briefly on the CEA from 1965 to 1966, says that he
regarded the controls ". . . to have been pretty much of a
flop. It was too easy to circumvent them and it was really
designed to make the balance of payments look good than for
it to be good. All of these measures delayed the coming to

terms with the reality of the American exchange rate."[95]

By the end of 1968 the CEA seemed to be moving toward Eckstein's view. They confessed that they found it ". . . hard to see, even in retrospect, any preferable strategies in U.S. policies to correct the deficit. The eclectic, ad hoc measures that were taken involved certain costs. But they maintained the strength of the dollar and the health of the world economy."[96] And yet, the report concluded, "work must go forward on the problems of liquidity, confidence and adjustment."[97]

Other Bureaucratic Agencies

No other agenices are likely to have taken a strong interest in capital controls. Whatever attitudes they adopted would have been a function of other interests.

The State Department was ideologically in favour of an internationalist position (i.e., minimum restrictions on trade and capital flows), but it also did not take much interest in economic policy. To the extent that State thought about the matter it probably favoured the controls. Firstly, because the general European reaction to the controls was positive (especially considering the alternative of trade restrictions), and State's position on balance of payments policy was to take the line of least European resistance.[98] Secondly, since State had an organizational interest in

preventing foreign aid being cut, it was doubtless happy to
see other items bear the cost of adjustment.

The Department of Defense was also in favour of
controls for the same reasons: it did not want its own
deficit producing activities cut. One interesting exception
to this overall organizational interest was the case of
Defense Secretary McNamara who, according to Gardner Ackley,
was "more violent in his denunciation of the whole idea of
capital controls than any other subject. . ."[99] McNamara
had, of course, been at Ford when Eisenhower's Treasury
Secretary Anderson tried to persuade Ford not to buy Ford
(U.K.) in 1960, for balance of payments reasons. At this
time, however, the balance of payments situation was not such
a serious threat to defense expenditure, and McNamara could
afford to indulge his previous interests.

The Bureau of the Budget, although playing an important
role in the fiscal policy "troika" (with Treasury and the CEA),
had little to do with the controls beyond being sceptical
as to whether they would work and frustrated at being unable
to get reliable data on capital flows in the first place.[100]
The Bureau seems to have found little to commend in any aspect
of balance of payments policy during this period. A former
officer in the Bureau's international division writes despair-
ingly of a lack of "careful preparation of staff papers for
review by agencies prior to taking positions on policy

181

matters," resulting in "Hurriedly called Cabinet level meetings
to discuss poorly analyzed proposals."[101]

Kennedy's Secretary of Labor, Arthur Goldberg, was
closer to the throne than most of his successors and may
have had some influence on the IET proposal, although in
which direction it is difficult to determine. One might
expect Labor to be in favour of restricting capital exports
on employment grounds, yet the Department's traditional approach
has been to look at structural market imperfections rather
than macroeconomic policy.

The Congress

Neither the House nor the Senate had any positive
policy input into the decision-making process on the capital
controls. The passing of the IET was basically a process
of "educating the Congress," as Stanley Surrey recalls.[102]
The voluntary controls did not require any legal form, and
the 1968 program was promulgated by Executive Order. There
were several reasons for this lack of influence: the low
level of effective private interest group pressure on Congressmen, a paucity of knowledge on the subject in the
Congress, the diffuseness of opinions within that body,
and the fact that from 1963 to 1968 Democrats had both the Presidency and a majority in both Houses. Hence, on the only measure to come to a vote (the IET), the voting was basically

along party lines. The use of an Executive Order for the
FDIP was probably indicative more of the need for speed than
of any great shift of opinion in Congress away from controls.
To the extent that there was any general sentiment in the
Congress, it was in favour of controls, particularly insofar
as the balance of payments problem was seen as the fault of
other countries not "cooperating" with the United States.

There was very little Democratic dissent against the
controls. The IET was passed by Mills' Ways and Means
Committee in 1964 with no difficulty--Dillon had taken the
trouble to privately explain the bill to Mills.[103] The
only Democrats to protest the voluntary program were Senators
Vance Hartke and Eugene McCarthy, who believed it would
reduce international liquidity and aggravate Britain's balance
of payments crisis at that time.[104] The 1968 program was
acclaimed by Democratic leaders in both Houses: Proxmire
(". . . exactly the kind of decisive and comprehensive
action called for. . ."), Reuss, Mills, Mansfield, Sparkman,
Smathers, Carlson, Bennett and Ullman.[105]

Republican opposition to the controls was weak and
divided. In 1964 a Critical Issues Council (chaired by
H. C. Wallich) suggested an "intensification" of the current
balance of payments measures.[106] The following year a
Republican Coordinating Committee condemned capital controls
as "ultimately self-defeating."[107] Senator Javits was the

most vocal public critic of the controls, although his
opposition was somewhat half-hearted: he first proposed a
"capital issues committee" as an alternative to the IET,[108]
as well as an "international conference."[109] and finally
settled on a pronouncement that the United States was
"drifting toward a new and dangerous form of isolationism."[110]
He continued to submit statements to Congressional
committees whenever the IET came up for renewal. The only
other prominent Republicans to take a stand on the issue were
Senator Dirksen, who was the only Republican to vote for
the IET, and Senator Bennett (the ranking Republican on the
Banking and Currency Committee), who praised the 1968 program.[111] Republicans in general, however, hit hard at the
1968 program for forcing the private sector to bear the brunt
of balance of payments adjustment.

Of the Congressional committees which considered such
questions, the Joint Economic Committee was the most fertile.
During the early 1960's Chairman Reuss favoured direct controls
on capital outflows for three reasons: Western Europe should
find its own capital, foreign investment reduced U.S. exports,
and it also led to foreign resentment.[112] He was critical
of Kennedy's "over-indulgent policy toward the EEC" and
recalled that "Had we in 1961, as I advocated, instituted the
controls on capital movements. . . we could have brought our
payments into balance much, much earlier and have launched

international monetary reforms much, much earlier."[113] Under
Reuss' guidance the JEC was moving from its advocacy of
direct capital controls to a more radical position,
first expressed in Committee reports in 1965, for a more
flexible exchange rate system. Reuss' earlier position (viz.,
barring new foreign securities issues in the United States
and direct screening of foreign direct investments[114]) was
only the means to a more far-reaching reform.

The one place where coherent Republican dissent did
appear was in the minority reports submitted with the
House Ways and Means Committee reports on the IET (and
each two-year extension). A group of Republicans, apparently
led by Thomas B. Curtis (Missouri) doggedly attached minority
reports to every Committee report on the original IET and
each extension of the bill. They made three major points.
Firstly, the IET was so full of loopholes that it would not
have much effect; the Candian exemption especially irritated
this group. Secondly, the IET "deals with a symptom, not the
underlying causes of the balance of payments problem" (viz.,
government expenditures), and does so in a way which "will
be detrimental to the position of the United States as
leader of the free world in the economic struggle against the
Communist bloc" (by abandoning the U.S. role as capital
supplier to the Free World).[115] Thirdly, they pointed to the
longer term benefits of foreign investment (debt servicing

remittances in this case). After 1965 these minority reports

included a brief condemnation of the voluntary programs.

What particularly incensed Republicans was the use of

Vietnam as a blanket excuse for all these programs:

> The question is whether this administration has used the
> time it has bought at such high cost to find a permanent
> and fundamental solution to the balance of payments
> problem. Furthermore, we have little confidence that the
> extension of the IET will spur the administration on to
> making the basic efforts that are needed to eliminate
> the deficit, including a reappraisal of U.S. foreign
> military expenditure overseas, and no avoidance of infla-
> tion at home. . . Vietnam may be in this picture to some
> degree, but the underlying problem is more than just
> Vietnam.[116]

Thus, while Congress did serve as forum for criticism

and new ideas it did not have any positive influence on

policy, barring the attachment of minor amendments to the IET.

Whatever power it had was negative--in the sense that Congress

would deny the use of alternative adjustment measures, such

as deflation (although whether Congress was responsible for

the failure to enact a tax surchage in 1966 and 1967 is

itself a major question). Since the end of the controls in

1974, Congressional sentiment has swung in favour of con-

trolling U.S. foreign investment, yet the issues now are not

primarily related to the balance of payments. During the

period 1963-1968, the Congressional role in U.S. capital

controls fits the image presented by James Robinson in 1962:

because Congress lacks the information and organizational

capacity to make quick decisions, its role in foreign policy has shifted away from initiation to legitimation and occasional amendation of executive policies.[117] It was not until after 1969 that there was a more bipartisan shift in Congress against the controls.

Conclusion

Taking the period 1963 to 1968, it was suggested in chapter four that U.S. policy-making on the sub-issue of capital export controls appeared to be perfectly consistent, in a predictive sense, with a constrained rational choice model. Yet an examination of intra-governmental politics indicates that disaggregation is necessary to explain what a rational choice perspective merely predicts. This explanation is twofold: during the Kennedy Administration international monetary policy was determined by the Treasury, or, to be more exact, by Dillon and Roosa; under President Johnson, power shifted to the White House, specifically to a group of NSC advisors around Francis Bator.

Dillon and Roosa saw capital controls as a temporary expedient until more fundamental adjustments were achieved which would maintain the Bretton Woods system in its existing form. Treasury became more pro-control under Fowler, but also lost influence vis-à-vis the White House, though retaining its dominance over Commerce and, to a lesser extent, the Federal Reserve. While Bator continued to promote the policy

of controls, his rationale was quite different: he saw
them as a holding operation until the structure of the
system itself was changed, to incorporate SDR's and a more
flexible exchange rate regime.

No other governmental actors had any positive policy
input. Their power was mainly negative: the Fed resisted
making the VFCR mandatory, Commerce probably slowed down
the introduction of the FDIP, and Congress may have helped
force the tightening of controls by its alleged reluctance
to raise taxes.

It might be noted that this explanation does not conform to a strict "bureaucratic politics" model, as defined
by Allison. Some positions were quite predictable (e.g.,
Commerce and the Fed). Yet others were much more personality
dependent--Treasury's shift to a pro-control position seems
to have been largely a question of Fowler's own personal
background. Secondly, during the Johnson Administration
bureaucratic positions were largely over-ridden by Presidential intervention in the form of Bator. Domestic politicization appears to dominate bureaucratic politics as a
policy determinant.

This chapter completes that portion of this thesis
which is directed to the domestic origins of the capital
controls in the period 1963 to 1968. The most important domestic
factors directly leading to the controls have been revealed

to revolve around the predominance of the Treasury under Kennedy and its decline under Johnson, as the source of decision-making on balance of payments policy shifted to the White House. While international influences have been brought into this explanation, they have so far been treated primarily as constraints on domestic policy-making. The following chapter will attempt to examine, in a more systematic fashion, the role of international influences during the formative period of U.S. capital controls.

CHAPTER VII

THE INTERNATIONAL FRAMEWORK: FOREIGN ATTITUDES

AND REACTIONS TO U.S. POLICY

In a very real sense the balance-of-payments adjustment problem--both for the world and for the United States-- in the 1958-67 period can be characterized as a struggle, both intellectual and real, to get the surplus countries of Western Europe to recognize that chronic surpluses were bad and to get the United States to reocgnize that chronic deficits were bad. For far too long, we continued to say three things: (a) our deficit was good for the world; (b) it really was not very important anyway; and (c) at the same time we apologized for being in deficit. For far too long, Western Europe continued to say: (a) the United States should correct its deficit; (b) Europe had no responsibility for taking compensating action; and (c) proper demand management in the United States would do the whole job.[1]

The question of to what extent the decisions to impose capital controls were a result of pressures originating outside of the United States is a particularly difficult one to answer, since international financial diplomacy generally takes place in a form which is difficult for students of the subject to uncover. As The Economist has put it: "In financial diplomacy the usual way of doing things is for a finance minister or central banker to amble across to a colleague after a dinner party to inquire casually what would be the reaction if his government did this or that."[2] This problem of analysis is particularly acute in the case of U.S.

capital controls since, with a few exceptions, they were not
the subject of formal inter-governmental representations
resulting in official statements of policy, as in the
case of the long negotiations leading to the SDR agreement
of 1967. While several countries (notably Canada and Japan)
took clear stands on the question of U.S. capital exports,
the attitude of the most influential group of countries
on this issue, Western Europe, was much more ambivalent and
ambiguous.

Since the international aspect of capital controls was
primarily a European-American dialogue, this group will be
examined first. Canada and Japan will then be considered,
as the countries which achieved much of what they desired
with regard to the capital controls. Less developed countries
were largely exempted from the controls. A fourth group of
countries was that which neither desired the controls, nor
achieved any significant concessions (e.g., Australia).
Finally, consideration will be given to the possible influence
of international organizations, both formal (e.g., the International Monetary Fund) and informal (e.g., the OECD's
Working Party Three).

Western Europe

The 1960's was a period of increasing European
pressure on the United States to take action to correct its

balance of payments deficit. Yet it was the European

countries which contributed most to the problem: the huge

outflows of portfolio capital in 1962-3 was largely to European

sources, and Europe was a major recipient of both U.S. bank

loans and direct investment. Hence the ambivalence of Euro-

peans on the balance of payments in general and, more specifi-

cally, on the subject of U.S. capital outflows: they wanted

the United States to correct its deficit, but by some means

which would not have any adverse effects on Europe. As Paul

McCracken suggested to a Senate committee in 1965: "There

is this sort of schizophrenia that one can detect abroad, in

being very concerned about our seeming inability to deal with

our balance of payments deficit, and yet at the same time

a little fearful that we might deal with it rather effectively,

and then what?"[3]

Insofar as there was a collective European mind on

the subject of U.S. balance of payments policy in 1962-3, the

consensus was to prescribe monetary deflation, since this

was the instrument which European governments themselves

used for the same problem. Realizing that this policy was

not going to be implemented, European governments and finan-

cial circles publicly accepted the IET with guarded relief:

> The reaction of official financial circles in Western
> Europe is that we have taken a step beneficial to our
> balance of payments, and that the program which the
> President announced on July 18 . . . will increase
> rather than reduce confidence in the dollar.[4]

While Europeans hoped that they would now be spared
from Roosa's schemes to use the dollar's leverage as a
reserve currency to exact more financing measures from them,
they were also sceptical as to whether the IET would work, due to
transfer effects and run-off sales of foreign held U.S.
securities. The latter phenomenon did in fact occur, foreign
holdings of U.S. stock declining until the third quarter of
1967.[5] The Economist's editors feared that world liquidity
would be adversely affected;[6] an opinion shared by few
Europeans at that time.

While there was no direct European pressure to impose
the IET,[7] European policies were indirectly responsible insofar as the IET resulted from large European debt offerings
in New York, the European refusal to take corrective measures,
and possibly the lack of success of the Kennedy Round at this
time.

The Western European move to currency convertibility
in 1958 marked the beginnings of a large outlfow of U.S.
portfolio capital, adding to the already large flows to Canada
and Japan. It was a rapid expansion of this outflow
beginning in the fourth quarter of 1962 which influenced the
timing of the IET, according to Dillon: ". . . we found
that the time had come when we just had to act, because
we could not stand a drain of this volume. . ."[8] At the time
the decision to impose the IET was made, it was known to the

Treasury that several hundred million dollars of new debt offerings from Europe and Japan were ready for placement.[9] Dillon was especially concerned about foreign government issues purely for domestic use (i.e., no direct transfer benefits to the United States), as they did not arise from any need for foreign exchange and merely reflected an interest rate differential.[10] The magnitude and distribution of these flows is reflected in Table 7.1

Table 7.1

Selected Net Outflows of U.S. Private Capital

Other than Direct Investments

(annual averages, $ millions)

	1959-61	1962-64
Transactions in foreign securities	698	917
Europe	180	91
Canada	293	481
Japan	37	95
Claims by U.S. nonbanks	882	1484
Europe	57	543
Canada	95	56
Japan	436	489

SOURCE: R. C. Bryant and P. H. Hendershott, "Financial Capital Flows in the Balance of Payments of the U.S.: An Exploratory Empirical Study," Princeton Studies in International Finance, no. 25, 1970, p. 18.

The figures in Table 7.1 indicate that the propensity
of U.S. policy-makers to blame Europe for these portfolio
outflows was somewhat unfair. What particularly irritated
Dillon and Roosa was that the Europeans were failing to develop
their own capital markets by maintaining stringent controls
on capital outflows. Borrowers who would not be accommodated
in local markets had nowhere to go but New York. Hence one
of the stated purposes of the IET was to force the Europeans
to develop their own long-term debt and equity markets.[11]
Lest the message be unclear, Federal Reserve Board member
Mitchell stated publicly that "If these countries are unwilling
to open their capital markets, possibly we should look
toward tax measures that might help to remedy this unbalanced
position."[12] Yet, European governments either did not receive this signal or did not take it seriously.

Other European-American problems may have also helped
produce the IET. According to Stein, European resistance to
tariff negotiations combined with the French veto of
Britain's entry into the EEC helped push the United States
to the IET.[13] In addition, one can discern the beginnings
of a deliberate linkage of defense and economic policy.
Testifying on the IET, Dillon noted that only Germany and
Italy were purchasing U.S. equipment to the extent necessary
to fully offset the balance of payments effects of U.S. NATO-
related expenditures.[14] In the following year (before the

Congressional approval of the IET), the Joint Economic Committee published a report which blamed U.S. payments problems
on certain NATO countries which were "enjoying more or less
a free ride."[15]

While official European reaction to the IET was simply
ambivalent, the directly affected groups were more sharply
divided. Investment and merchant bankers had a great deal
to gain in the forced development of national capital markets
and the Euro-markets.[16] Commercial banks in general were less
happy: they liked the oligopolistic, segmented structure
of the European capital markets and did not want to develop
long-term securities markets (either nationally or off-
shore) preferring to lend short-term to industry, therefore
retaining more control. The most extreme example of this
situation was that of West Germany, where three banks dominated the industry, performing both commercial and merchant
banking functions. Furthermore, the integration of capital
markets in Europe and the development of offshore markets would
(and did) attract competition from U.S. banks.

From the point of view of the borrower, the IET was
a double blow: not only was the New York market a cheaper
source of funds, but it could handle larger public offerings,
which many European markets could not. Borrowers faced a
"crowding out" problem compounded by the IET's effect of
pushing Japanese borrowers into the European markets.[17] The

situation eased as the offshore Eurobond and Eurodollar markets expanded to take placements which could not be made in
national markets, and as U.S. long-term bank loans to foreigners expanded. Yet the relief was temporary, since the
1965 restraint program brought U.S. corporations to the Euromarkets and the Gore Amendment applied the IET to long-term
bank loans.

There was little progress in developing an integrated
European capital market, partly because, beneath their official approval of the IET, European reactions differed both
between and within countries. England stood to benefit from
the IET, since it had not been a large borrower in New
York, and also since London was the obvious alternative as
an international offshore financing center. So did
Luxembourg, for the same reason. The same was true for
France: French firms had been discouraged from borrowing
in New York, and there were aspirations of making Paris the
new financial center of Europe.[18] However, the West
German government was probably not as happy, since the IET
posed a threat to the structure of the German banking
industry. The unhappiest major country of Europe was Italy,
having both a severe balance of payments problem and a high
degree of dependence on external capital sources.[19] Capital
market integration was a dead letter, among members of the
EEC.

European reaction to the VFCR was similar: they
believed that their own use of monetary policy for internal
balance was being thwarted by a more expansive monetary policy
in the United States.[21] While disappointed that the United
States was not using monetary restraint, they could accept
capital controls as an alternative. The extent of European
influence was probably no more than that attributed to it by
Fowler: "They can't tell us what to do, but we do feel
an obligation to try to make them understand why our policies
seem to be right from our point of view. . ."[22] The basic
issue, Fowler said, was whether the United States should have
to raise interest rates (primarily long rates) or whether
Europe should lower its rates, and while he "recognized" the
European concern about inflation, they could better solve it
with "sounder" fiscal policies rather than pressuring the United
States to exercise undue monetary restraint.[23] The day
after the announcement of the voluntary programs in 1965, Dillon
reported European disappointment to the President,[24] which
suggests that if there were any inter-governmental consultation,
it had been minimal.

While the reaction of European bankers was similar, they
probably welcomed the VFCR program as a means of protecting
their own relatively inefficient commercial banking system.
Some may have realized that the VFCR would eventually increase
competition from American commercial banks by forcing them

to establish local branches.[25] The President of Germany's largest bank, the Deutsche Bank, reportedly feared this effect.[26]

There were no significant national differences in reactions to the VFCR. Britain, the country that one might expect to oppose the VFCR, since it followed the recent Sterling crisis of 1964, was given special recognition in the VFCR guidelines, which requested banks to be lenient with special cases such as the U.K. (but still remaining within the bank's overall limit). In addition, the depth and sophistication of the City offered numerous ways of mitigating the effects of the VFCR; as a Bank of England official put it: "It doesn't matter to me whether Citibank is evading American regulations in London. I wouldn't particularly want to know."[27]

More important than both the IET and VFCR were the controls on direct investment, particularly since Europe was the specific target of both the voluntary and later the mandatory FDIP. During the 1960's a number of issues were debated with regard to the dangers of U.S. direct investment: foreign controlled enterprise may thwart governmental planning, drive smaller European firms out of business, stimulate inflation in areas of labor shortage, and make Europe dependent on U.S. technology.[28] Those who believed these arguments naturally favoured U.S. controls on direct investment outflows, failing to realize that the purpose of the controls was to shift the financing of such investment to Europe rather than reduce the magnitude of investment.

As the financing issue became more salient, a new argument emerged: U.S. firms were simply buying existing enterprises and financing the takeover in Europe. This was a powerful political argument, though economically mis-leading. Takeovers did constitute about 25 percent of U.S. direct investment in Europe from 1963 to 1968,[29] but even if this were 100 percent financed in Europe there must have been some element of value-added or risk preference in-volved (i.e., a benefit to Europe), otherwise the European capital supplier would have acquired the enterprise himself.

However, the benefits of foreign investment were readily apparent to most European countries. The numerous laws, regulations and treaties which gave much scope for gov-ernments to use administrative discretion in shaping their policies toward U.S. investment, allowed European politicians to publicly criticize American investment while actually encouraging it. Most European countries, including France, had special agencies in the United States to attract U.S. investment (e.g., the French Industrial Development Agency in New York), and offered a variety of incentives for particularly attractive investments.[30] Insofar as the U.S. controls may have caused problems, those countries affected

could themselves make regulations covering local financing
and repatriation of capital or dividends; all except West
Germany had some regulations of this kind. France, the U.K.
and Sweden required American firms to bring in most of
their capital from outside the country.[31] Thus, there
was no consistent European pressure on the United States
to restrict direct investment outflows, save for the last few
months of 1967, and even then European proponents of such
measures saw them as only a temporary substitute for more
fundamental adjustments (viz., deflation by the United
States). The distribution and relative importance to
different countries of U.S. investment may be seen in Table
7.2.

The countries which were most active in attracting
U.S. investment were the U.K., Italy and the Benelux group.
With the exception of Italy, this is reflected in the per cap-
ita figures of Table 7.2. Britain has, despite exchange
restrictions which have inconvenienced U.S. corporations,
encouraged U.S. investment. At a time when de Gaulle was
calling for pan-European restrictions on U.S. investment,
Chancellor of the Exchequer Maudling pointedly reiterated
Britain's disagreement with this view,[32] probably because
of fears that Britain's exclusion from the EEC would deflect
U.S. investment to the Six. Following the 1965 program,
Prime Minister Wilson visited the United States but did not

Table 7.2

U.S. Direct Investment in Selected

European Countries

	A	B	U.S. share (%) of . . .
U.K.	6703	6.5	total foreign capital, '68 = 67.1
Germany	3774	2.9	foreign cap. invest., '61-9 = 47.4
France	1910	1.5	foreign gross invest., '62-8 = 25.8
Switzerland	1436	9.8	n.a.
Italy	1272	1.7	productive capital inflow, '56-69 = 40.8
Netherlands	1073	4.2	no. of foreign subsid. = 45.4
Den./Norw./Sweden	915	1.9	foreign direct inv., mid-60's = 45*
Belg./Lux.	963	4.6	value foreign projects, '59-69 = 56*
Spain	587	2.3	approved invest. with > 50% foreign equity, '59-69 = 38.1

KEY: A = total value, $ million, end 1968
B = book value as % of per capita GNP, 1968
* = estimate only

SOURCE: Hellman, Challenge to U.S. Dominance, pp. 319, 327-9, 337.

protest the controls, though he did express fears about the

effect on world liquidity.[33] However, the British Treasury

was concerned, and put new restrictions on foreign borrowing

in the U.K. The United States protested (via a message
from the Federal Reserve to the Bank of England), but was
told "politely" that Britain's problem was more serious.[34]
The French government had taken similar action, forcing
American companies in these countries to look for investment finance in Germany, Holland and Belgium. Again, in 1968,
Britain was hurt by the new controls both because of its
desire for U.S. investment and because the new program could
partly offset the British devaluation.

The Dutch and Belgian governments were also enthu-
siastic about U.S. investment, and could, lacking Britain's
currency problems, offer more attractive incentives. Following
the 1965 program, the Dutch set up a special office in New
York to keep attracting U.S. investment. Belgium resorted
to more tax concessions and subsidies. Throughout the
1960's Belgium and Holland competed with incentives for U.S.
investment.[36]

The position of the West German government was more
complex: both U.S. adjustment and less U.S. investment in
Germany were favoured, but capital controls were not considered the right method. Bundesbank President Blessing and
Governor Emminger made it clear that monetary policy was the
only sensible option for the United States.[37] On the question
of U.S. investment, the government was concerned about both
inflation (due to Germany's labor shortage) and about competitive

takeovers. While a few larger takeovers were indirectly prevented, the preferred strategy of the government was to encourage integration in and subsidize the industries involved.[38] Thus, the German government was not, in principle, in favour of pressuring the United States to impose more stringent capital controls. And, of course, Germany had a special relationship with the United States which would have inhibited pressure tactics in any case—a relationship symbolised by the letter from Blessing (on behalf of the government) to Governor Martin, pledging that Germany would not convert any dollar reserves into gold, on the understanding that U.S. troop levels in Germany would be maintained—a formalization of what was already in practice.[39] This is not to say that Germany did not favour mandatory controls in the wake of the 1967 Sterling crisis. Indeed, Emminger may even have visited the United States to advise on the FDIP.[40] However, U.S. controls were not a general policy objective of the German government.

The case of France would appear to be quite different, as the French government gained the reputation of being the most active campaigner against U.S. investment. Yet, primarily for domestic political and economic reasons, this policy could not be consistently pursued.[41] During 1963 and 1964, French officials and businessmen actively campaigned against American investment, doubtless provoked by Chrysler's acquisition of

Simca by raising its equity holding from 25 percent to 63 percent in January 1963. The French government could have blocked this takeover, as it did others, but chose instead to ask other EEC members to take a joint stand in formulating controls on U.S. investment.[42] The major French manufacturing association, the Patronat, supported the government, fearing the competitive power of U.S. corporations.

Failing to get the rest of the EEC behind France, de Gaulle held his famous press conference of 3 February 1965 where he called for a return to the Gold Standard. The speech had been preceded by large French sales of dollars for gold in January 1965.[44] At the same time, however, French policy on U.S. investment became separated from French international monetary policy: U.S. investment was again encouraged, while the government attacked U.S. dominance of the Bretton Woods system by other means. A report by the Minister of Industry, Maurice-Pokanowski, established criteria for judging foreign investments which, when they were proved too harsh, were changed in 1966 (under Finance Minister Debré) to make France more attractive to U.S. investors.[45]

This attempt to decouple foreign investment policy from systemic policy was only partly successful, and U.S. investment per capita remained the lowest in Western Europe (see Table 7.2). The difficulty was evidenced in France's

subsequent actions, which helped force the United States
into mandatory capital controls. Once the FDIP was
announced, French officials allegedly "sneered outright" at
the inadequacy of the program[46] and yet feared that the program would shift speculative pressure onto the Franc, itself
weakened by domestic economic and political problems. While
publicly belittling the program, Premier Debré privately informed Undersecretary of State Katzenbach that the French
government would, if necessary, block financial transfers
from U.S. companies in France.[47]

Below the level of national governments the reaction
of European businessmen was similar to bankers' reactions to
the VFCR: what was initially welcomed as an impediment to
U.S. competition turned into a curse, as U.S. corporations
moved into the Euro-markets, driving up interest rates and
crowding out European borrowers. U.S. corporations were
able to do this partly because of the backing of the parent
company (i.e., the attraction of size for the European
bond buyer) and because debt offerings were often given the
added attraction of convertibility into the common stock
of the U.S. parent.[48] European bankers were suggesting that
their central banks regulate the timing and size of U.S.
debt offerings.[49]

American investment bankers responded by pointing out
that European banks themselves were doing about 70 percent

of the Euro-underwriting, and in any case, "If a Swiss banker
would rather buy Amoco 5-3/4s than Copenhagen 6-1/4s,
that's too bad. It's just competition."[50] Evelyn
de Rothschild protested bitterly about such crowding out--the
day after his own London bank had participated in underwriting
a $50 million issue by General Electric.[51] These European
fears were probably exaggerated. An IMF study in 1966
suggested that little crowding out was really happening,
estimating that 60 percent of U.S. Euro-issues were being bought
for unlisted Swiss bank accounts and 15 percent from sources
in Hong Kong, the Middle East, the Bahamas and the U.K.
(i.e., presumably non-European funds which would not have been
used to buy European securities anyway).[52]

In examining European national and sub-national reactions to the various capital controls, it would appear that
at least up to 1967, these reactions were ambivalent and
divided. Yet during 1967, the major European governments
gradually coalesced around a position which forced the
United States to resort to more stringent controls by linking
the continuance of the Gold Pool, the activation of SDRs and
the holding of dollar reserves to some kind of more vigorous
balance of payments program by the United States. Since the
United States could not be pushed in any other direction (deflation being the preferred European remedy for the United
States), they ended up focusing on capital controls--not

because they actually wanted to keep U.S. capital out,
but because there was no other acceptable alternative. Deaf
to U.S. threats of "unilateral action,"[53] attempted
counter-linkages to NATO, and pleading assertions that surplus
countries have to adjust too, European pressure built up to
a point where the U.S. plan to merely continue the voluntary
program had to be discarded.

The SDR issue brought France and Germany together
in their insistence that the SDR plan be linked to further
U.S. adjustment measures. While the French insisted that the
U.S. deficit must have "disappeared" and the Germans only
referred to "diminution," there was little to distinguish in
the conditions they stated for the SDR plan at the Rio
meeting of the IMF in September 1967.[54]

The Gold Pool offered a similar bargaining linkage.
France withdrew from the Pool in June 1967 and the remaining
members eventually exacted a pledge to take action from the
United States, in exchange for staying in. Undersecretary
Deming's meeting with other Pool members on 10 December 1967
produced rumours of "new moves" by the United States. The
United States was proposing various measures to strengthen
the Gold Pool; what the Europeans wanted was U.S. deflation.
Agreement to keep the Gold Pool in operation was made condi-
tional on firm action by the United States.[55]

The final arm-twister was provided by European dollar

holdings (though France only had $600 million left by
December) and the short-term swap lines (on which the New York
Fed had about $1.5 billion outstanding to European central
banks by February 1968). As The Economist put it, European
central banks were willing to keep holding dollars only
". . . in return for a really firm assurance. . ." on balance
of payments policy: ". . . the Americans were left in no
doubt that this time they would have to deliver fast."[56]
And since they could not and would not deliver a fast
deflation, the Europeans settled for capital controls. One
central banker explained it to Business Week quite simply:
"If one has to choose between a payments deficit and restraint
of capital exports, it should be the latter."[57]

At the beginning of December 1967, the U.S. position
"ruled out" mandatory capital controls, asked for more support
in the Gold Pool, and, as concessions, offered only the
prospect of a tax increase with a slight tightening of the
voluntary controls guidelines. The United States claimed
it was willing to let the system break down rather than go
further. By the third week in December, agreement
was apparently reached in Basel, between the United States,
the U.K., Germany, France, Belgium, the Netherlands, Italy
and Switzerland; the United States offered the mandatory
program and the Europeans agreed to keep supporting the dollar.[58]

Canada

Canada was the only country, other than those designated "less developed," to be exempted from nearly all aspects of the controls. This may be attributed to U.S. recognition of the sensitivity and vulnerability of the Canadian economy, and the willingness of the Canadian government to make certain compensating changes in its own policies.[59]

The immediate effect of the IET on Canada was devastating: Canadian stocks fell sharply, trading in Canadian bonds came to a halt, and the Canadian dollar fell, despite heavy support by the Bank of Canada. The tax was seen as having a deflationary effect.[60] The initial Canadian interpretation was that the failure to exempt Canada from the IET was in retaliation for recent Canadian moves to block takeovers by foreign interests (via a tax on the sale of securities to foreigners).[61] However, Dillon's assertion that it was simply a misinterpretation is probably correct:

> With respect to Canada, our expectation was that the interest equalization tax would reduce the level of Canadian borrowing but not below amounts necessary to supplement Canadian earnings from other sources in financing its current account deficit. It had not been our expectation that the tax would eliminate Canadian borrowing in the United States.
> The proposal was, however, interpreted by Canadian financial circles as, in the absence of a substantial rise in all Canadian interest rates, effectively closing the U.S. capital market completely to Canadian borrowing, leaving Canada without sufficient income to finance its current account deficit.[62]

In a telephone conversation with Hayes (of the New York Fed), several days before the announcement of the IET, Dillon said that the State Department would "explain" the situation to the Canadians. He obviously had not anticipated the Canadian reaction.[63] The result was a top level Canadian representation to Washington, consisting of L. Rasminsky (Bank of Canada), C. S. A. Ritchie (Canadian Ambassador to the United States), A. Plumptre (Assistant Deputy Minister of Finance) and A. E. Ritchie (Assistant Undersecretary for External Affairs). After negotiations with Dillon, Roosa, Surrey and Ball, a compromise was reached. Canada would manipulate its own interest rates to ensure that her dollar reserves did not increase beyond a predetermined level, and would ensure that Canada would not be used as a means of evading the application of the IET to other countries.[64]

Other, less explicit, concessions were extracted from Canada. During the saga of the "Mercantile Bank Affair" (the acquisition by Citibank of Mercantile), U.S. government protest notes against the Canadian Bank Act of 1966 (to prevent such takeovers) made pointed references to Canada's access to U.S. capital markets:

> In view of the important interrelationships of capital markets in the two countries and the substantial benefits derived by Canadian banks from operations in the United States, it is hoped that the Government of Canada would agree that it is undesirable to avoid placing unnecessary restrictions on such mutually beneficial activities.[65]

The Canadian government replied that it was not
fair to make this a bilateral issue, since the proposed Bank
Act was to apply to all foreigners.[66.] Conveniently forgotten
was the Canadian bilateral repsonse to the IET.

A similar compromise was reached on the VFCR program: Canada was exempted in return for lowering its
ceiling on dollar reserves $100 million below the IET level.[67]
Again, the exemption was not announced with the program, but
came after negotiations. This may be due to the problem that
the Canadians (like the Europeans before the IET) were
curiously deaf to threats of coming action. During the latter
part of 1964 U.S. officials had been warning Canada to hold
down its bank borrowing in the United States, but had been
ignored.[68]

Canadian responses to the voluntary and mandatory
direct investment controls were also examples of delayed
response. With regard to the voluntary program, Secretary
Connor asked U.S. companies to allow Canadian subsidiares
only enough funds for operating expenses.[69] In a country
where 46 percent of manufacturing industry, 62 percent of
petroleum and natural gas and 52 percent of the mining
industry was controlled by U.S. companies,[70] the macroeconomic effect of such a policy would have been tremendous.
It was not until March 1966 that the U.S. government stated
that subsidiaries in Canada were not required to follow the

letter of the guidelines.[71]

The 1968 FDIP again included Canada at the outset.
The immediate effect was to put severe pressure on the Canadian
dollar, part of which was speculative and part repatriation
of funds by U.S. subsidiaries. Canada retaliated by asking
banks to refuse loans to American subsidiaries if the money
was to be used to meet the FDIP rules.[72] The United
States eventually exempted Canada from both the FDIP and the
VFCR, for the immediate reason that a devaluation by Canada
could touch off a chain of devaluations and pull the U.S.
dollar down.[73]

Canada had little to do with the inception of any
of the U.S. controls programs. Not consulted prior to their
announcement, the most Canada could do was to bargain for
exemptions. Canada was important in policy-making only insofar as capital flows to Canada contributed to the situation
which was seen to require capital controls.

Japan

The case of Japan falls somewhere in between that of
Europe and Canada: while Japan had a strong interest in
U.S. portfolio capital, it had an interest in the international
monetary system more akin to that of Europe. The bargaining pattern, however, was closer to that of Canada, mainly
because of the asymmetry of strength in this issue area.

The announcement of the IET hit Japan in much the same
way that it hit Canada: stocks fell in what The Economist
described as selling that "reached panic proportions."[74]
The Japanese response was to send Foreign Minister Ohira to
Washington to ask for an exemption on three grounds: the
IET would damage the Japanese economy; Japan has a "special
dependence" on the U.S. economy; and, thirdly, the IET
would hurt the ruling Liberal Democratic Party politically.
Before Ohira's departure, Finance Minister Tanaka had publicly
suggested that Japan would have to reconsider its international
trade and monetary policies--later clarifying the point by
declaring that trade with Communist China would be increased.
Ohira met with both Dillon and Kennedy, and was refused any
concessions on the IET.[75]

Both the Treasury and the State Department had talks
with their Japanese counterparts. Dillon refused to budge,
believing that the Japanese had no persuasive reason for
getting an exemption. George Ball was inclined to be more
lenient, but could only tell the Japanese that Canada would
be "closely watched" and reiterate to Dillon the Japanese
fear of being explicitly singled out by name in the IET
legislation.[76]

The immediate failure of the Japanese to obtain concessions was probably due to the lack of credibility of its
threats, its own inability to make as good an economic case

as the Canadians, and its lack of close relations with U.S.
interest groups and the subunits of the U.S. government.[77]
To be sure, the latter factor might not have helped even had
it existed. Strong transnational and transgovernmental links
do not appear to have helped the Canadians a great deal.[78]
In addition, the Japanese position was weakened by the fact
that their own long-term capital markets were almost totally
closed to foreigners, and remained so until 1972.

Japanese companies were forced to go to Europe for
long-term finance, the first Japanese securities to be
offered in Europe since World War Two appearing in December
1963. The solution was not satisfactory for the companies
or for the governments involved. Firstly, Japanese companies
could only borrow at rates of about 1 percent over New York
rates. Secondly, European governments made it clear that they
did not welcome Japanese borrowing at a time when their own
borrowers were being turned away from New York.[79] Finance
Ministers Tanaka and Giscard d'Estaing met to discuss the
floating of Japanese debt securities in the highly restricted
Paris capital market. This attempt to play on French ambitions
to build an international finance center failed.[80] Giscard
rebuffed Tanaka's approach, doubtless realizing that France
did not have the capacity to play this role.

The Japanese eventually got a partial exemption in
February 1965 (up to $100 million per year) for reasons which

appear to be similar to the ones Japan cited in its original

request for exemption in 1963:

> Despite an improvement in Japan's external posi-
> tion, the country continues to be heavily dependent on
> foreign capital and currently accounts for almost one-
> fourth of foreign lending of U.S. banks. In view of the
> softness of European capital markets for Japanese issues
> and the impact of our voluntary restraint program on
> bank lending, continued access to the U.S. capital market--
> even if limited--is necessary to sustain confidence in
> the yen.
> This exemption thus serves the double purpose of
> providing continued Japanese access to our financial
> markets at a time of reduced other availabilities and as
> a symbol of U.S. readiness to extend assistance in case
> of need. We believe that a sound functioning of the
> international monetary system necessitates that Japan,
> as the leading financial center in the Far East and
> one that is playing a greater role in regional develop-
> ment assistance efforts, continue to maintain the
> international value of its currency on a sound basis.[81]

For these same reasons, the VFCR guidelines made

special mention of Japan, asking banks to take note of

Japan's special situation: Dillon had assured the Japanese

that the February 1965 balance of payments message of the

President would not mention Canada without mentioning

Japan.[82] It is doubtful whether Japan suffered much from the

VFCR. Much of the bank lending to Japan was for trade

financing (e.g., the Australian-Japanese wool trade) which

could be shifted to U.S. branches overseas.

Japan was not worried by any of the U.S. controls on

direct investment. On the contrary, the United States has

been trying unsuccessfully to the present date to open up

Japan to U.S. investment. Secretary Fowler attempted to

wring concessions out of the Japanese at a ministerial conference in early 1965, with no success. Secretary Connor
later suggested that the United States use the VFCR as a
"bargaining chip" to open up Japan.[83] This was obviously
unsuccessful, the Japanese fear of competition being greater
than any retaliatory measures the United States was prepared
to threaten. With the threat of trade restrictions on
Japanese exports, some moves were made to loosen up foreign
investment regulations, though not enough to allow Dow
Chemical to establish a subsidiary in 1975, to compete with
Japanese chemical manufacturers.[84]

Australia

As the one other remaining developed country to be included in the capital controls, Australia is an example of
a small ally with no big influence. Unlike Japan or
Canada, Australia got no special treatment in any of the
controls.

Australia had been the major supplier of governmental
public placements in the New York long-term debt market
prior to the IET (see Table 7.3). After the Canadians had
come and gone, Australian Ambassador Beale made a rather
belated appeal for an exemption to Dillon, who refused,
pleading that Congressional opinion would not take any more
exemptions.[85]

Table 7.3

Public Long-Term Debt Offerings of Foreign

Governments, Registered with the SEC,

1 January 1961 to 15 July 1963

($ million)

Registrant	Amount
Australia	137.1
Norway	71.2
Denmark	63.0
Belgium	54.0
City of Montreal	50.4
New Zealand	43.9
Mexico	35.0
Japan	26.9
European Coal & Steel Community	24.8
City of Milan	19.8
Finland	12.3
	538.3

SOURCE: Derived from information supplied by U.S.
Treasury for the record; House, Committee on Banking and Currency, Recent Changes in Monetary Policy, 1963, pp. 177-178.

NOTE: During the same period, private placements by foreign
governments (for which the SEC does not give the geographical
distribution) totaled $801 million; ibid., p. 170.

Why, then, did Australia not protest more resolutely?

Firstly, aside from governmental borrowings, U.S. portfolio

capital was not important to private industrial development

in Australia. U.S. investment had been rising rapidly, from
25.4 percent of long-term capital inflows in 1954 to 40 percent
in 1963; the comparable figures for the U.K. declined from
64.5 percent to 44.7 percent during the same period. However,
almost all of this was direct investment and therefore un-
affected by the IET. With the exception of Broken Hill
Proprietary (a mining company), there was little American
portfolio investment in the Australian private sector.
Secondly, foreign investment had become a political issue di-
viding the ruling Liberal-Country Party coalition, the latter
urging more control on foreign investment. Thirdly, there
was at the time an excess supply of loanable funds within Australia and the government had a high level of reserves.[86]
In September 1963, however, the Australian government barred
citizens from acquiring stock in foreign companies, though
probably as a precautionary measure rather than explicit
retaliation.[87]

The importance of direct investment did stimulate an
Australian reaction to the 1965 program, though again it
was somewhat belated. It was not until March that Prime
Minister Menzies announced that he would ask President Johnson
to ease the curbs, which he did by sending Treasury Minister
Harold Holt to the United States. Holt returned empty-
handed, having been told by President Johnson that he
doubted any adverse consequences would befall Australia.

Menzies reportedly intended to take the matter up with
President Johnson on his next visit, though there is no evidence that he did.[88] Australian opposition petered out
rapidly because U.S. companies continued to invest
heavily in Australia with offshore financing, and because
a public position in favour of foreign investment was a
politically difficult position for a Liberal politician
to take, since it drew fire from both the Labour and Country
Parties.

The Deputy Prime Minister, Country Party leader McEwan,
probably favoured U.S. capital outflow restrictions, since
he believed that foreign investment was a result of a lack
of Australian enterprise and initiative. In addition to
the Country Party's purely nationalistic reasons for opposing
foreign investment, it had quite rational economic and
political ones: capital inflows made it more difficult for
farm interests to argue their case for devaluation, and at
the same time accelerated the urban growth that was causing
the slow decline of the Country Party's electoral base. Thus,
in its position as an indispensable coalition partner, the
Country Party was a powerful brake on any efforts by the
government to protest U.S. capital outflow restrictions.

There was, in addition, a certain political reti-
cence in dealing with the United States. As the situation in
Vietnam worsened in 1965, Australia felt more in need of

ANZUS than ever, and this may well have had the psychological effect of discouraging Australian protests.

The government did take some measures to mitigate
the adverse effects of U.S. controls, namely by requiring foreign
controlled companies to "consult" with the Reserve Bank
before borrowing in Australia. These guidelines were made
more explicit in 1968, making it clear that approval would
be refused if the funds were borrowed to facilitate remittances out of Australia.[89]

Following the 1968 FDIP, Australia went through the
motions of protest. Prime Minister McEwan asked Undersecretary Rostow (during the latter's Far Eastern tour to
"explain" the program) for "special consideration," saying
Australia was entitled to "special reciprocal treatment"
because of its close relationship with the United States as
a major purchaser of U.S. defense equipment.[90] Again,
however, several factors served to mute the Australian
reaction. Firstly, Australia was put into schedule B of the
FDIP, giving it a higher investment allowance than Western
Europe. Secondly, the base period for the FDIP (1965-66)
favoured Australia since it was a year of high U.S. direct
investment, no doubt the result of U.S. firms rushing to
beat the guidelines of the voluntary program. Thirdly, the
political dependency factor may have been operating, since
the war in Vietnam was not going well and American efforts

to push the South Vietnamese army to the forefront of the fighting may have encouraged an Australian low profile at the time. Fourthly, the Prime Minister at the time was Country Party leader McEwan (following the death of Holt in 1967), who had been critical of his government's open door policy to foreign investment for many years. His successor, in February 1968, was John Gorton, a Liberal politician whose more nationalistic attitude to foreign investment was a sharp break from his party's tradition.

Less Developed Countries

This group did not oppose the capital control programs, since, with a few exceptions, all such countries were exempted. Indeed, for this reason the LDC's had every reason to favour the programs since they were the indirect beneficiaries. Hufbauer suggests that Latin America, in particular, benefited from the programs, noting that the growth rate for U.S. private investment in Latin America rose from 5.8 percent in 1953-63 to 8.7 percent in 1963-70, while in Western Europe it declined from 15.2 percent to 8.3 percent. Changes in growth rates of GDP cannot account for this change since they remained relatively constant in both areas.[91]

International Organizations

Such organizations were, in their capital raising function, exempted from the IET. What is more important in

this context is the extent to which pressures from within such
organizations may have promoted the U.S. capital controls.
The major organizations involved were the International
Monetary Fund (IMF), the organs of the European Economic Com-
munity (EEC), the Organization for Economic Cooperation and
Development (OECD), the more informal Group of Ten, and the
Bank for International Settlements (BIS).

The IMF has tended to follow rather than lead events
in the international monetary system. Per Jacobsson, IMF
Director until September 1963, did not see U.S. capital outflows as a problem:

> I have been asked for many years, however, what might
> be the result if interest rates were to be reduced in
> the United States in a period of recession, while
> rates remained high or were even increased in Europe.
> I have replied that there probably would be an outflow
> of funds, although the central banks would not appreciably
> reduce, and might even increase, their dollar balances.
> At the same time it was, however, likely that in such a
> situation the current account of the U.S. balance of
> payments would be strengthened by increased exports to
> Europe. That is exactly the position today, . . .[92]

His successor, Pierre-Paul Schweitzer (formerly Deputy-
Governor of the Bank of France) was similarly optimistic before
he entered office, expressing confidence that the U.S. balance
of payments would improve and scepticism about plans to
expand international liquidity.[93]

However, Schweitzer evidently was carried away by the
organizational mission of the IMF, inspired by its former
Research Director Edward Bernstein, whose plan was to increase

liquidity in the system through increases in and more flexible use of the IMF quotas. With this preoccupation, the IMF did not directly concern itself with the capital controls. Bernstein favoured the capital controls, he claimed, because he believed they were working. It is more likely that he favoured them because he saw the correction of the U.S. deficit as making the liquidity issue more urgent.[94] This view was representative of the internationalist pro-U.S. opinion in the IMF. Schweitzer also favoured the controls, because, he said, they were better than deflation.[95] He naturally tended more to the European view (having overcome his earlier optimism) that some U.S. adjustment was a pre-requisite to liquidity based reform of the system.

In any case, the IMF's concern with liquidity rather than adjustment effectively removed it from the capital controls debate. Insofar as capital controls did get discussed, the IMF was merely a forum for the expression of national views. In 1966, for example, Secretary Fowler used the annual meeting of the IMF to warn his European colleagues of more drastic capital controls if they did not adopt the appropriate monetary policies.[96]

The EEC tended to reflect the balance of national powers within it. During the first half of the 1960's it reflected the French view that international monetary reform must await correction of the U.S. deficit, and that such an adjustment was entirely the responsibility of the United States. The emphasis at this time was on excess liquidity in the United States. The 1964 Annual Report of the Monetary Commission of the EEC, supported by the Vice-President of the Commission of the EEC (Robert Marjolin) recommended monetary deflation for the United States.[97] Earlier, de Gaulle had suggested that the EEC adopt some joint retaliatory measure against the IET, but such a measure did not receive the support of the other members of the Community.[98]

On the question of direct investment, the EEC Commission took a moderate stand: members should coordinate their investment policies but not impose any drastic restrictions on U.S. investment.[99] After 1965 it tended to adopt a balance between the extreme French demand for a return to the gold standard and the members more sympathetic to the United States by adopting the position (spelt out in a communiqué in January 1967) that international monetary reform should be preceded by the elimination of the deficits of reserve currency countries. The President of the Monetary Committee suggested that U.S. capital outflow controls could effectively do this.[100]

While the IMF and the EEC, as institutions in their own right, were of little importance, the overlapping group consisting of the OECD's Working Party Three, the Group of Ten and the Bank for International Settlements, were important forums for putting pressure on the United States to impose

controls, especially during 1967. Again, however, though
these groups had more policy influence, they tended to represent an aggregation of national interests rather than any
autonomous transgovernmental force.[101]

The meetings of Working Party Three tended to be
technical discussions rather than negotiating forums.[102] Yet
these technical discussions did provide the participants with
the opportunity to assess other national policies. During
the Kennedy period, the meetings ". . . chastened somewhat
further any remaining hopes by some members of the Administration for more sweeping or decisive action on the monetary
front."[103]

The relevance of the Working Party was twofold. Firstly,
it was a channel of communication. The French government used
its prior knowledge of the IET, gained from the Working Party,
to "leak" the news to journalist Paul Fabra in order to
sabotage the IET and/or embarrass the United States. The
plot failed, since The Economist's European editor, Fred
Hirsch, did not believe the story, and Fabra had been told not
to give it to Le Monde, since it would then be obvious from
where the leak had come.

Secondly, it was a forum for the construction of joint
statements based on predetermined national positions. This
tended to produce anodyne statements which could be all things
to all parties. The famous 1966 report on adjustment illustrates

this with its qualified endorsement of capital controls:

58. It is agreed, in general, a high degree of freedom for international capital movements is desirable. There is, however, some acceptance that measures to affect capital movements may in some circumstances be needed in the interests of internal monetary policy. In practice, moreover, there can develop large-scale movements of both short and long-term capital, sometimes prompted by relative tax advantages or differences in the structure of capital markets, which are not such as more fundamental economic considerations would indicate as desirable, and where the use of direct measures to influence them may be appropriate. The effectiveness of many such measures, notably of an incentive or persuasive nature, may, however, tend to diminish as time passes. Furthermore, since it is generaly considered desirable to liberalize capital movements to the greatest extent compatible with internal policy objectives, increasing reliance on controls over capital movements would normally indicate that other action was needed to affect the capital account; e.g., more active use of monetary policy, fiscal changes, or action to improve the efficiency of financial institutions. Alternatively, adjustments might be sought on the side of the current account.[104]

It was in the Group of Ten, where finance ministers and central bankers met, that the strongest pressures on the United States originated. It was here that the political pressure gradually built up on the United States in November and December of 1967.

At the same time, the meetings of central bankers at the Bank for International Settlements reinforced these pressures. The BIS did differ from the Group of Ten meetings insofar as it did have an organizational existence of its own. As a central bank for central banks it had, through the 1960's, followed the predictable line (in its annual reports) that the best cure for a deficit was monetary deflation, though

it did endorse the IET and the 1965 program as appropriate
temporary measures.[105] It was not until the latter part of
1967 that it turned to capital controls as those members of
the BIS who were also in the Gold Pool met at Basel to
pressure the United States to take drastic adjustment measures.

Conclusion

International influences on the U.S. capital controls
programs increased during the period 1963-68, notably
during 1967. Geographically, the only direct causal pressure
for these controls came from those Western European countries which had decided that capital controls were better
than no adjustment at all. None of the countries involved
advocated this policy for domestic political reasons (i.e.,
resentment of U.S. investment), since by 1967 even the most
nationalistic among them had realized the costs of discouraging
U.S. investment in general. These European motives were
apparently misperceived in the United States, since the post-
1968 policy of "benign neglect" was premised on the assumption that a renewed outflow of capital to Europe would force
these countries to accept exchange rate changes. The United
States overestimated the extent of European opposition to
U.S. investment, or at least underestimated the value which
the Europeans placed on U.S. capital inflows. In addition
to this direct advocacy of the policy by late 1967, one might
also attribute an indirect policy influence to Europe, since

it was this region which was responsible for a large part
of the environment which necessitated controls: the
high level of portfolio flows to Europe in the early 1960's
(and the unwillingness or inability of these countries to
take corrective measures), the encouragement of direct investment, the conversion of dollar reserves into gold, and the
speculative backwash after the Sterling devaluation.

The other major affected countries (Canada, Japan,
Australia, and the less developed areas) did not have any direct causal influence on the policy. Their roles were
restricted to attempting to influence the way in which the
policies were implemented. They did not, as did Europe,
bargain with the United States over the decision of whether
or not to impose controls, but merely bargained for concessions insofar as they as individual countries were affected
by the controls. They were dealt with essentially as an
afterthought to a policy determined by other factors.

With regard to the level of interaction at which these
influences occurred, the direct causal pressures on U.S.
policy appear to have been at an interstate rather than
transgovernmental or transnational interaction.[106] Even in
areas where one might expect to find areas of autonomous
transgovernmental interactions, these do not seem to have
exerted any critical influence on policy. The U.S.-Canadian
Balance of Payments Committee established in 1963 is one such

example. In this case the policy questions were negotiated
at too high a level of both governments for such bodies to
have any influence independent of their respective governments.[107] Another case is the meeting of central bankers
at the Bank for International Settlements, an excellent
opportunity for relatively independent institutions to agree
on a common policy to press on their home governments. Yet,
from what is known about BIS meetings in late 1967, they
reflected the same kinds of pressures being put on the
United States that were occurring in other forums, that is,
that the United States must take drastic action in return for
continued cooperation in the support of the dollar, the continuation of the Gold Pool and the activation of SDRs.[108]

In the case of transnational interactions, there is little
evidence of any direct policy influence. Again, however, the
existence of international capital markets as a transnational
phenomenon influenced the type, form and evolution of the
controls. For example, the ability of banks to substitute
long-term loans for debt securities forced the extension of
the IET to cover such loans.

This dominance of interstate politics reflects another
dimension of the same phenomenon which accounts for the declining importance of bureaucratic and interest group politics
in the domestic aspect of policy-making on this issue: politicization. As the issue of capital controls became more contentious,

policy-making rose to the Executive branch level, while the number and intensity of international influences. were also enhanced. This rising level of salience and controversiality of the issue of capital controls is also reflected in the circumstances under which the controls were gradually removed as the first step in the strategy of "benign neglect."

CHAPTER VIII

THE DENOUEMENT: THE 1968 PROGRAM AND THE BALANCE
OF PAYMENTS POLICY OF THE NIXON ADMINISTRATION

Following the introduction of the 1968 program, the
policy-making environment began to change. Firstly, the
higher level of domestic politicization of the issue, which
had previously been reflected only in a horizontal executive
level power shift from Treasury to White House, also produced
a greater degree of vertical politicization, as even large
foreign investors found their interests substantially
affected. This private opposition to the controls is quite
consistent with the major studies of the controls which indicate that, in the longer term, they are ineffective instruments
of balance of payments policy. The second major change came
in 1969 when the decision was made to gradually remove the
controls as the first step in the compellence strategy of
"benign neglect," designed to force the Western European
and Japanese governments to revalue their currencies.

Direct Investors and the 1968 Program

The FDIP produced protest from business which was, as
Weil and Davidson note, "immediate, violent and long."[1] In
1973 a Federal Court in Washington ruled that the Executive

Order, under which the controls were imposed, was without legal authority, since the Order incorrectly invoked the Trading with the Enemy Acts of 1917.[2] This was, however, too late to help those firms immediately affected in 1968; and the FDIP itself had been largely dismantled by 1973.

Large companies could, as they had under the voluntary program, borrow internationally to finance direct investment. Yet the conditions under which they had to do this became increasingly irksome under the FDIP for a variety of reasons. Higher debt/equity ratios for subsidiaries created capitalization problems. Even ITT was driven to complain that the repatriation requirement of the FDIP was seriously undermining its competitive positon in foreign markets. What ITT objected to was not so much the restrictions on transfers of capital abroad (since ITT could easily borrow internationally), but the repatriation of subsidiary earnings according to a specific formula. The forced repatriation of earnings would also eventually affect the subsidiary's capacity to borrow by depleting its equity capitalization.[3] Other large foreign direct investors were similarly affected: while they could borrow to finance investment, the capacity of subsidiaries to do this would be weakened by earnings repatriation.[4]

Even without the repatriation problem, international borrowing became more costly during 1968. The rush of U.S. corporations into the Eurobond market drove interest rates

up sharply from previous levels and widened the gap
between Eurobond and U.S. domestic corporate bond yields.[5]
Part of this higher cost was due not only to the greater
volume of borrowing, but to the inability of U.S. corporations
to act as guarantors of loans to their subsidiaries, since
the FDIP prohibited the transfer of funds abroad in support
of such guarantees.

Convertible debt issues offered a way of obtaining lower
cost finance, but even these became more difficult. Both
the uncertain direction of the stock market in the United
States and the possibility of a fall in the value of the
dollar made convertibles less attractive to buyers. Earlier
in the year, large U.S. corporations could raise up to $50
million in convertible Eurodollar bonds. By the fall, Mobil
Oil was having difficulty selling $35 million of convertible
debentures.[6]

Another difficulty for large foreign investors was the
choice of 1965-66 as the base period for the FDIP allowance. The effect of this was to penalize those firms which
had been brought into the earlier voluntary program (i.e.,
the largest 500-600 foreign investors). This inequity was
later removed, but as Sanford Rose noted, ". . . The companies
have never quite got over it. A residue of ill will and
bruised feelings unquestionably lingers."[7]

During the early months of the program some companies

were able to exploit the inexperience of OFDI officials, or problems with the regulations, to obtain specific exemptions. As OFDI built up its staff, it became more stringent in the terms it exacted for any concessions granted. Companies which, for example, pleaded that they could not repatriate earnings for political reasons, were often forced to borrow in the international capital markets and repatriate this borrowing. The Westavco Corporation, a paper products company, received permission to retain $1.25 million of earnings in Brazil, provided that it borrow the same amount in the Eurodollar market.[8]

The companies found themselves squeezed between the United States and other governments which did not react favourably to increased borrowing by U.S. subsidiaries. As several countries increased restrictions on local borrowing, more U.S. subsidiaries were forced into the international capital markets, increasing the cost of this source of finance. One U.S. construction company had its local borrowing allowance suddenly cut 40 percent by the exchange control authorities of a European country.[9] This particularly hurt companies which were shifting operations into countries where they had low previous levels of investment. Kennecott Copper, for example, was in the process of building up its Australian operations but had a low base point allowance in that country owing to the newness of the investment.[10]

Hence the OFDI regulations forced it to attempt to borrow
most of its capital locally, but these borrowings were in
turn scrutinized by the Reserve Bank of Australia to make sure
that they were not to be used to facilitate any repatriation
of funds to the United States.

There were ways of getting around even the tight
FDIP. One method was the parallel loan. The most widely
cited example of this ploy was that arranged between Raytheon,
which needed sterling for its U.K. operations, and British
Petroleum, which needed dollars for a U.S. subsidiary. Each
parent company simply lent equivalent amounts to the local
subsidiary of the other company. When this kind of deal
began to take a triangular form, OFDI had to step in and
require prior authorization. An example of the triangular
arrangement was ITT's loan to the U.S. branch of a British
insurance company in exchange for a loan to ITT(U.K.). The
difference was that the insurance company then used the loan
to buy U.S. equities, which OFDI frowned upon, since the
stock could then be sold and the capital repatriated to
the U.K.[11]

Smaller and newer foreign investors, as with the
previous controls. suffered even more from the 1968 program.
This was especially the case for companies which found it
difficult to borrow internationally because of the nature of
their activities. Construction companies, for example, found

European bankers unwilling to accept a fixed, illiquid asset
as collateral for a loan, especially if the asset was located
in an area of political instability.[12] The new element in
the FDIP was that even large corporations began to suffer
from the controls.

In March 1970, the U.S. Council of the International
Chamber of Commerce took a survey of 60 major foreign investors
to determine the effects of the FDIP.[13] The report expressed
concern about the effects of the program even on large international corporations. Firstly, the large volume of international borrowing caused by the FDIP not only made long-range
planning difficult, since expected future costs of international borrowing became more important, but was pushing
some companies to the limi of their borrowing capacity.
Two companies reported that they had had to actually disinvest
to comply with the program. Others reported retaliatory host
government restrictions on local borrowing, specifically
mentioning Mexico and Venezuela.

Secondly, the large corporations engaged in raw
materials extraction found the three-fold area schedule of
the FDIP highly constrictive. What good, they asked, was a
higher allowance in the place where they extracted the
material, if they could not fully market it because these
markets were in areas with lower investment allowances?

Finally, the report cited instances of how the FDIP

reduced exports from the United States, and claimed that any

new gain to the balance of payments accounts was of little real

meaning:

> . . . actual experience with the program has displayed
> to businessmen the mere bookkeeping character of the
> balance of payments "advantages" alleged as the raison
> d'etre of the controls. Under the controls the government
> makes a crucial distinction between liabilities of a
> bank's New York headquarters and those of its branches
> in London and Paris, and similarly between dollar funds
> available to a company in the United States and dollar
> funds available to it abroad. These largely fictitious
> distinctions are maintained at the cost of the noted
> disadvantages to business operations abroad and crippling
> disadvantages to the normal further development and contin-
> ued functioning of the United States' international capital
> and money markets.[14]

The International Economic Policy Association,

National Association of Manufacturers, the Machinery and

Allied Products Institute and other trade organizations

submitted protests to various Congressional committee

hearings: particularly the Joint Economic Committee's hearings

on the President's Economic Report for 1968 and the House

Foreign Affairs Committee's hearings on the FDIP. The common

theme of the protests was that the FDIP was causing grievous

injury to foreign investors, large and small, and not helping

the balance of payments.

The Results: Analysis and Criticism

The reactions of individual firms suggests that the

control programs produced three types of phenomena. Firstly,

financing was shifted out of the United States. In its

immediate effects this benefited the balance of payments (reducing the outflow of the items selected) without depriving investors of the capacity to acquire foreign financial and real assets. However, this balance of payments gain could have been offset by substitution within the capital account. To the extent that capital assets are substitutable, the lower outflows of certain items could have been offset by larger outflows of other items. Convertible Eurobonds are a case in point: a reduction in direct investment may be offset as foreigners convert the debt into stock, sell it, and repatriate the funds as a portfolio outflow from the United States. Thirdly, there are transfer effects onto the current account. Even if the controls did not reduce the acquisition of foreign assets, but simply moved the financing out of the United States, there could still be adverse transfer effects insofar as this effect is affected by the source of finance for the purchase of the asset. Furthermore, there undoubtedly was some reduction in the acquisition of foreign assets even if only because of the cost and inconvenience of foreign financing.

1. Effects: The International Debt Shift

This was an argument commonly used to defend the direct investment restrictions (though it is applicable also to the IET and VFCR) against the accusation that a reduction in foreign

investment reduces both visible (e.g., exports) and invisible
(e.g., dividends) benefits to the balance of payments. Even
if the debt incurred abroad is guaranteed by a U.S. parent
corporation, there is still a balance of payments gain in
shifting the structure of U.S. liabilities to foreigners (i.e.,
a direct investment outflow which would end up as a short-term
liability of the banking system or the U.S. government is
converted into a long-term liability of a U.S. corporation).
This became a standard governmental defense of the controls.[15]

There was a large increase in foreign borrowing by
corporations ($?.5 billion of long-term debt was outstanding
by the end of 1971) and an increase in the deposit liabilities of overseas branches of U.S. banks. In the case
of direct investment, it has been suggested that U.S. corporations borrowed even more than they needed to comply with the
FDIP,[16] though this does not necessarily mean that their
investment would not have been greater in the absence of
controls.

In the short term, this debt or liability shift was
the most immediate effect of the controls. It was certainly
the primary effect experienced by foreign investors. The
controls were, therefore, successful in their immediate
purpose of shifting long-term financing (the IET and FDIP)
and bank loans (the VFCR) out of the United States. For
the same reasons, a sudden removal of the controls would

produce large outflows, at least for a short period of time.[17]

2. Effects: Asset Substitution

Over the longer term, however, much of this immediate success of the controls was lost via substitution within the capital account. Hewson and Sakakibara, in an econometric study of the controls, found that their balance of payments effects were completely offset within the capital account, primarily through reductions in liquid liabilities to foreigners.[18] There are a number of ways in which substitution can occur. The precise reuglations of the IET, VFCR, and FDIP were often changed in attempts to cope with this problem.

While the controls attempted to separate national and international capital markets, the resort by U.S. corporations and banks to foreign funds tended to bring the markets closer. Hence the most obvious form of substitution: an increase in borrowing by corporations (or in deposit liabilities of banks) in foreign capital markets will increase interest rates, drawing liquid liabilities out of the United States and diverting future potential inflows of capital away from the United States. In addition, there were numerous indirect forms of substitution. A large California bank which wished to lend to a Japanese company, but was prevented by the VFCR, simply made the loan to the local subsidiary of the Japanese company, which then transferred the funds bank to its head office. The exempted countries also acted as substitution vehicles. In 1968, for example, large amounts of funds shifted from Canada to Europe. This may have been due to the effect of Canada's exemption from the FDIP in shifting funds to Canada, which left more Canadian loanable funds available to foreigners.[19]

3. Effects: The Current Account

Finally, the effects of the controls were partly offset over a longer period of time by transfer effects onto the current account. The preponderant trend in empirical studies of the subject is to suggest that controls on foreign investment have a negative impact on the current account. Wiesner point to this problem with regard to the IET.[20] Lees suggests that the VFCR hurt U.S. exports.[21] Others have elaborated on Machlup's famous "transfer gap" article and examined the effect of direct investment controls on U.S. imports and exports. Morawetz conducted an econometric study from which he concluded that financial transfers in aggregate have little effect on imports but do stimulate exports.[22] Directing his attention specifically to direct investment and exports, Horst found that foreign investment and U.S. exports are, in the aggregate, complementary.[23]

These transfer effects assume that controls did result in some reduction in the ownership of the targeted foreign

assets (e.g., because of higher borrowing costs), not merely
a shift in the source of financing. However, even if there
was merely a shift in financing, there could still be negative
current account effects. A loan from a local foreign bank
might, for example, be tied to local procurement of capital
or input goods in place of U.S. exports. In 1969, Occidental
Oil claimed that it had been required to make substantial foreign
puchases of goods and services in exchange for loans, particularly
in local capital markets.[24] A large foreign asset owned by
the local branch of a U.S. bank rather than by the head
office might be worth less to the balance of payments insofar
as local costs absorb part of the potential remittance to the
United States.

Thus, in considering these three types of reactions
to capital controls (shifting sources of finance, substitution
and transfer effects), the weight of the literature suggests
that controls are effective in the short term. They do produce obvious reductions in the items selected. Over a long
period of time, however, substitution within the capital
account and transfer effects onto the current account whittle
away the initial benefits. This conclusion is significant
insofar as it provides a twofold rationale for the removal
of the controls. Firstly, the short-term effect of removing
the controls would be to produce a large capital outflow in
the items controlled (for the same reason that controls will

reduce these items) and in other current and capital account
items (e.g., servicing or buying the debt built up by subsidiaries during the controls). This short-term outflow effect could be manipulated for policy purposes. Secondly, the
conclusion provides a common-sense rationale for the removal
of the controls as a longer-term policy: they simply did
not help the balance of payments for more than a short period
of time.

The Removal of the Controls: Domestic Politics

The Johnson Administration did not give any
signs of changing its direct control strategy for the balance
of payments during 1968. Fowler urged the next Administration
not to dismantle any parts of the program, and in November
Johnson approved the extension of the FDIP into 1969.[25] Given
the build-up of private oppositon to the controls, and the
increasing weight of economic analysis condemning capital controls, the Johnson strategy, which appeared to be that of trying
to stop any change in the international monetary system, was
an ideal election year target for a Republican candidate.
Candidate Nixon was able to present himself as a President
who would make radical changes in the international monetary
system; a rather unfair accusation, since the Bator-Fowler
strategy had been designed to do this by getting SDR's in place.

Opposition to controls on ideological grounds fitted in

well with the belief of Republican economists (at that time!)
that controls of any kind simply do not work. Most of the
incoming Administration were "free-market" men. Secretary
of the Treasury designate, D. M. Kennedy, declared that he
had worked "most of my life" to reduce barriers to international trade and capital flows;[26] he was at the time
chairman of Continental Illinois National Bank. Similarly,
chairman designate of the CEA, Paul McCracken, declared that
"We set up some machinery at Bretton Woods to achieve a more
liberal international trading system. We have to be careful
that we don't start giving up our liberal system to preserve
the machinery."[27] Declarations to this effect became a
permanent part of statements on international economics, despite
some notable deviations from the policy.

There may also have been a certain "election payoff"
element, as one Johnson Administration official (among others)
has suggested.[28] Nixon's pre-election speeches on the
subject made reference to the dubious legality of the controls
and he pledged to remove them at the earliest possible opportunity. Private opposition to the controls was strong and
long lasting. The Williams Commission (which included some
of the country's largest foreign investors) recorded its
condemnation of the controls, though the controls had been
greatly weakened even before the Commission was established
in 1970.[29]

In any case, the newly elected President directed the
Treasury to study ways of removing the controls. Commerce
Secretary Stans made new appointments to his advisory
committee on the controls: "The Committee will advise the
Secretary on steps to simplify the OFDI and on further
means of relaxing the program as balance of payments conditions
permit."[30] For 1969, the controls were eased considerably;
the direct investment target was raised by $250 million,
the threshold below which an investment was uncontrolled
was raised, and companies could now choose to calculate allowances on the basis of earnings rather than the 1965-66 base
period.[31]
  All of these factors can be seen at least implicitly
in Nixon's message to Congress on the balance of payments in
April 1969:

> . . . the problem of regaining equilibrium in the
> U.S. balance of payments cannot be solved with expedients
> that postpone the problem to another year. We shall
> stop treating symptoms and start treating causes, and
> we shall find our solutions in the framework of freer
> trade and payments.
> "Fundamental economics" call for:
> - creating the conditions that make it possible to
>   rebuild our trade surplus.
> - ultimate dismantling of the network of direct
>   controls which may seem useful in the short run but
>   are self-defeating in the long run.
>   . . .
> - In international investment we will review our own
>   regulations and tax policy to assure that foreign
>   investment in the U.S. is not discouraged; for example,
>   we move now to eliminate from our laws the prospective
>   taxation of interest on foreign-held bank deposits.
>   . . .

Accordingly, I have begun, gradually but purposefully, to dismantle the direct controls which only
mask the underlying problem.
    Specifically:
    First, I have today signed an Executive order (11464)
reducing the effective rate of the interest equalization
tax from 1¼ percent to ¼ of 1 percent.
                    . . .
    Second, I have approved a recommendation to relax
somewhat the foreign direct investment program of the
Department of Commerce. This means that most firms
investing abroad will have substantially more freedom
in planning these investments.
                    . . .
    Third, I have been informed by Chairman Martin of
modifications in the Federal Reserve program which will
provide more flexibility for commercial banks, particularly
smaller and medium-sized banks, to finance U.S. exports.[32]

Each of the factors cited above--rational economic analysis,

election politics, ideology--might have been sufficient to

explain the removal of the controls. However, beginning in

April 1969 the relaxation of the controls was accelerated.

This was due to an entirely new factor: linkage politics

within the international monetary issue area.

    International economics had already been linked to other

issues (e.g., NATO burden sharing), and the Europeans had

linked SDR's, the Gold Pool, and the dollar "overhang" to U.S.

balance of payments adjustment. There was, therefore, ample

precedent for attempting to use the removal of the controls

to obtain concessions desired by the United States. Bator

had suggested the possibility of demonetizing gold or imposing

capital controls so stringent that the Europeans would find

the effects sufficiently painful to stop obstructing system

reforms, but rejected both.[33] In general, however, Bator
(and other members of the Johnson Administration) were against
tactics of linkage which produced confrontation. By the
end of the Johnson Administration, the Bator strategy of
moving to an SDR based system with more easily adjustable
exchange rates had run out of steam because of the unwillingness of the Administration to try tactics which might force
its major trading partners to revalue their currencies.
At a time when pressure for some kind of system-level change
was growing from within the United States, and even within
the government (notably from the Joint Economic Committee[34]),
a new tactic was clearly in order.

This tactic came to be known as "benign neglect":
deliberately allowing the balance of payments to deteriorate.
The European and Japanese governments would be forced to
either accept revaluation of exchange rates, inflate or impose controls; the first two were unacceptable and the third
had little success. The only major alternative would be to
attempt to exchange their excess dollar reserves for gold.
Since dollar liabilities to foreigners exceeded U.S. gold
reserves, this latter course of action would precipitate a
break-down of the system. The result would be much the same
in the end, since the United States would be forced to float
the dollar against gold. Bator had seen this latter option
(viz., demonetizing gold and letting the dollar float) but

rejected it: "As long as there is a chance for a reasonable, cooperative solution by consensus, it is wrong for a great power to settle matters by 'force majeure.'"[35] Benign neglect was an attempt to find a middle course between the Johnson policy of trying to persuade others to cooperate and the alternative extreme of taking unilateral action which would leave them with no choice. The goal was the same for all three courses of action; only the tactics differed.

Benign neglect originated in a Republican pré-election task force in 1968, chaired by Professor Gottfried Haberler. As Haberler himself explains it, the policy had three aspects: U.S. macro-economic policy should be guided by domestic economic objectives only; the balance of payments should not be corrected with artificial controls; and, finally, the United States should not try to devalue the dollar but leave it to other nations to revalue.[36]

.   The actual task force report did not express the policy quite in this way. It recommended a movement towards freer trade and capital movements, a "flexible" gold policy, and unilateral U.S. action if all else failed. The consensus among the group was that the best tactic would be to begin dismantling the capital controls; this was, at the time, the only low-confrontation option available, since domestic priorities dictated a deflationary monetary and fiscal policy. If the removal of the controls set off a "gold rush," the

report suggested, the United States should suspend convertibility and keep going with benign neglect.[37] Inconvertibility
would be a last resort; as one of the task force's economists
put it:

> Perhaps rather than going inconvertible the best response
> would be to take off the capital controls. This would
> be a clear political act on the /part of the/ United
> States to make it clear that we are going to be following
> a passive policy until such time as the international
> community decided they want to follow such other
> reasonable alternative.[38]

In April 1969 a group of U.S. officials (including
Houthakker of the CEA and Volcker from the Treasury) visited
European financial officials. They were told by the individual
countries, as well as by EEC Commissioner for Monetary Affairs,
that if the United States devalued, so would Europe. Since
this had been the expected response, the Europeans were
then told that the United States would begin dismantling its
capital controls.[39] It was then, during a speech delivered
at the University of Bonn, that Houthakker made the first
official declaration of benign neglect, explaining it in
exactly the same terms as did Haberler several years later:
macroeconomic policy for domestic objectives, no controls,
and let other countries reach their own decisions on how and
when to reach a cooperative solution with the United States.
He went on to explain that some variability of exchange
rates was required and that the U.S. decision to remove the
controls "should not be underrated," leaving it to his

audience to deduce the precise implications of his talk.[40]

Between 1965 and 1968, the source of international monetary policy shifted from the Treasury to the White House staff. During the first two and a half years of the Nixon Administration, policy was largely determined by the CEA. This was partly by default, as the White House was not very interested in this area and partly because Treasury appears to have been confused and divided on policy at this time. The Council on International Economic Policy was not established until 1971, and even then had very limited jurisdiction and influence under two directors, Peter Flanigan and Peter Peterson.

The Nixon system of foreign policy decision-making made Kissinger the "prime official" in foreign policy.[41] However, the President had little interest in foreign economic issues (except where they had domestic political aspects), though he did give explicit approval to both the dismantling of the controls (in April 1969) and to benign neglect (in June 1969).[42] Kissinger had little interest in economics, domestic or foreign, at this time. In the first years of the Administration, when economics came up, "Henry's eyes tended to glaze over," as one friend put it.[43] However, there were members of Kissinger's NSC staff who took an interest in such things.

Fred Bergsten, Kissinger's Assistant for International

Economic Affairs, was very much in favour of removing the
capital controls, but rejected benign neglect: he liked the
tactic but not the strategy. He rejected controls as bad
eocnomics (i.e., there are too many loopholes and they don't
help the balance of payments in the long term) and bad politics:
". . . The primary objective /of removing controls7 would be
to signal clearly to the world that we do not intend to rely
on controls to achieve adjustment."[44] Yet he rejected benign
neglect as too belligerent a strategy--it simply emphasized
U.S. hegemonial power and antagonized those to whom it was
directed.[45] His preference was to look for more cooperative
ways to move to a system of international control over liquidity
and adjustment. Finding benign neglect too extreme a tactic,
he naturally also rejected the subsequent "August 1971" tactic
to reach the same goal.[46]

Yet Bergsten, like most other NSC staffers, had no
power--though, unlike many others, he stayed on until May 1971.
The State Department took a position similar to that of
Bergsten: controls were not a viable long-term economic
policy, but a tactic which could lead to confrontation was
undesirable. State did want international monetary reform,
fearing that continued monetary conflicts would undermine the
NATO alliance, but wanted a more cooperative tactic.[47] However, State, like Bergsten, had no effective policy input in
this field.

Therefore, the only potentially effective opposition
to either removing the controls or benign neglect (or both)
would have to have come from Treasury or the Federal Reserve.
Yet both were divided on the subject of controls, though fairly
unified in their rejection of benign neglect. While benign
neglect remained the dominant policy, it caused "endless em-
barrassment" for the Treasury and the Fed in dealing with their
foreign counterparts.[48]

Most of the accounts of U.S. international monetary
policy during this period attribute an overwhelming dominance
to the Treasury, particularly through the sub-Cabinet level
Volcker Group, chaired by Undersecretary of the Treasury
for International Affairs, Paul Volcker.[49] Treasury did
regain some power it lost in the post-Dillon era, but from
1969 to 1971, it did not effectively rival the CEA as a
source of policy. Treasury's policy had been to tie the
removal of the controls to an improvement in the balance of
payments, as the Europeans had demanded in 1967. Decontrol
in April 1969 (when the balance of payments was deteriorating)
was a reversal of Treasury's tactics. Treasury accepted the
need for exchange rate changes, but not the strategy of
benign neglect via decontrol.[50]

Undersecretaries Deming and Volcker frequently told
Congressional committees that the capital controls could not
be quickly removed because the balance of payments deficit

had to be eliminated first.[51] Volcker made similar statements
in urging House and Senate Committees to renew the IET in
1969.[52] The Deming-Volcker line reflected the "old" Treasury
view held during the Johnson Administration. The new Secretary of the Treasury, D. M. Kennedy, expressed himself very
much in favour of removing the controls, though probably more
for ideological reasons than for approval of benign neglect.
This division within Treasury greatly weakened its bureaucratic
power in this area, until Connally arrived on the scene in
1971.

The Federal Reserve opposed benign negelct, but was
divided on controls. According to Houthakker, the Fed did
understand benign neglect and did not like it because it
offended their foreign colleagues.[53] It is likely that they
did understand the goal, but did not approve of it. Chairman
Martin later said that the first devaluation in 1971 had been
the sign of a profound "failure" of American policy.[54] Other
members of the board, such as S. J. Maisel, favoured the
goal of exchange rate change, but disliked the strategy of
benign neglect.

The Fed was divided on tactics as well as strategy.
Brimmer and Dewey Daane were against the removal of the controls:
Daane because he wanted fixed exchange rates and Brimmer because the control program (not only the VFCR but the voluntary
direct investment program from 1965 to 1967) was, as one

contemporary put it, "Brimmer's Baby." Brimmer's argument
against decontrol was that it would lead to "a substantial
outpouring of funds"[55]--which was precisely the object of
benign neglect. Martin, as was indicated in chapter six, did
not favour controls, but he favoured exchange rate changes
even less. Thus, what Houthakker saw as the Fed simply not
knowing what was going on, was more likely a situation of the
Fed Board being divided on strategy and tactics.

The Commerce Department, as before, had little influence. In any case, Commerce was suffering some cognitive
dissonance on the decontrol question. On the one hand,
Commerce retained its overall ideological dislike of controls;
but on the other, it had developed an institutional mission.
OFDI's director, C. E. Fiero, suggested the controls should
be continued indefinitely, since the current account does not
adjust quickly enough to capital account changes, so that
U.S. controls are necessary for "world financial stability."[56]
Furthermore, the leadership of Commerce apparently did not
understand benign neglect. Like the Fed, they opposed any
rapid decontrol on the grounds that a massive capital outflow
would result. K. N. Davis, Assistant Secretary for Domestic and International Business, publicly attacked those who,
in his opinion, were saying that the balance of payments
did not matter.[57] The CEA tactic, to act as if the balance
of payments did not matter, was apparently not comprehended.

Thus, during the first two years of the Administration the CEA reigned supreme in international monetary policy because of lack of interest, understanding or unity on the part of potential alternative sources of policy. It was not until Connally became Treasury Secretary that benign neglect began to lose favour, or at least the specific tactic (i.e., decontrol) by which it was being implemented began to be seen as inadequate to the task.

The Removal of the Controls: International Tactics

Benign neglect by decontrol had one major fault as a tactic: it didn't work because the Europeans were not sorry to see the controls removed. The Houthakker-Volcker mission to Europe in April 1969 confirmed the European refusal to accept exchange rate changes, though Germany and Italy were sympathetic and the U.K. "lukewarm" to the idea of exchange rate discussions. When told that the United States would therefore begin to remove its capital controls, Houthakker and Volcker were rather surprised to find that there was very little opposition.[58] Belgium, Spain and Ireland had been officially requesting exemptions from the FDIP; the U.K. and Italy wanted U.S. capital, and the French needed it. Only the Netherlands, West Germany and Switzerland were concerned about the possible effects of capital inflows on their exchange rates and domestic rates of inflation. The former two were, however, also sympathetic to U.S. aims and Germany, in particular, was reluctant to openly resist U.S. policy.

The Europeans were, in aggregate, not sorry to see the controls removed for several general reasons. The general macroeconomic benefits (employment, income, etc.) were readily apparent. At the micro-level, the controls were causing considerable congestion in the Euromarkets, higher interest rates and the crowding out of smaller European borrowers. In addition, there were several unique events which probably made U.S. capital markets more attractive. The political events of 1968 in France and Czechoslovakia simulated large inflows of European portfolio capital into the United States: foreign purchases of U.S. securities jumped from $849 million in 1967 to $2126 million in 1968. This same instability and tight capital market conditions was shifting U.S. capital flows toward Asia, Africa and Latin America.[59]

In 1969, the situation worsened as the U.S. deflation took large amounts of liquid capital out of Europe to the United States.[60] The confluence of all these circumstances not only made European governments less resistant to U.S. capital inflows, but made them eager to activate the new SDR scheme.[61] In 1967 it was the Europeans who were delaying activation to force the United States to control capital outflows. Finally, the movement towards European Monetary

Unification in 1969 may have made certain weak currency
countries even more eager for U.S. capital, if they were to
be capable of staying in the EMU's "snake."

Thus, while the Europeans generally rejected the
goal and the compellence strategy of benign neglect, they
had good reason to welcome the specific tactic being employed.
The particular situations of several countries deserve
closer attention.

The most obvious effect on Britain of the FDIP was to
make it harder for the 1967 devaluation to improve the U.K.
balance of payments. The situation then went from bad to
worse. Britain was forced to request a $2 billion stand-by
credit from the Group of Ten in September 1968, and in the
following month announced a deflationary "mini-budget."[62]
This, on top of the capital-diverting effect of Britain's
exclusion from the EEC in November 1968, made long-term
capital inflows vital to Britain 's economic health.

Even before the events of May 1968, observers were
predicting that France would be hard hit by a slowdown in
U.S. investment.[63] While the French government was officially
contemptuous of the inadequacy of the U.S. program, privately
there was some consternation: the economy had a deflationary
gap of about 7-8 percent and the balance of payments deficit
had been expected to widen even before the FDIP was announced.
A resumption of capital inflows would be one of the few ways

France could avoid the devaluation which the government had
rejected. In an effort to mitigate the effects of the FDIP,
Finance Minister Debre had a "very frank" discussion with
Undersecretary of State Katzenbach, in which he stated France's
opposition to any special terms for the U.K. (i.e, diverting
U.S. capital from France) and warned that any large repatriation of profits by U.S. companies affected by the FDIP
would be forcibly prevented.[64] The French financial daily
Le Nouveau Journal, predicted that French industry would suffer
heavily because profit margins were too low to allow them
to borrow at the higher interest rates induced by the FDIP.[65]

Following the May riots, France's situation worsened.
In November the government announced cuts in government
spending, exchange controls and tax changes to encourage
exports. Thus, by 1969, France was hardly in a position
to do anything but welcome U.S. investment, both for balance
of payments reasons (though the franc still had to be
devalued) and for domestic reasons. After May 1968 French
policy on U.S. investment was relaxed, and after de Gaulle's
resignation in 1969, Premier Chaban-Delmas announced that the
government would only intervene where there was danger of an
entire sector falling under foreign control.[66] Since then,
the French government has taken out annual special advertising
supplements in Business Week to announce that:

Needless to say, foreign investors are really

welcome. Many that have already joined us in France
will tell you that their corporate objectives and the goals
of the French government are not only compatible, but can
work to our mutual advantage.[67]

The attitude of the German government was more complex.

Sympathetic to the U.S. desire for exchange rate changes,

Germany offered little resistance to the removal of the U.S.

controls. There are several other reasons which may have

muted German opposition to decontrol. Firstly, Germany was

recovering from a mild recession during 1968, and the FDIP

was seen to be hampering this recovery. Secondly, the kind

of capital inflows which Germany was trying to prevent were

short-term, destabilizing flows; long-term direct investment

inflows were welcomed for the same macroeconomic reasons that

they were welcomed in other countries, particularly since the

1967/68 recession had resulted in unusually large outflows

of long-term capital from Germany in 1968/69. Portfolio and

direct investment outflows increased from DM 2.4 billion in

1967 to DM 7.2 billion in 1968 and DM 11.5 billion in 1969,

falling back to DM 4.5 billion in 1970. A third reason why

Germany may have welcomed decontrol is that the OECD was

urging it to reflate the consumer sector of the economy,

to help the balance of payments of its less fortunate partners;[68]

such a policy was anathema to policy-makers for whom the rule

was recovery led by investment in the capital goods sector

for export growth.

Other countries which welcomed U.S. capital (e.g.,
Spain, Ireland, Belgium, Italy) had no reason to oppose
decontrol. With the exception of Italy, however, these
countries were not important in the success or failure of
benign neglect. The other country of importance was Japan,
which rejected the strategy of benign neglect (not wanting
to revalue the yen), but had no reason to oppose the tactic
of decontrol since Japan could, by itself, regulate undesirable
capital inflows. Indeed, threats to remove Japanese exemptions were more likely to be successful; in February 1970 the
IET was restored on portfolio flows to Japan.[69]

Thus, while the governments whose policies were critical
to the success of benign neglect rejected its goals, they
welcomed the tactic of decontrolling capital flows. In
addition, they pretended not to understand the goal of
benign neglect; this enabled them to enjoy the benefits of
U.S. capital inflows while avoiding the crux of the issue by
criticizing the United States for having no coherent adjustment policy. The 1971 report of the Bank for International
Settlements criticized the United States for not having any
plan to cure the deficit. This was, according to Houthakker,
pure hypocrisy, since the BIS understood very well what the
United States was trying to do.[70]

Epilogue: August 1971 and After

By 1971 it was clear that benign neglect was not working. Only the Deutschemark had been revalued by a small amount in 1969. The unilateral suspension of dollar convertibility into gold, the import surcharge and other measures were not, as some commentors saw it, a dramatic change in policy. The Haberler report of 1968 mentioned such action as a last resort. As one of the practitioners of benign neglect put it: "The drastic actions taken by John Connally while he was Secretary of the Treasury were a departure from the tactics, though not the strategy, of benign neglect."[71] What the August 1971 policy had done was to make benign neglect explicit: foreign central banks were being told that they would hold dollars whether they liked it or not. The subsequent realignment of exchange rates delayed the process of removing the capital controls. Under Treasury Secretary Shultz, the strategy of benign neglect returned and, subject to other influences, the controls were finally removed in January 1974.

It required more than a lack of response by Europe and Japan to force a shift to a more vigorous compellence strategy. The rise of John Connally provided a powerful boost to the opponents of benign neglect.[72] Curiously, many of those who joined the anti-benign neglect movement were not thinking of exchange rate changes. Peter Peterson,

director of the Council on International Economic Policy
and former President of Bell and Howell, was probably
thinking of tariffs. Dewey Daane of the Federal Reserve
Board constantly attacked benign neglect during the spring
of 1971, on the grounds that diplomatic repercussions would
lead to trade and capital flow restrictions by other countries.[73]

By 1971 capital controls were no longer an important
issue, save for the few foreign securities dealers who duti-
fully testified to the House Ways and Means Committee
against the IET during its extension in 1971. The focus of
policy was not directly on exchange rates, specifically on
what kind of exchange rate alignment should be advocated and
the specific measures to be used.

At the resulting Smithsonian Agreement in December
1971, as a part of the Euro-Japanese revaluation plus U.S.
devaluation compromise, the United States formally announced
that the capital controls would be continued.[74] This was
partly a diplomatic concession to the Europeans, and partly
because the French government was asking for more stringent
controls on U.S. capital outflows.[75] At this stage, preventing further revaluation of the franc was more important
to President Pompidou than the benefits of U.S. investment,
particularly when the investment consisted of relatively
liquid assets.

During 1972 the strategy of benign neglect was resumed

under Treasury Secretary Shultz. As The Economist noted:
". . . The U.S. is once again being forced by the inertia of
its allies, particularly the Europeans, to suggest its own
solutions to the economic problems. . ."[76] In February 1973
the dollar was again devalued, and, to emphasize the U.S.
insistance on the move toward flexible exchange rates as the
major international adjustment measure, Shultz announced
that the last vestiges of the capital controls would be removed
by the end of 1974.

The end came sooner, in February 1974. The reason for
the sudden and complete removal of all the controls was that,
as a result of the oil crisis and a trade surplus in 1973 (the
trade deficit in 1972 had been $7 billion), the dollar was
appreciating rapidly, threatening to offset the results of
the two devaluations and the 1973 currency floats.[77] In
addition, the United States wanted to facilitate the recycling
process by making it easier for the huge amounts of oil
money flowing in to flow out again.[78]

The removal of the controls aroused great fears among
Eurobankers that there would be a great rush of lending and
underwriting activity back to the United States, killing
off the Eurobond and Eurodollar markets. This has not been
the case. The U.S. capital market still carries the disadvantage of withholding tax and S.E.C. registration
requirements, and even without these legal obstacles it would

take some time for U.S. investors to become familiarized
with foreign securities, and for dealers to develop the
infrastructure for researching, rating and marketing them.
The Euromarkets, on the other hand, are still virtually
unregulated (save for some moral suasion on the part of the
Bank of England with regard to shareholders in consortia
banks); Eurobonds can be issued free of tax in bearer form;
and no reserves are required on Eurodollar deposits. Furthermore, the Euromarket has the advantage of political and
cultural proximity to its users (especially those in the
Middle East) and direct links to the growing, Singapore-based
Asian-dollar market.[79] Thus, even though capital itself will
eventually flow around most kinds of barriers, the location
of the institutions which direct this activity is still
highly sensitive to environmental constraints.

Conclusion

The removal of the controls over the period 1969-74
has two aspects. Firstly, domestic political change in the
form of corporate resistance to the FDIP, election politics
in 1968 and the general economic ideology of the Republican
Party, all provided an element of domestic politicization
which supplemented the Treasury to White House power shift,
maintaining the capital control issue at a fairly high level
of salience and controversiality. This domestic politicization

is not inconsistent with the general consensus among economists, that the controls did not help the balance of payments
over the longer term. By 1968 the controls reached an
escalation threshold; the short-term effectiveness of the
controls reached a corporate "pain threshold" and the salience
of the controls as a policy instrument reached a level sufficient to make them a national economic issue.

Secondly, the international dimension of the problem
changed. Prior to 1969 capital controls had only been a
part of U.S. international monetary strategy insofar as
European demands for some "real," unilateral adjustment by
the United States were accepted as a prerequisite for maintaining
the Bretton Woods system and putting into effect certain minor
changes (e.g., SDR's). Even those, such as Bator, who looked
to more far-reaching changes in the system did not see a
role for capital controls beyond being part of a holding
operation to prevent the balance of payments deteriorating
further while the Europeans were persuaded to move toward an
SDR-based system with more exchange rate flexibility. In 1969
controls, or decontrol, became part of an active compellence
strategy to use against the Europeans the same linkage that
had been used against the United States in 1967, namely,
the linkage between system maintenance or change and the
U.S. deficit. Yet the tactic did not work in reverse
because the European situation had changed: in 1967 they

wanted U.S. adjustment more than they wanted U.S. capital;
in 1969-70 the priority was reversed. Hence the specific
tactic of benign neglect did not provide any incentive
to comply with U.S. objectives.

CHAPTER IX

CONCLUSION

The principal purpose of this thesis was to explain
why the United States chose to implement, during the 1960's,
a balance of payments policy of the kind it had been committed
to discouraging since the end of the Second World War.
Capital controls were implicit in the norms of the Bretton
Woods system as it had developed to the end of the 1960's, but
from the standpoint of U.S. foreign economic policy objectives,
such controls could be justified only as a temporary expedient.
It has been suggested that the reasons for the choice of capital
controls by U.S. balance of payments policy-makers may be
found in a complex interplay of both domestic and international
political factors. What is especially salient in the evolution of the U.S. capital control program is that its
sources and objectives changed during the decade of its operation. Starting as a primarily domestic bureaucratic policy
response dictated by Treasury dominance of balance of payments policy, capital controls became part of a wider international strategy with its source more in the Executive
branch of government than in bureaucratic policy preferences.
The key to this shifting locus of authority is politicization:

what began as a temporary balance of payments measure became
part of a long struggle by the United States first to maintain
the existing international monetary system, then to find a
suitable stopgap measure while a new system was being negotiated, and finally, to force the principal allies of the
United States to accept certain changes in the structure of
the system.

This process of politicization had its origins in the
norms and values of the Bretton Woods system. The original
Anglo-U.S. disagreement on the structure of the system was
expressed in the differences between the Keynes Plan (to
emphasize liquidity in the system) and the White Plan (focusing
on domestic adjustment rather than liquidity). The result
was an agreement which paid lip-service to both imperatives,
yet did not provide any effective means for implementing either
of them. The newly created International Monetary Fund
could provide liquidity, but only in small amounts and on
terms that were not acceptable to most potential borrowers.
Neither was there any effective mechanism for coaxing
countries to use macroeconomic policy to adjust as an
alternative to financing payments imbalances. The only way
out of this dilemma was to give tacit approval to current
and capital account controls, particularly the latter.

The United States compromised in accepting a practice
inconsistent with its stated international economic policy

for two major reasons. Firstly, compromise was necessary in order to make the system work: the United States provided the system's primary collective good (viz., an international reserve asset of relatively stable value with respect to gold), leaving it to other countries to adjust their external balances vis-à-vis the United States. The ironic flaw in this arrangement was that it implied a confusions of ends and means, since the purpose of the international financial system is to facilitate the exchange of real goods and services and factors of production. The imposition of restrictions on trade and capital flows in order to maintain the international payments sytem resulted in a contradictory situation, the nature of which became more painfully obvious when the United States itself chose to adopt capital account controls during the 1960's.

The second reason for the American concession was power: the United States could afford to compromise on economic issues because its global position was assured by an overwhelming military preponderance in the political sphere.[1] Concessions did not detract from the ultimate economic power of the United States, in the sense of its ability to control events and outcomes by determining the structure of the system, and indirectly supported U.S. military power by providing an incentive for its Western allies to cooperate in world politics. There was a relationship of what Baumgartner and Burns call "multiplexity": the exchange of valuables in the economic sphere for valuables in another sphere.[2] Had the United States insisted on a totally open international economy, its allies would have been less useful in the political sphere insofar as their recovery would have been delayed. Furthermore, the sooner Europe and Japan recovered economically, the sooner they would be in a position to conform to the economic as well as the military policy imperatives of the United States.

The problem here was that by the time Europe had reached the stage of recovery where it could conform to the spirit of both Bretton Woods and U.S. foreign economic objectives the United States was itself reaching the point where it could no longer do so. Just as the system reached the point where economic power was roughly congruent with the policy imperatives of the structure, this point was passed as the dollar shortage became a dollar glut. White the United States still retained its power to change the structure of the system, the policy imperatives of the existing system required it to take action to correct its own balance of payments deficit. The processes of the system were, by the 1960's, weakening rather than reinforcing U.S. power.

This erosion of U.S. power within the structure of the existing system was hastened by a higher degree of inter-dependence between the advanced industrial economies, evidenced

by the deterioration in the U.S. capital account as direct
and portfolio investment flows responded to the European-Japanese
economic recovery and growth which had been encouraged by
the United States. This increased level of sensitivity to
international economic conditions helped produce the politicization of policy responses that ultimately forced the United
States to exercise its power to change the structure of the
system. The emergence of a relatively equal distribution of
economic power (in terms of policy responses within the
existing structure) created the conditions whereby "sensitivity" interdependence politicized or enhanced disputes
about events and outcomes to the extent that the United
States felt obliged to exercise its ultimate control, to
act in the realm of "vulnerability" interdependence.[3] It
was this process of politicization of policy responses
during the 1960's that caught up with and changed the nature
of the U.S. capital controls from an instrument with which
to limit "sensitivity" interdependence to a means of exercising
control over "vulnerability" interdependence.

Why did the United States not act to change the structure of the system in the early 1960's, and avoid a decade
of debilitating stop-gap measures? For a number of reasons,
that have been dealt with in the chapters above, structural
change (viz., an exchange rate change by the United States)
was not part of the existing paradigm which dominated

international monetary policy.[4] It was the politicization
of the issue which gradually introduced and made acceptable
the option of structural change.[5] The course of this process is reflected in the history of the U.S. capital control
programs. The implementation of the controls up to 1971 was
indicative of an unwillingness to resort to unilateral measures,
though the idea of structural change was being gradually
introduced.

This may be seen in the three basic phases of the
program. During the period 1963-65 controls were primarily
a bureaucratic, Treasury-dominated choice of a means to
protect the existing system against adverse conditions which
were seen to be temporary. From 1965 to 1968, locus of
authority shifted to the White House and the purpose of the
controls developed into a holding operation to be maintained
until the SDR scheme was in place as the foundation stone of
a new system. Finally, in the period 1969-71, capital controls
became part of a deliberate compellence strategy to force
other nations to accept exchange rate changes.

These changes in the nature of the program can be seen
as the result of politicization which was both domestic
and international in origin. Domestic politicization was
responsible for the successively higher levels at which the
issue was discussed, resulting in a reduction in the purely
bureaucratic element in the policy choices and an enhanced

role for the preferences of the President and his immediate circle of advisors. The year 1965 was the threshold point in this process, largely as a result of the departure of two dominating personalities, Dillon and Roosa, and the rise of a new group of Presidential advisors around Francis Bator. Subsequently, under the Nixon Administration the bureaucratic politics element appears to have re-emerged with the intra-mural disputes over both the tactic of removing the controls and the strategy of benign neglect. However, the level of decision-making remained essentially at a higher level than during the days of almost total Treasury dominance in the early 1960's. This was in part due to the increased opposition of private interests to controls after 1968.

Concurrently, the issue was also being politicized in an international sense. From 1963, when the IET was imposed as a unilateral measure without any significant policy input from other countries, the controls increasingly became the subject of international dispute as Western Europe exerted influence in the direction of a more stringent control program during 1967. In the following phase, from 1969 to 1971, the controls remained an international issue--both because benign neglect in general was either misunderstood or disliked (or both) and because the controls in particular were no longer viewed with favour.

Thus, politicization, both domestic and international,

may be seen as the key intervening variable which explains
the changing policy framework for this aspect of international
monetary politics. Rather than attempting to apply a single
decision-making model, one must see this case study as an
explanatory problem requiring the linking of several of the
currently popular modes of explanation. Politicization
resulted in a transition from what one might call a situation
of "domestic bureaucratic imperialism" to one of "internationalized
Executive politics." While these characterizations lack
brevity and elegance, they may reflect more accurately the
complexity of real policy decisions than would an attempt to
characterize the explanation offered in this thesis as
primarily bureaucratic politics, interest group politics,
Presidential politics, or as a rational actor model.

It is this underlying trend of politicization which is
reflected in the causal importance of the elements selected
for treatment in each chapter. Chapter three established
the basis for a political explanation, namely that there is
no obvious policy recommendation in the economic theory on
the subject. Chapter four illustrated how the policy decision
is perfectly consistent with a model of rational political
choice in an international state policy framework. Such
an explanation, focusing on the norms and values of state
policy, implies a high level of politicization of the issue,
such that the policy-making process goes on above

intra-governmental dissension. For this reason, the state
policy framework was judged to be more applicable to this
issue from the mid-1960's. Chapters five and six support
this judgment, analysing the pattern of domestic interest
aggregation. Domestic private interest groups were, as
chapter five indicates, relatively inactive on the issue of
capital controls. This inactivity established a permissive
environment which made it possible for bureaucratic politics
to play a role limited by the politicization of the problem.
Bureaucratic factors declined in importance after 1965, not
because of the arousal of interest group attention, but
because Executive level attention was drawn to the issue.
While intra-mural disagreements again became more noticeable
after 1968, policy-making authority never fell back from the
Executive to the purely bureaucratic level.

Chapters seven and eight show how the international
dimension of the capital control problem grew from a factor
of negligible importance in 1963, to a significant exogenous
pressure on U.S. policy in 1967, and finally to an integral
part of that policy in 1969. This international politicization
reinforced the domestic politicization process in focusing
the issue on Executive level decision-makers. There was, it
has been noted, a revival of domestic interest politics over
the issue after 1968, both from private interests and bureaucratic groups. However, by this time the capital control

policy was locked into an international strategy, such that
a revival of domestic political interest in the subject was
not a critical influence on policy-making.

These phenomena--domestic and international politiciza-
tion--are symptomatic of a system undergoing change. The
case of U.S. capital controls was, albeit, only one element
in this process of change; yet it does illustrate the way
in which this transformation took place and the consequences
of the change. The study may also be the basis for further
reflections on some of the current questions for debate among
political economists.

It has become very much the vogue to suggest that the
nation-state as an explanatory concept is obsolete. The
political institutions relating to international finance are,
it has been suggested, ". . . carried forward by an irre-
pressible evolutionary process. . .,"[6] and ". . . the true
logic of the global economy. . ."[7] is outpacing the political
structure. The relationship between politics and economics
is a reciprocal one in which the causal effects are not unam-
biguously in one direction. While it is largely true that
the structure of the Bretton Woods system made the process of
break-down virtually inevitable as the economic power relationships between the key participants changed, the way in
which change occurred was preeminently political.

Even among those who do not see international economic

change in a historicist fashion, there is a tendency to
see fundamental changes which are not obviously supported
by this case study. Morse, among others, sees the politics
of "power and position" being superseded by the politics of
"wealth and welfare."[8] The U.S. capital controls were a
problem which involved both power and welfare, the former
being generally a more important determinant policy if not
the underlying trend of that policy.

These questions of economic determinism and welfare
versus power politics converge in the debate over whether
and to what extent the world is "interdependent." Both
the economic determinist and the "wealth and welfare"
political economist suggest that the responsiveness of
national economies to incremental changes in other countries
is rising. This case study supports this hypothesis, reflected
in both the development of the U.S. capital account problem
and the difficulty in successfully dealing with it.

However, in considering the extent to which interdependence exists in the form of mutual economic vulnerability, both of these schools of thought have little to
say, since here what is at stake is more a question of political
choice relating to the ability of a state to change the structure of the system. The political choices examined in this
case study suggest the conditions under which this type of
interdependence may be successfully exploited.

The entire period of capital controls has often been
seen as one of the decline and fall of American dominance
over the world monetary system. What this case study suggests
is that the capital controls were indicative of a temporary
slippage of hegemonial power. Ultimately these controls
were a means by which the United States re-established its
power over the international monetary system. The dollar
is, once again, the key vehicle currency in international
trade and finance, and the policies of the United States
are the major determinants of the overall trends not only in
international trade policies but in the domestic macroeconomic policies of many countries. The dollar is likely
to remain the strongest currency for the foreseeable future,
thereby determining the exchange rate and, indirectly, the
general thrust of the macroeconomic policies of the other
major trading nations.

CHAPTER I

1. Henry Kissinger, interviewed by Business Week, 13 January 1975, p. 76.

2. The term "capital" is used here to denote both direct investment flows (i.e., capital as a real factor of production) and portfolio or financial capital in the form of various types of securities. "Long-term" is used in the normal sense, referring to capital flows having a maturity of more than one year.

3. G. Modelski, "Some Continuities in the Structure of World Politics," Harvard University, November 1973, p. 6 (mimeo.).

4. A. Inkeles, "The Emerging Social Structure of the World," paper prepared for presentation at the International Political Science Association Meeting in Montreal, Canada, August 1973, p. 15 (mimeo.).

5. The Bretton Woods Agreement did not specifically endorse capital controls, but neither did it contain any articles recommending that they not be used, except in the extreme case of exchange control, which, it was assumed, would be gradually dismantled as circumstances permitted.

6. The net liquidity concept assumes that the net balance on current account items, long-term capital flows and non-liquid short-term capital flows are the autonomous items in the balance of payments account which must be offset by accommodating transactions.
    For an explanation of balance of payments concepts, see R. M. Stern, The Balance of Payments (Chicago: Aldine, 1973), chapter 1.

7. E. L. Morse, Foreign Policy and Interdependence in Gaullist France (Princeton: Princeton University Press, 1973), p. 3.

8. J. D. Hogan, The U.S. Balance of Payments and Capital Flows (New York: Praeger, 1967); A. Cairncross, Control of Long-Term Capital Movements (Washington: Brookings Institution, 1973); the U.S. capital controls programs

have also been the subject of numerous monographs and journal articles, almost all of a technical economic nature.

9. These terms are here used in the sense defined by Nye and Keohane: "transnational relations" consists of "transnational interactions," where at least one actor is non-governmental, and "transgovernmental interactions," which occur between sub-units of different governments. See. R. O. Keohane and J. S. Nye, Transnational Relations and World Politics (Cambridge, Mass.: Harvard University Press, 1972), introduction and conclusion.

CHAPTER II

1. An interesting exposition on this theme is contained in R. N. Cooper, The Economics of Interdependence (New York: McGraw Hill, 1968), chapters 1 and 2. Cooper's argument is that a reasonable degree of autonomy (defined as "the ability to carry out objectives of domestic economic policy") under a fixed exchange rate system requires some sacrifice in sovereignty (the formal ability of a political unit to make its own decisions).

2. Brief histories of the Bretton Woods Agreement and its evolution are contained in Cooper, ibid., part 1 and W. M. Scammell, International Monetary Policy, 2nd ed. (London: Macmillan, 1964), chapters 5, 6, 7, 11. A survey of the balance of payments problems of the major trading economies is contained in B. J. Cohen, Balance of Payments Policy (Harmondsworth: Penguin, 1969), chapter 4.

3. A concise explanation of the theoretical problems of a gold exchange standard is contained in H. G. Grubel, The International Monetary System (Harmondsworth: Penguin, 1969), chapter 7.

4. A detailed account of the 1960 Gold Crisis is contained in F. Hirsch, Money International, revised ed. (Harmondsworth: Penguin, 1969), pp. 281-288.

5. The distinction between stock and flow measures of balance may be found in Cohen, Balance of Payments Policy, pp. 36-40. Examples of the line of argument cited here are: R. Vernon, "A Sceptic Looks at the Balance of Payments," Foreign Policy, 5, Winter 1971-1972; and H. S. Houthakker, testimony, U.S., Congress, Joint Economic Committee, The Balance of Payments Mess, Hearings before the Subcommittee

on International Exchange and Payments, 92d Cong., 1st sess., 1971, p. 259.

6. A recent review of the issues in balance of payments accounting may be found in P. H. Kuwayama, "Measuring the United States Balance of Payments," Federal Reserve Bank of New York, Monthly Review, August 1975.

7. P. T. Bauer and A. A. Walters, "Economists and the Dollar Problem," Lloyds' Bank Review, April 1975, p. 25.

8. R. Triffin, Gold and the Dollar Crisis (New Haven: Yale University Press, 1961). A Condensation of the book appears in H. G. Grubel (ed.), World Monetary Reform (Stanford: Stanford University Press, 1963), chapter 1.

9. Committee for Economic Development, National Objectives and the Balance of Payments Problem (New York: CED, February, 1960); Committee for Economic Development, The International Position of the Dollar (New York: CED, May 1961).

10. CED, National Objectives, p. 3.

11. U.S., Congress, Joint Economic Committee, Factors Affecting the United States Balance of Payments, Compilation of studies prepared for the Subcommittee on International Exchange and Payments, Joint Committee Print, 87th Cong., 2d sess., 1962.

12. The particular studies mentioned from the compendium cited in the previous footnote are: S. E. Harris, "The U.S. Balance of Payments: The Problem and Its Solution;" Robert V. Roosa, "Assuring the Free World's Liquidity;" J. Vanek, "Overvaluation of the Dollar: Causes, Effects and Remedies;" H. S. Houthakker, "Exchange Rate Adjustment;" and P. W. Bell, "Private Capital Movements and the U.S. Balance of Payments."

13. Walter S. Salant, et al., The United States Balance of Payments in 1968 (Washington, D.C.: The Brookings Institution, 1963).

14. Hal B. Lary, Problems of the United States as a World Trader and Banker (New York: National Bureau of Economic Research, 1963).

15. U.S., President, Public Papers of the Presidents of

the United States, John F. Kennedy, 1961, pp. 57-66.

16. Ibid., 1963, pp. 574-584.

17. Ibid., Lyndon B. Johnson, 1965, pp. 170-177.

18. Ibid., p. 171.

19. The VFCR program is outlined in"Guidelines for Banks and Nonbank Financial Institutions," Federal Reserve Bulletin, March 1965.

20. Statement of Secretary Connor; U.S., Congress, Senate, Committee on Banking and Currency, Balance of Payments-- 1965, Hearings before the Subcommittee on International Finance, 89th Cong., 1st sess., 1965, pp. 186-188.

21. "Guidelines Tighten on Foreign Investment," Business Week, 11 December 1965, p. 12.

22. Statement by the President Outlining a Program of Action to Deal with the Balance of Payments Problem, 1 January 1968, in U.S., President, Public Papers, Lyndon B. Johnson, 1968, pp. 8-13.

23. Ibid., Richard M. Nixon, 1969, p. 267.

CHAPTER III

1. Max Weber, The Theory of Social and Economic Action (New York: The Free Press, 1964), chapter I.2.

2. See D. M. Winch, Analytic Welfare Economics (Harmonds- worth: Penguin, 1971), chapter 1.

3. The neo-classical and optimal foreign investment litera- ture is surveyed in R. M. Stern, The Balance of Payments, chapters 8 and 9 (from which the discussion below is largely derived) and, more rigorously, in A. Takayama, International Trade (New York: Holt, Rinehart and Winston, 1972), pp. 452-461.

4. A. E. Jasay, "The Social Choice Between Home and Overseas Investment," Economic Journal, vol. 70, 1960; reprinted in J. H. Dunning, ed., International Investment (Harmonds- worth: Penguin, 1972). Jasay's argument is based on the proposition that increases in the capital stock abroad will affect the marginal productivity of capital at home, and thus make the problem indeterminate. Only

if overseas investment raises the marginal productivity of domestic capital can one presume that capital will be over-exported.

5. Thus concludes Thomas Horst, "American Exports and Foreign Direct Investments," Discussion Paper no. 362, May 1974, Harvard Institute of Economic Research, p. 5 (mimeo.).

6. A typical example of this line of thought is D. A. Snider, "The Case or Capital Controls to Relieve the U.S. Balance of Payments," American Economic Review, vol. 64, 1964; reprinted in Dunning, International Investment.

7. P. B. Musgrave, Taxation of Foreign Investment, Harvard University, 26 February 1975 (mimeo.).

8. R. Gilpin, U.S. Power and the Multinational Corporation (New York: Basic Books, 1975), chapter 7.

9. R. Manning, "A Nash-Cournot Model of Taxation of International Capital Movements," Economic Record, March 1974.

10. N. S. Fielecke, "The Welfare Effects of Controls over Capital Exports from the United States," Essays in International Finance, no. 82, Princeton University, 1971.

11. Fielecke makes the point here that capital flows caused by differing fiscal-monetary policy mixes in different countries are not necessarily inefficient as long as interest rate differentials are accompanied by marginal efficiency of capital differentials. A financial capital flow will thus equalize interest rates and the marginal efficiencies of capital. However, Johnson has pointed out that the corollary of this point of view is that each country's rates of investment and saving should be adjusted to achieve real transfers equal to financial transfers. Since this may have undesirable effects on the composition of output, there is no reason to suppose that this policy is superior to controlling capital movements (although here the emphasis shifts back to national welfare); see H. G. Johnson, "Theoretical Problems of an International Monetary System," in R. N. Cooper (ed.), International Finance (Harmondsworth: Penguin, 1969), pp. 315-318.

12. C. P. Kindleberger, The World in Depression, 1929-1930

(Berkeley and Los Angeles: University of California Press, 1973), pp. 54-57.

13. E. Depres, C. P. Kindleberger and W. S. Salant, "The Dollar and World Liquidity--A Minority View," The Economist, 5 February 1966, pp. 526-529.

14. Ibid., p. 527.

15. J. H. Makin, "On the Success of the Reserve Currency System in the Crisis Zone," Journal of International Economics, February 1972.

16. R. A. Mundell, "The Crisis Problem," in Monetary Problems of the International Economy (Chicago: University of Chicago Press, 1968); Mundell's model is described in H. G. Johnson, "Theoretical Problems of the International Monetary System," in Cooper, International Finance, pp. 372-330.

17. A more rigorous treatment of price versus income theories of adjustment may be found in Stern, Balance of Payments, chapter 4 and 6.

18. This presentation is drawn from R. E. Caves and R. W. Jones, World Trade and Payments (Boston: Little, Brown, 1973), chapter 22.

19. Ibid., pp. 459-460.

20. R. Mundell, International Economics (New York: Macmillan, 1968), chapter 15.

21. R. Vernon, "The Economic Consequences of U.S. Foreign Direct Investment," in Commission on International Trade and Investment Policy, United States International Economic Policy in an Interdependent World (Washington: Government Printing Office, 1971), vol. I, p. 945.

CHAPTER IV

1. See, for example, H. A. Simon, "Rational Choice and the Structure of the Environment," in R. E. Emery (ed.), Systems Thinking (Harmondsworth: Penguin, 1969).

2. The idea that informational problems lead to decision-making on normative grounds is a common-sense proposition which may be found in a more elaborate form in J. H. de Rivera, The Psychological Dimension of Foreign Policy

(Columbus: C. E. Merrill, 1968), especially chapters 2, 3.

3. Weber, Theory of Social and Economic Action, chapter 1.2.

4. R. Jervis, The Logic of Images (Princeton: Princeton University Press, 1970).

5. L. L. Farrar, "The Limits of Choice: July 1941 Reconsidered," Journal of Conflict Resolution, March 1972.

6. Jervis, Logic of Images.

7. Ibid., pp. 20-21.

8. Ibid., p. 26.

9. Cited in G. L. Weil and I. Davidson, The Gold War, (New York: Holt, Rinehart and Winston, 1970), p. 73.

10. Jervis, Logic of Images, pp. 28-40.

11. Ibid., p. 26.

12. The policy of "benign neglect" is discussed at greater length in chapter eight.

13. Jervis, Logic of Images, p. 142.

14. Ibid., p. 174.

15. Farrar, "The Limits of Choice."

16. Klaus Knorr, Power and Wealth (New York: Basic Books, 1973), p. 3.

17. F. Perroux, "The Domination Effect and Modern Economic Theory," Social Research, vol. 17, 1950; reprinted in K. W. Rothschild, ed., Power in Economics (Harmondsworth: Penguin, 1971), pp. 56-57.

18. H. G. Aubrey, The Dollar in World Affairs (New York: Praeger, 1964), p. 217.

19. C. P. Kindleberger, "The Politics of International Money and World Language," Essays in International Finance, no. 61, August 1967, Princeton University.

20. F. M. Heller, "The Framework for Investigating Direct Manufacturing Investment Overseas," Law and Contemporary Problems, Winter 1969, p. 5.

21. See, for example, Depres, Kindleberger and Salant, "The Dollar and World Liquidity."

22. These models are described in Cohen, Balance of Payments Policy, chapter 3.

23. See, for example, W. W. Heller, New Dimensions of Political Economy (New York: W. W. Norton, 1966); and A. M. Okun, The Political Economy of Prosperity (New York: W. W. Norton, 1970).

24. Seymour E. Harris, Economics of the Kennedy Years and a Look Ahead (New York: Harper and Row, 1964), p. 171.

25. These measures are described in U.S., Treasury, Maintaining the Strength of the Dollar in a Strong Free World Economy (Washington: Government Printing Office, January 1968), part 5.

26. L. Dudley and P. Passell, "The War in Vietnam and the United States Balance of Payments," Review of Economics and Statistics, November 1968; reprinted with testimony in U.S., Congress, Joint Economic Committee, A Review of Balance of Payments Policies, Hearings before the Subcommittee on International Exchange and Payments, 91st Congress, 1st sess., 1969, p. 115.

27. B. J. Cohen, Vietnam: The Impact on American Business, A Study Commissioned by the Institute for Policy Studies for the Businessmen's Educational Fund, 1969 (mimeo.).

28. Snider, "The Case for Capital Controls. . .," p. 362.

29. Aubrey, writing in 1963, (The Dollar in World Affairs, p. 250) feared that this would be the result of capital controls.

30. This theme is emphasized in Cairncross, Control of Long-Term International Capital Movements, chapter 3.

31. G. Wright and M. A. Molot, "Capital Movements and Governmental Control," International Organization, Autumn 1974, p. 673.

32. Interview with C. P. Kindleberger, Cambridge, Mass.,
    6 June 1975.

33. One such official was Stanley S. Surrey, Assistant Sec-
    retary of the Treasury for Tax Policy, 1961-1969; inter-
    viewed, Cambridge, Mass., 18 June 1975.

34. Seymour E. Harris, Economics of the Kennedy Years and a
    Look Ahead (New York: Harper and Row, 1964), p. 330.

35. According to Paul Samuelson, recorded interview by J.
    Pechman, 1 August 1964, John F. Kennedy Library, Oral
    History Program, p. 94.

36. See T. C. Sorensen, Kennedy (New York: Harper and Row,
    1965), p. 406.

37. Kennedy's concern about U.S. gold losses is cited by
    several first-hand observers; see R. V. Roosa, The Dollar
    and   World Liquidity (New York: Random House, 1967),
    pp. 4-15; also A. M. Schlesinger, A Thousand Days
    (Boston: Houghton Mifflin, 1965), p. 131.

38. Interview with Paul Samuelson, Cambridge, Mass.,
    19 June 1975.

39. J. Tobin, The New Economics One Decade Older (Princeton:
    Princeton University Press, 1974), pp. 28-29.

40. Sorensen, Kennedy, p. 405.

41. Schlesinger, A Thousand Days, pp. 655-656.

42. M. Michaely, The Responsiveness of Demand Policies to
    Balance of Payments (New York: Columbia University Press,
    1971), p. 273.

43. U.S., President, Public Papers, John F. Kennedy, 1963,
    p. 575.

44. Schlesinger, A Thousand Days, p. 620.

45. Harris, Economics of the Kennedy Years, pp. 148-149.

46. Sorensen, Kennedy, p. 408.

47. Paul Samuelson (interviewed, Cambridge, Mass., 19 June
    1975), among others, has confirmed this impression of
    Kennedy's view of devaluation.

48. D. Ellsberg, "The Quagmire Myth and the Stalemate Machine," in Papers on the War (New York: Simon and Schuster, 1972).

49. Roosa, The Dollar, pp. 6-7.

50. Schlesinger, A Thousand Days, p. 655.

51. See especially A. A. Stein, "Balance of Payments Policy in the Kennedy Administration," Papers of the Peace Society International, vol. 23, 1974; also S. E. Rolfe and J. L. Burtle, The Great Wheel (New York: Quadrangle, 1973), chapter 7.

52. Sorensen, Kennedy, p. 412.

53. I. M. Destler, Presidents, Bureaucrats, and Foreign Policy (Princeton University Press, 1974), p. 96.

54. Statement of Secretary Dillon; U.S., Congress, Committee on Ways and Means, Interest Equalization Tax Act, Hearings on HR 8000, 88th Cong., 1st sess., 1963, pp. 72, 129.

55. Cairncross, Control, p. 31

56. New York Times, 25 July 1963, p. 36.

57. Business Week, 11 May 1963, p. 90.

58. Business Week, 15 June 1963, p. 40 and 6 July 1963, p. 34.

59. New York Times, 22 January 1963, p. I.

60. Ibid., 11 May 1963, p. 28; 1 July 1963, p. 33.

61. U.S., President, Public Papers, John F. Kennedy, 1963, p. 580.

62. Ibid., pp. 581-582.

63. Ibid., p. 580.

64. New York Times, 1 October 1963, p. 1.

65. Brief descriptions of balance of payments policy during the Johnson Administration may be found in Rolfe and Burtle, The Great Wheel, chapter 8; and Brian Johnson, The

Politics of Money (London: John Murray, 1970), pp. 259-263.

66. Destler, Presidents, p. 95.

67. M. J. Golden, "The 'No-Tax Decision' of 1966," in Griffenhagen-Kroeger, Cases on a Decade of United States Foreign Economic Policy, 2 vols. (San Francisco, 1974), p. 334.(Prepared for the Murphy Commission.)

68. Professor L. R. Klein argues that the effect of a tax boost in 1966 would have been negligible, see Soma Golden, "Johnson Administration Exonerated by New Study of Blame for Inflation," New York Times, 30 December 1975, pp. 31, 36.

69. The President's views on monetary policy at this time may be found in L. B. Johnson, The Vantage Point (New York: Holt, Rinehart and Winston, 1971), p. 445.

70. Quoted in Business Week, 14 January 1967, p. 36.

71. Quoted in J. L. Knipe, The Federal Reserve and the American Dollar (Chapel Hill: University of North Carolina Press, 1965), p. 166.

72. U.S., President, Public Papers, Lyndon B. Johnson, 1965, p. 177.

73. Ibid., p. 173.

74. Business Week, 6 January 1968, p. 29.

75. Johnson, The Vantage Point, pp. 443-444.

76. Not least of all, by Francis Bator himself (interviewed in Cambridge, Mass., 24 June 1975); also see Henry Brandon, The Retreat of American Power (New York: Delta, 1972), p. 233; Statement of C. F. Bergsten (formerly of the National Security Council Staff) in U.S., Congress, Senate, Committee on Banking, Housing and Urban Affairs, Extension of the Council on International Economic Policy, Hearings before the Subcommittee on International Finance, 93d Cong., 1st sess., 1973, p. 30; Bruce Brittain, "Two Monetary International Decisions," in Griffenhagen-Kroeger, U.S. Foreign Economic Policy, parts I and II; Tobin, The New Economics, p. 30.

77. Francis M. Bator, "The Politics of International Money," Foreign Affairs, October 1968.

78. Ibid., p. 67.

79. Ibid., p. 52.

80. Ibid., p. 60.

81. Ibid., p. 65.

82. Business Week, 5 September 1964, p. 43.

83. New York Times, 11 February 1965, p. 57.

84. Business Week, 30 January 1965, p. 110.

85. U.S., President, Public Papers, Lyndon B. Johnson, 1965, p. 173.

86. Business Week, 3 July 1965, p. 67.

87. Quoted in New York Times, 18 August 1965, p. 1.

88. Business Week, 27 November 1965, p. 111.

89. Ibid., 17 December 1966, p. 50.

90. Testimony of Henry Fowler; U.S., Congress, Joint Economic Committee, The 1967 Economic Report of the President, Hearings, 90th Cong., 1st sess., 1967, p. 212.

91. Johnson himself has noted that the Kennedy Round took a good deal of his own attention that year; see The Vantage Point, p. 312.

92. Interview with Joseph W. Barr, Cambridge, Mass., 15 October 1975.

93. New York Times, 17 November 1967, p. 71.

94. Statement of Federal Reserve Board member A. Brimmer; Joint Economic Committee, Review of Balance of Payments Policies, 1969, p. 165.

95. New York Times, 19 November 1967, p. 1.

96. Interview with Stanley S. Surrey.

97. Business Week, 13 January 1968, p. 20.

98. New York Times, 12 January 1968, p. 15.

99. Statement of Undersecretary of the Treasury for Monetary Affairs, F. L. Deming; Joint Economic Committee, Review of Balance of Payments Policies, 1969, p. 177.

100. See testimony of Acting Commerce Secretary H. J. Samuels; U.S., Congress, Joint Economic Committee, 1968 Economic Report of the President, Hearings, 90th Cong., 2d sess., 1968, p. 128.

101. Testimony of C. Stewart of the Machinery and Allied Products Institute; U.S., Congress, House, Committee on Foreign Affairs, Foreign Direct Investment Controls, Hearings before the Subcommittee on Foreign Economic Policy, 91st Cong., 1st sess., 1969, p. 61.

102. Interview with Joseph W. Barr.

103. Rivera, Psychological Dimensions, p. 79; Rivera's citation is to Kurt Lewin. Principles of Topological Psychology (New York: McGraw Hill, 1936).

104. Schlesinger, A Thousand Days, p. 623.

CHAPTER V

1. See Mancur Olsen, The Logic of Collective Action (Cambridge, Mass.: Harvard University Press, 1964).

2. C.E.D., The International Position of the Dollar, p. 52.

3. Business Week, 25 May 1963, p. 168; 5 August 1967, p. 132; 6 January 1968, p. 102.

4. New York Times, 4 March 1963, p. 36; 31 July 1963, p. 28.

5. Ibid., 19 July 1963, p. 1.

6. Ibid., 9 December 1963, p. 57.

7. See H. S. Reuss, recorded interview by R. J. Grele, 12 and 15 December 1965, John F. Kennedy Library, Oral History Program, p. 68; also S. E. Harris, recorded interview by A. Schlesinger, 16 and 17 June 1964, John F. Kennedy Library, Oral History Program, p. 53.

8. These may be found in House, Committee on Ways and Means, Interest Equalization Tax Act, 1963, and subsequent extension acts of 1965, 1967, 1971 and 1973.

9. Statement of M. E. Richardson; ibid., 1963, pp. 157-158, 162-163.

10. Statement of I. W. Burnham, III of Burnham & Co.; ibid., p. 258.

11. Statement of R. A. Gilbert of the Investor's League; ibid., pp. 176-177.

12. See, for example, statement of the American Bankers Association, in U.S., Congress, Joint Economic Committee, January 1964 Economic Report of the President, Hearings, 88th Cong., 2d sess., 1964, p. 9.

13. New York Times, 10 March 1965, p. 55.

14. Information supplied by the U.S., Treasury, in U.S., Congress, House, Committee on Banking and Currency, Recent Changes in Monetary Policy and the Balance of Payments, Hearings, 88th Cong., 1st sess., 1963, p. 169.

15. R. A. Bauer, I. de Sola Pool and L. A. Dexter, American Business and Public Policy, 2nd ed. (Chicago: Aldine, 1972), pp. 279, 286, 281.

16. Statement of Secretary Dillon; House, Committee on Banking and Currency, Recent Changes in Monetary Policy, p. 152.

17. Business Week, 16 March 1963, p. 136.

18. For a general survey of the growth in Wall Street activities during the 1960's, see John Brooks, The Go-Go Years: When Prices Went Topless (New York: Ballantine, 1973).

19. New York Times, 21 January 1966, p. 67.

20. Kuhn, Loeb & Co., Kuhn, Loeb (New York: n.p., 1975), pp. 20, 27.

21 Dillon, Read & Co., Dillon, Read (New York: n.p., 1974), pp. 14, 25-26.

22. Quoting ABA Vice President C. Walker, New York Times, 11 February 1965, p. 57.

23. New York Times, 11 February 1965, p. 57. David Rocke-
    feller (Chase Manhattan) and Gabriel Hauge (Manufacturers
    Hanover) voiced concern over monetary policy; R. Rierson
    (Chief Economist at Bankers Trust) questioned aid and
    military expenditure.

24. The idea of suspending gold convertibility had been raised,
    and condemned, at an ABA meeting in 1967; Business
    Week, 5 August 1967, p. 108.

25. New York Times, 7 April 1967, p. 51, and 12 April 1967,
    p. 65.

26. This quasi-bargaining relationship between the
    regulator and the regulated is examined in Martin
    Mayer, The Bankers (New York: Ballantine, 1976),
    part 4.

27. Business Week, 9 October 1965, p. 53.

28. Ibid., 13 March 1965, p. 146.

29. Memos of telephone conversations with Hayes (15 January
    1965) and Martin (10 February 1965); C. Douglas
    Dillon, personal papers, John F. Kennedy Library.

30. End of December figures supplied by Governor Brimmer;
    Joint Economic Committee, Review of Balance of Payments
    Policies, 1969, p. 167.

31. F. A. Lees, International Banking and Finance (London:
    Macmillan, 1974), p. 223.

32. See Mayer, Bankers, chapter 2.

33. Quoted in F. Freidel, FDR: Launching the New Deal (Boston:
    Little Brown, 1973), p. 203.

34. Sorensen, Kennedy, p. 408.

35. New York Times, 3 January 1968, p. 67.

36. This diagram is adapted from one presented by Janet
    Kelly, "American Banks in Britain" (Ph.D. dissertation,
    Johns Hopkins University, 1975), p. 260.

37. On the rapid overseas exapnsion of U.S. banks during the
    1960's, see J. C. Baker and M. G. Bradford, American
    Banks Abroad (New York: Praeger, 1974).

38. The mechanics of foreign branch banking are described in Mayer, Bankers, chapter 17; Lees, International Banking, chapters 5, 8, 11; and Stuart W. Robinson, Multinational Banking (Lejden: Sijthoff, 1972), especially pp. 224-241 on the VFCR and IET.

39. Statement of Governor Brimmer; Joint Economic Committee, Balance of Payments Policies, 1969, pp. 162-163.

40. The ramifications of the Edge Act are discussed in Lees, International Banking, chapter 6.

41. See B. S. Quinn, The New Euromarkets (London: Macmillan, 1975), chapter 4.

42. New York Times, 12 April 1965, p. 52.

43. National Industrial Conference Board, U.S. Production Abroad and the Balance of Payments (New York: NICB, 1966) and Judd Polk, "U.S. Exports in Relation to U.S. Production Abroad" in Bela Balassa (ed.), Changing Patterns of Foreign Trade and Payments, revised ed. (New York: Norton, 1970), pp. 61-71; Mr. Polk wrote this essay for the Joint Economic Committee, in his capacity as Research Director of the U.S. Council of the I.C.C.

44. Written statements supplied by MAPI and NAM; U.S., Congress, Joint Economic Committee, January 1965 Economic Report of the President, 89th Cong., 1st sess., 1965, part 4.

45. See R. A. Musgrave, "Tax Policy," Review of Economics and Statistics, May 1964, p. 127.

46. New York Times, 11 February 1965, p. 57.

47. G. Wright and M. A. Molot, "Capital Movements and Governmental Control," p. 677.

48. Senate, Committee on Banking and Currency, Balance of Payments--1965, 1965, p. 964.

49. Samuelson, recorded interview, Kennedy Library, pp. 94-95, 98.

50. Business Week, 11 May 1963, p. 90.

51. Testimony of Secretary Dillon; Joint Economic Committee,

1965 Economic Report, pp. 104-105.

52. Reprinted in Senate, Committee on Banking and Currency, *Balance of Payments - 1965*, pp. 521-522.

53. *New York Times*, 1 September 1963, III, p. 1.

54. "Rushing to Span the Globe," *Business Week*, 8 August 1964, pp. 19-21.

55. *Business Week*, 20 February 1965, p. 20.

56. R. Heller and N. Willatt, *The European Revenge* (London: Barrie & Jenkins, 1975), p. 33. The study they refer to is undoubtedly U.S., Department of Commerce, Bureau of Economic Analysis, *U.S. Direct Investment Abroad 1966* (Government Printing Office, 1972).

57. H. S. Houthakker, "The United States Balance of Payments: A Look Ahead," Commission on International Trade and Investment, vol. I, p. 41.

58. R. Ablin, "The Maturity Effect, Rates of Return and the Course of U.S. Foreign Investment," *Journal of International Economics*, February 1976, pp. 1-20.

59. F. H. Fleck and R. Mahfouz, "The Multinational Corporation: Tax Avoidance and Profit Manipulation via Subsidiaries and Tax Havens," *Swiss Magazine for Political Economy*, 2, 1974.

60. S. M. Robbins and R. B. Stobaugh, *Money in the Multinational Enterprise* (New York: Basic, 1973), p. 70. A minimum flotation of about $25 million, in addition to credit rating, discriminated against smaller companies.

61. See Quinn, *New Euromarkets*, p. 241, for a comparison of the cost of borrowing in the floating rate market and the Eurobond market.

62. Ibid., p. 202.

63. *Business Week*, 25 September 1965, p. 154, and 2 October 1965, pp. 107-108.

64. Quinn, *New Euromarkets*, p. 203.

65. Ibid., p. 49.

66. Robbins and Stobaugh, Money in the Multinational Enterprise, pp. 50-51.

67. Bauer, Pool, Dexter, American Business, p. 229.

68. D. Harms, "An Analysis of the U.S. Voluntary Restraint Program: Its Effect on U.S. Balance of Payments and Private U.S. Industry," (D.B.A. dissertation, George Washington University, 1968), p. 160.

69. These were firms which could sell on their "name" in Europe but did not have good credit ratings in the United States; see Quinn, New Euromarkets, pp. 206-207.

70. Testimony of F. C. Fenton; Senate, Committee on Banking And Currency, Balance of Payments - 1965, p. 961.

71. There is a wealth of literature on this subject; see, for example, R. E. Caves, "International Corporations: The Industrial Economics of Foreign Investment," Economica, February 1971; R. Vernon, "The Economic Consequences of U.S. Foreign Direct Investment," in Commission on International Trade and Investment, vol. I, pp. 929-953.

72. T. Horst, "American Investments Abroad and Domestic Market Power," in C. F. Bergsten, T. Horst and T. Moran, American Multinationals and American Interests (Washington, D.C.: Brookings Institution, forthcoming), chapter 7.

73. This is suggested, en passant, by P. B. Musgrave, "Direct Investment Abroad and the Multinationals: Effects on the U.S. Economy," Harvard Law School International Tax Program, 25-26 February 1975, p. 13. (Mimeo.)

74. See J. H. Dunning, "Technology, U.S. Investment and European Economic Growth," in Dunning, International Investment, pp. 377-409.

75. R. L. Tonneden, Foreign Disinvestment by U.S. Multinational Corporations (New York: Praeger, 1975), pp. 128-130.

76. See testimonies in House, Foreign Affairs Committee, Foreign Direct Investment Controls, 1969.

77. Nat Goldfinger, Director of Research at the AFL-CIO, ably summarizes the labor point of view in "A Labor View of Foreign Investment and Trade Issues," in Commission

on International Trade and Investment, vol. I, pp. 913-928.

78. Minority statements of I. W. Abel (United Steelworkers) and F. E. Smith (International Association of Machinists and Aerospace Workers), in ibid., vol. III, p. 339. The statements rejected the Report's conclusion that capital controls were ineffective and against the U.S. national interest.

79. Musgrave, "Direct Investment Abroad and the Multinationals," p. 12.

80. U.S., Congress, Senate, Committee on Finance, Implications of Multinational Firms for World Trade and Investment and for U.S. Trade and Labor, Committee Print, 93d Cong., 1st sess., 1973, chapter seven.

81. Statement of Nat Goldfinger on behalf of the AFL-CIO; House, Committee on Ways and Means, Interest Equalization Tax, 1963, pp. 421-423.

82. Statement of S. H. Ruttenberg, AFL-CIO; U.S., Congress, Joint Economic Committee, Outlook for the U.S. Balance of Payments, Hearings before the Subcommittee on International Exchange and Payments, 87th Cong., 2d sess., 1962, p. 31.

83. Statement of Nat Goldfinger; U.S., Congress, Joint Economic Committee, Guidelines for International Monetary Reform, Hearings before the Subcommittee on International Exchange and Payments, 89th Cong., 1st sess., 1965, p. 187.

84. Joint Economic Committee, 1965 Economic Report, part 4.

85. New York Times, 5 January 1968, p. 69.

86. An obvious example is R. J. Barnet and R. E. Müller, Global Reach (New York: Simon & Schuster, 1975), who would see capital flows controlled for reasons of equity, both between and within countries.

87. P. A. Samuelson, "Economic Frontiers," in New Frontiers of the Kennedy Administration, Task Force Reports Prepared for the President (Washington, D.C.: Public Affairs Press, 1961), pp. 27, 29, 36.

88. Quoted in Business Week, 26 March 1963, p. 26.

89. Interview with Samuelson.

90. Harris, "U.S. Balance of Payments," in Joint Economic Committee, Factors Affecting the Balance of Payments, 1962, p. 25; also testimony in Joint Economic Committee, 1965 Economic Report, part 2, p. 9.

91. J. K. Galbraith, "The Balance of Payments: A Political and Administrative View," Review of Economics and Statistics, May 1964.

92. Interview with Samuelson.

93. Statement of Triffin; U.S., Congress, Joint Economic Committee, Contingency Planning for U.S. International Monetary Policy, Statements submitted to the Subcommittee on International Exchange and Payments, 1966, p. 118.

94. Salant, The U.S. Balance of Payments in 1968, p. 153.

95. Depres, Kindleberger, Salant, "The Dollar and World Liquidity;" Aubrey, The Dollar in World Affairs, pp. 193-205; P. B. Kenen, "The International Position of the Dollar," in B. J. Cohen (ed.), American Foreign Economic Policy (New York: Harper and Row, 1968) pp. 55-56.

96. G. N. Halm, "International Financial Intermediation: Deficits Benign and Malignant," Essays in International Finance, No. 68, Princeton University, 1968, p. 17.

97. H. G. Johnson, "The Efficiency and Welfare Implications of the Multinational Corporation," in C. P. Kindleberger (ed.), The International Corporation (Cambridge, Mass.: M.I.T. Press, 1970), pp. 53-54.

98. See H. G. Johnson, "The Monetary Approach to the Balance of Payments," Social Science Research Council, International Monetary Research Programme (London: London School of Economics and Political Science, n.d.).

99. F. Machlup, International Payments, Debt and Gold (New York: Scribner's Sons, 1964), part 5; and "The Transfer Gap of the United States," Reprints in International Finance, No. 11, Princeton University, 1968.

100. F. Machlup, Remaking the International Monetary System (Baltimore: Johns Hopkins Press, 1968), p. 108.

101. Cooper, The Economics of Interdependence, chapter five.

102. Aubrey, Dollar in World Affairs, pp. 55-56; P. W. Bell, prepared statement; Joint Economic Committee, Outlook for the Balance of Payments, 1963, pp. 125-126.

103. B. J. Cohen, "Voluntary Foreign Investment Curbs: A Plan That Really Works," Challenge, March/April 1967.

104. H. Magdoff, "Imperialism Without Colonies," in R. Owen and B. Sutcliffe (eds.), Studies in the Theory of Imperialism (London: Longmans, 1972), p. 162.

105. A. Stadnichenko, Monetary Crisis of Capitalism (Moscow: Progress Publishers, 1975), p. 138.

106. E. Mandel, Europe vs. America (New York: Monthly Review Press, 1972), chapters 1, 5.

107. The "agenda setting" role of multinational actors is discussed in J. S. Nye, "Multinational Corporations in World Politics," Foreign Affairs, October 1974, pp. 159-161.

CHAPTER VI

1. G. Allison, Essence of Decision (Boston: Little, Brown, 1971), chapter 5.

2. Ibid., p. 162.

3. Ibid., p. 166.

4. For example, the two volumes of economic cases prepared for the Murphy Commission; see Griffenhagen-Kroeger, Cases on a Decade of United States Foreign Economic Policy.

5. L. C. Pierce, The Politics of Fiscal Policy Formation (Pacific Palisades: Goodyear Publishing Co., 1971), p. 202.

6. S. J. Maisel, Managing the Dollar (New York: Norton, 1973), p. 207.

7. Hirsch, Money International, revised ed., p. 446.

8. Statement of C. Stewart, Machinery and Allied Products Institute; House, Committee on Foreign Affairs, Foreign Direct Investment Controls, 1969, p. 48.

9. Schlesinger, Thousand Days, p. 652.

10. D. S. Green /formerly of the Bureau of the Budget7,
    "Government Organization for Policymaking and Execution
    in International Trade and Investment," in Commission
    on International Trade and Investment Policy, vol. 2,
    p. 420.

11. Statement of Secretary Dillon; House, Committee on
    Ways and Means, Interest Equalization Tax Act, 1963,
    p. 72.

12. J. K. Galbraith, "The Balance of Payments: A Political
    and Administrative View," p. 119.

13. Sorensen, Kennedy, p. 409.

14. Statement of Secretary Dillon; U.S., Congress, Joint
    Economic Committee, International Payments Imbalances,
    Hearings before the Subcommittee on International Economic
    Policy, 87th Cong., 1st sess., 1961, p. 24.

15. Roosa's own remarks about "abstract theory" may be found
    in R. N. Roosa, "Movements of Long-Term Capital and the
    Adjustment Process," Review of Economics and Statistics,
    May 1964. Harris' remark is in Seymour Harris, recorded
    interview, Kennedy Library, p. 36.

16. J. M. Keynes, The General Theory of Employment, Interest
    and Prices (London: Macmillan, 1936), p. 383.

17. Roos'a basic ideas may be found in his two major works:
    The Dollar and World Liquidity (New York: Random
    House, 1967) and Monetary Reform for the World Economy
    (New York: Random House, 1965).

18. Statement of Undersecretary Roosa; U.S., Congress,
    Joint Economic Committee, The United States Balance of
    Payments, Hearings, 88th Cong., 1st sess., 1963, p. 146.

19. Interview with Paul Samuelson.

20. Remarks of R. V. Roosa at the Monetary Conference of the
    American Bankers Association, Rome, Italy, 17 May 1962
    (reprinted in Joint Economic Committee, Factors Affecting
    the U.S. Balance of Payments, p. 332).

21. Seymour Harris, recorded interview, Kennedy Library, p.
    48.

22. Roosa, Dollar and World Liquidity, pp. 9, 29-30.

23. Remarks of R. V. Roosa at the annual convention of the American Bankers' Association at Atlantic City, N.J., 25 September 1962 (reprinted in Joint Economic Committee, Factors Affecting the Balance of Payments, pp. 335-336).

24. Testimony of Secretary Dillon; House, Committee on Banking and Currency, Recent Changes in Monetary Policy, 1963, pp. 100-101.

25. Douglas Dillon, personal papers, Kennedy Library, p. 2.

26. Testimony of Secretary Dillon; Joint Economic Committee, 1965 Economic Report, p. 96.

27. Harris says it was clearly "thought up by Roosa" (recorded interview, Kennedy Library, p. 52). Surrey claims Dillon was more directly responsible (interview with Surrey).

28. New York Times, 14 March 1963, p. 4.

29. A summary of the report, dated 18 March 1963, may be found in the Department of Commerce Records, roll 12, John F. Kennedy Library.

30. Business Week, 6 July 1963, p. 34.

31. Harris, recorded interview, Kennedy Library, p. 53.

32. Testimony of Secretary Dillon; Joint Economic Committee, U.S. Balance of Payments, 1963, pp. 55, 70.

33. Testimony of Secretary Dillon; Senate, Committee on Banking and Currency, Balance of Payments--1965, 1965, p. 57.

34. New York Times, 12 February 1965, p. 38.

35. Kermit Gordon, recorded interview by J. Pechman, 1 August 1964, John F. Kennedy Library, Oral History Program, p. 431.

36. Bruce Brittain, "Two Monetary International Decisions," in Griffenhagen-Kroeger, p. 225.

37. Quoted in New York Times, 28 April 1966, p. 61.

38. G. C. Hufbauer and M. Adler, Overseas Manufacturing Investment and the Balance of Payments, U.S. Treasury Department Tax Policy Research Study No. 1 (Washington, D.C.: Government Printing Office, 1968).

39. Statement supplied for the record by Undersecretary Deming; U.S., Congress, House, Committee on Ways and Means, Interest Equalization Tax Extension Act of 1967, Hearings on HR 3813, 90th Cong., 1st sess., 1967, p. 80.

40. This study is summarized in N. K. Bruck and F. A. Lees, "Foreign Investment, Capital Controls and the Balance of Payments," The Bulletin, No. 48-49, April 1968, pp. 37-39.

41. Treasury Department, Maintaining the Strength of the United States Dollar, pp. 91-102.

42. Information supplied in interviews with Stanley Surrey and Francis Bator. President Johnson makes a reference to "A special team headed by Secretary Fowler /which/ worked night and day throughout the last half of December. . ."(The Vantage Point, p. 317).

43. Sanford Rose, "Capital is Something that Doesn't Love a Wall," Fortune, February 1971, p. 101.

44. Interview with N. S. Fielecke, Boston, Mass., 9 June 1975.

45. Knipe, Federal Reserve and the American Dollar, pp. 170-171.

46. Statement of Chairman Martin; U.S., Congress, Joint Economic Committee, January 1963 Economic Report of the President, Hearings, 88th Cong., 1st sess., p. 342.

47. See J. S. Little, "The Impact of the Euro-dollar Market on the Effectiveness of Monetary Policy in the U.S. and Abroad," New England Economic Review, March/April 1975, especially pp. 17-18.

48. Statement of former Fed Board Chairman Martin, Remarks delivered to the Institute of Politics (Harvard University), 12 November 1975. In the course of his remarks Mr. Martin also revealed that "my life has revolved around gold."

49. Chairman Martin, written reply for the record; House, Committee on Banking and Currency, Recent Changes in

Monetary Policy, p. 70.

50. Maisel, Managing the Dollar, pp. 207-208.

51. Public speech, quoted in The Economist, 5 January 1963, p. 45.

52. Memorandum, 10 July 1963; Dillon, personal papers, Kennedy Library.

53. Business Week, 27 July 1963, p. 19.

54. Testimony of Chairman Martin; U.S., Congress, Joint Economic Committee, January 1968 Economic Report of the President, Hearings, 89th Cong., 1st sess, p. 37. Martin made no secret of the fact that he shared this scepticism:

> The interest equalization tax is an example of the first approach /to capital flows/. Experience with this approach so far has indicated both its strength and weakness. It is generally agreed that a tax is more consistent with the principles on which our economy is based than would be the use of direct controls or an appeal to voluntary restraint. But a tax statute can hardly avoid some opportunities for legal escape, since it is extremely difficut, if not impossible, in legislative drafting to foresee all loophole possibilities. Too, embracing a tax with many exceptions and qualifica-tions could be so complicated to administer that its effectiveness would be seriously impaired.
> Exchange controls have not been tried in the past, except under wartime conditions, and I, for one, hope they will not be tried. By shifting decisionmaking in individual business transactions from participants to some Government agency, this approach would be repugnant to the principles of our economic system. Also, experience everywhere has shown that exchange regulations, if couched in general terms, can be avoided as easily as a special tax; and if elaborated in great detail, become so oppressive that they also hamper business activities beneficial to our payments situation. And once this route has been chosen, experience has demonstrated the difficulty of retracing one's steps toward free-dom from controls. Of the three methods of selective restraint, exchange controls are, in my judgment, the one that should not be seriously contemplated.

This leaves for comment the voluntary approach.
This method also has shortcomings. The person, individual, or corporate, adhering to a voluntary program,
may be penalized in favor of an uncooperative person.
But if widespread voluntary restraint can reasonably
be expected, the method has three advantages: First,
it leaves the ultimate decision to the market participants; second, it is flexible enough to take care
of changing circumstances and of the experience gained
in the process; and third, given the good faith of
all parties, it avoids the encumbrance of legalistic
interpretations of the "rules of the game."
(Statement of Chairman Martin; Senate, Committee
on Banking and Currency, Balance of Payments - 1965,
p. 107.)

55. See The Economist, 27 April 1968, p. 59; New York Times,
2 June 1965, p. 1 and 16 July 1965, p. 38.

56. Testimony of Chairman Martin; House, Committee on Banking
and Currency, Recent Changes in Monetary Policy, p. 28.

57. See his statement in Senate, Committee on Banking and
Currency, Balance of Payments - 1965, pp. 917-924.

58. Maisel, Managing the Dollar, p. 215.

59. K. Gordon and Walter Heller, recorded interview by J.
Pechman, 1 August 1964, John F. Kennedy Library, Oral
History Program, p. 380.

60. Statement of G. W. Mitchell; Joint Economic Committee,
1963 Economic Report, p. 385.

61. Brimmer was a major opponent of the dismantling of the
controls after 1969; source: interview with H. S.
Houthakker, Cambridge, Mass., 3 July 1975.

62. Quoted in Business Week, 27 April 1963, p. 94.

63. Memorandum, 16 July 1963; Dillon, personal papers, Kennedy Library.

64. New York Times, 8 October 1964, p. 63.

65. Federal Reserve Bank of New York, Annual Report 1964,
p. 7.

66. Maisel, Managing the Dollar, p. 226.

67. Testimony of P. D. Seghers, President, Institute on U.S. Taxation of Foreign Income, in House, Foreign Affairs Committee, Foreign Direct Investment Controls, p. 160.

68. Letter from Secretary Hodges to President Kennedy, 25 July 1963, Commerce Department records, roll 7, Kennedy Library.

69. Business Week, 27 February 1965, p. 47.

70. Speech to the National Industrial Conference Board, cited in New York Times, 19 September 1968, p. 72.

71. F. Cutler and S. Pizer, "U.S. Trade with Foreign Affiliates of U.S. Firms," Survey of Current Business, December 1964, pp. 20-26.

72. Statement of J. G. Morton, Special Assistant to the Secretary of Commerce (1962-1967); House, Committee on Foreign Affairs, Foreign Direct Investment Controls, p. 5.

73. Mr. Behrman was Assistant Secretary of Commerce for Domestic and International Business, 1962-1964; see J. Behrman, "Foreign Investment Muddle: The Perils of Ad Hocery," Columbia Journal of World Business, Fall 1965.

74. Memorandum of telephone conversation between Connor and Dillon, 26 February 1965; Dillon, personal papers, Kennedy Library.

75. Interview with Stanley Surrey.

76. The Economist, 9 October 1965, p. 193.

77. Interview with Francis Bator.

78. For example, see Connors remarks cited in New York Times, 18 January 1966, p. 47, and Fowler's rejoinder, ibid., 4 February 1966, p. 41.

79. Remarks of D. F. Heatherington, Assistant Director, OFDI, in Milwaukee, 3 December 1968; reprinted in U.S. Department of Commerce News (no date), p. 1.

80. Business Week, 13 January 1968, p. 35.

81. Business Week, 27 February 1965, p. 47.

82. Ibid., 13 March 1965, p. 98.

83. Ibid., 2 October 1968, p. 41.

84. New York Times, 23 October 1966, p. 46.

85. A brief history of the CEA may be found in Lewis Beman, "The Chastening of the Washington Economists," Fortune, January 1976, pp. 158-166.

86. Salant, U.S. Balance of Payments in 1968.

87. W. W. Heller, New Dimensions of Political Economy (New York: Norton, 1966), p. 48.

88. Memorandum of telephone conversation, 17 February 1965; Dillon, personal papers, Kennedy Library.

89. Tobin's argument convinced Kennedy and half-convinced the Treasury; see recorded interview with Seymour Harris, Kennedy Library, p. 54.

90. J. Tobin, recorded interview by J. Pechman, 1 August 1964, John F. Kennedy Library, Oral History Program; see appendix note 3.

91. Ibid., note 3.

92. Council of Economic Advisors, Annual Report, January 1967.

93. Business Week, 6 January 1968, p. 19.

94. Okun, Political Economy of Prosperity.

95. Otto Eckstein, letter to the author, 15 July 1975.

96. CEA, Annual Report, January 1969, p. 146.

97. Ibid., p. 150.

98. On State's "Europeanist" orientation in this regard, see H. van B. Cleveland, The Atlantic Idea and Its European Rivals (New York: McGraw Hill, 1966), chapter three. Kennedy's Special Representative for Trade Negotiations in 1963 was opposed to the IET for the same reason—he was afraid it would anger the Europeans and prejudice the Kennedy Round (source: interview with N. S. Fielecke).

99. G. Ackley, recorded interview by J. Pechman, 1 August
1964, John F. Kennedy Library, Oral History Program,
p. 99. Tobin confirms that, in general, Defense (and
State) favoured any balance of payments policy which did
not affect their own special interests; see Tobin, New
Economics, pp. 30-31.

100. Interview with N. S. Fielecke (an employee of the Bureau
of the Budget in 1963).

101. Green, "Government Organization," in Commission on International Trade and Investment, vol 2, p. 423.

102. Interview with Stanley Surrey.

103. Memorandum of telephone conversation with Representative
Mills; Dillon, personal papers, Kennedy Library.

104. Joint statement by Senators Hartke and McCarthy; Senate,
Committee on Banking and Currency, Balance of Payments -
1965, p. 999.

105. New York Times, 2 January 1968, p. 16.

106. Ibid., 21 May 1964, p. 22.

107. Ibid., 9 September 1965, p. 55.

108. Statement of Senator Javits; Joint Economic Committee,
1964 Economic Report, p. 175.

109. Cited in New York Times, 4 September 1963, p. 19.

110. Statement of Senator Javits; Joint Economic Committee,
1965 Economic Report, p. 11.

111. New York Times, 28 July 1964, p. 35 and 2 January 1968,
p. 16.

112. H. S. Reuss, The Critical Decade (New York: McGraw
Hill, 1964), pp. 85-86.

113. H. S. Reuss, recorded interview, Kennedy Library.

114. U. S. Congress, Joint Economic Committee, U.S. Payments
Policies Consistent with Domestic Objectives of Maximum
Employment and Growth, Report of the Subcommittee on
International Exchange and Payments, 87th Cong., 2d sess.,
1962, p. 10.

115. U.S., Congress, House, Interest Equalization Tax of 1963, H. Rept. 1046 to accompany HR 8000, 88th Cong., 1st sess., 1964, pp. 76-83.

116. Statement of Representative Byrnes (Wisconsin); House, Committee on Ways and Means, Interest Equalization Tax Extension Act, 1967, pp. 34, 90.

117. James A. Robinson, Congress and Foreign Policy Making (Homewood, Ill.: Dorsey Press, 1962), chapter 7.

CHAPTER VII

1. Statement of Undersecretary Deming; Joint Economic Committee, A Review of Balance of Payments Policies, 1969, p. 1975.

2. The Economist, 29 March 1975, p. 36.

3. Testimony of Professor P. McCracken; Senate, Committee on Banking and Currency, Balance of Payments - 1965, p. 303.

4. Written reply to Congressman T. B. Curtis from Secretary Dillon; House, Committee on Ways and Means, Interest Equalization Tax, 1963, p. 106.

5. Business Week, 17 August 1963; New York Times, 24 July 1963, p. 37, 3 October 1963, p. 47, 4 September 1967, p. 32.

6. The Economist, 27 July 1963, p. 334.

7. Interview with Stanley Surrey. This is not to say that the Europeans were happy with the overall aims of U.S. policy. As Tobin notes, ". . . his /Roosa's/ holding strategy delayed any far-reaching international resolution or even discussion of the basic problems, an evasion which made the Europeans increasingly restless;" see Tobin, New Economics, p. 33.

8. Testimony of Secretary Dillon; House, Committee on Ways and Means, Interest Equalization Tax, 1963, p. 142.

9. Aubrey, Dollar and World Affairs, p. 53.

10. Statement of Secretary Dillon; House, Committee on Ways and Means, Interest Equalization Tax, 1963, p. 61

11. The Department of State prepared a full report of these restrictions; see "Government Restrictions on the Outflow of Private Capital Employed by Principal Capital Exporting Countries," reprinted in Joint Economic Committee, 1963 Economic Report, pp. 408-435.

12. Testimony of Governor Mitchell; ibid., p. 385.

13. Stein, "Balance of Payments Policy in the Kennedy Administration," pp. 119-120.

14. Testimony of Secretary Dillon; House, Committee on Ways and Means, Interest Equalization Tax, 1963, p. 128.

15. Cited and quoted in New York Times, 20 March 1964, p. 45.

16. See R. Larre, "Facts of Life about the Integration of National Capital Markets," Journal of Money, Credit and Banking, vol. 1, 1969, pp. 319-327.

17. See Lees, International Banking, p. 256.

18. New York Times, 20 July 1963, p. 23; 27 November 1963, p. 59.

19. Ibid., 20 July 1963, p. 30.

20. On the problem of integration, see S. E. Rolfe, Capital Markets in Atlantic Economic Relationships (Boulogne-sur-Seine: Atlantic Institute, 1967).

21. On the problem of differences in policy assignment between Europe and the United States, see Cohen, Balance of Payments Policy, p. 155 and Cleveland, Atlantic Idea, p. 79.

22. Testimony of Secretary Fowler; Senate, Committee on Banking and Currency, Balance of Payments - 1965, p. 1055.

23. Ibid.

24. Memorandum of telephone conversation with President Johnson, 11 February 1965, Dillon, personal papers, Kennedy Library.

25. The question of competition is discussed in J.-P. Koszul, "American Banks in Europe," in C. P. Kindleberger (ed.), The International Corporation (Cambridge, Mass.: MIT Press, 1970).

26. Testimony of C. P. Kindleberger; Senate, Committee on Banking and Currency, Balance of Payments - 1965, p. 379.

27. Quoted in Mayer, Bankers, p. 476.

28. See C. F. Karsten, "Should Europe Restrict U.S. Investments," in Cohen, American Foreign Economic Policy, pp. 233-234; also C. P. Kindleberger, American Business Abroad (New Haven: Yale University Press, 1969), chapter 3.

29. R. Hellman, The Challenge to U.S. Dominance of the International Corporation (New York: Dunellen, 1970), p. 257.

30. A comprehensive survey of European policies may be found in J. J. Boddewyn, "Western European Policies toward U.S. Investors," The Bulletin, Nos. 93-95, March 1974.

31. Ibid., pp. 40-41.

32. Business Week, 9 February 1963, p. 91.

33. Testimony of Secretary Connor; Senate, Committee on Banking and Currency, Balance of Payments - 1965, p. 913; Business Week, 17 April 1965, p. 40; the purpose of the visit was more to discuss Vietnam, see Harold Wilson, A Personal Record (Boston: Little, Brown, 1971), pp. 95-96.

34. Business Week, 6 November 1965, p. 151.

35. The Economist, 20 November 1965, Survey, p. xxviii.

36. Ibid., 26 October 1968, Survey, pp. xix-xx.

37. New York Times, 12 February 1965, p. 39; 17 March 1965, p. 73.

38. Hellman, The Challenge to U.S. Dominance, pp. 135-137.

39. Written reply of Governor Burns to Senator Javits; U.S., Congress, Joint Economic Committee, The 1971 Economic Report of the President, Hearings, 92d Cong., 1st sess., p. 277.

40. New York Times, 3 January 1968, p. 74.

41. See Henrik and Michele Schmiegelow, "The New Mercantilism in International Relations," International Organization, Spring 1975; P. J. Katzenstein, "International Relations and Domestic Structures," International Organization, Winter 1975, pp. 29-35; and Morse, Foreign Policy and Interdependence in Gaullist France.

42. Business Week, 26 January 1963, p. 100.

43. Ibid., 24 October 1964, p. 149, 6 December 1964, pp. 114-119.

44. New York Times, 9 January 1965, p. 1.

45. See Morse, Foreign Policy and Interdependence, p. 233; Business Week, 14 May 1966, pp. 44-45; and Hellman, Challenge to U.S. Dominance, pp. 131-133.

46. Business Week, 6 January 1968, p. 19.

47. Kindleberger, American Business Abroad, p. 59.

48. See Business Week, 18 June 1966, pp. 118-119; 5 March 1966, pp. 128-129.

49. Ibid., 2 April 1966, p. 116.

50. A "Wall Street investment banker," quoted in New York Times, 19 December 1965, III, p. 11.

51. Ibid.

52. D. Williams, "Foreign Currency Issues in the European Securities Markets," IMF Staff Papers, September 1966.

53. Such threats, the content unspecified, were made frequently by Fowler during 1967; e.g., in a speech to the American Bankers Association in March 1967, quoted in E. A. Birnbaum, "Changing the U.S. Commitment to Gold," Essays in International Finance, no. 63, Princeton University, 1967, p. 1.

54. See Morse, Foreign Policy and Interdependence, p. 240; also S. D. Cohen, International Monetary Reform 1964-69 (New York: Praeger, 1970), pp. 142-149.

55. See The Economist, 6 January 1968, p. 41; Business Week, 23 December 1967, pp. 11-12; New York Times, 16 December 1967, p. 1; 2 January 1968, p. 16.

56. The Economist, 23 March 1968, p. 78, also 3 February 1968, p. 98.

57. Business Week, 2 December 1967, p. 34.

58. Ibid., 9 December 1967, p. 106; 23 December 1967, pp. 11-12.

59. For a general survey of Canadian-American financial relations, see Wright and Molot, "Capital Movements and Government Control."

60. The Economist, 27 July 1963, p. 370.

61. Ibid., p. 356.

62. Written reply to Representative Multer from Secretary Dillon; House, Committee on Banking and Currency, Recent Changes in Monetary Policy, p. 165.

63. Dillon, personal papers, Kennedy Library.

64. New York Times, 21 July 1963, p. 1; 22 July 1963, p. 1; 25 July 1963, p. 36.

65. Text of U.S. government protest note, 7 April 1966; reproduced in J. Fayerweather, The Mercantile Bank Affair (New York: NYU Press, 1974), p. 412.

66. Ibid., p. 81.

67. Wright and Molot, "Capital Movements and Government Control," p. 677.

68. Business Week, 30 January 1965, p. 110.

69. New York Times, 17 March 1965, p. 65.

70. Figures for 1963; T. L. Powrie, "Foreign Direct Investment in Canada," in S. E. Rolfe and W. Damm (eds.), The Multinational Corporation in the World Economy (New York: Praeger, 1970), p. 92.

71. Wright and Molot, "Capital Movements and Government Control, p. 677.

72. Business Week, 27 January 1968, p. 31.

73. Ibid., 16 March 1968, pp. 29-32.

74. The Economist, 27 July 1963, pp. 373-374.

75. New York Times, 20 July 1963, p. 30; 31 July 1963, p. 33; 3 August 1963, p. 21; 4 August 1963, III, p. 1; 11 August 1963, p. 25.

76. Memo of telephone conversation; Dillon, personal papers, Kennedy Library.

77. See R. Keohane, "The Big Influence of Small Allies," Foreign Policy, no. 2, Spring 1971.

78. See Wright and Molot, "Capital Movements and Government Control," pp. 683-687.

79. New York Times, 11 December 1963, p. 69; 18 December 1963, p. 70.

80. New York Times, 9 September 1964, p. 61.

81. Undersecretary Deming's written reply to Representative Vanik; House, Committee on Ways and Means, Interest Equalization Tax Extension Act, 1967, p. 120.

82. Memo of telephone conversation with McGeorge Bundy, 9 February 1965; Dillon, personal papers, Kennedy Library.

83. Testimony of Secretary Connor; Senate, Committee on Banking and Currency, Balance of Payments - 1965, pp. 911-912.

84. Business Week, 16 March 1968, pp. 125-126; 4 May 1968, p. 100; The Economist, 1 November 1975, p. 82.

85. Memo of telephone conversation, 24 July 1963, Dillon, personal papers, Kennedy Library.

86. The Economist, 27 July 1963, p. 374.

87. New York Times, 6 September 1963, p. 37.

88. Ibid., 16 March 1965, p. 53; 2 April 1965, p. 45; 14 April 1965, p. 55.

89. D. T. Brash, "Australia as Host to the International Corporation," in Kindleberger, International Corporation, pp. 304-305.

90. New York Times, 6 January 1968, p. 39.

91. G. C. Hufbauer, "The Control of Capital Movements," U.S.
     Treasury Conference on Capital Control Programs, discussion
     paper no. 5, 7-8 December 1972, pp. 9, 22. (Mimeo.)

92. Per Jacobsson, International Monetary Problems, 1957-1963
     (Washington, D.C.: International Monetary Fund, 1964),
     p. 174.

93. Quoted in Business Week, 15 June 1963, p. 152.

94. See E. M. Bernstein, "U.S. Balance of Payments and In-
     ternational Liquidity," reprinted in Joint Economic Com-
     mittee, Guidelines for International Monetary Reform,
     1965, p. 231.

95. New York Times, 25 February 1966, p. 40.

96. Ibid., 8 October 1966, p. 157.

97. Report of the Monetary Committee reprinted and Marjolin's
     comments reprinted in Senate, Committee on Banking and
     Currency, Balance of Payments - 1965, pp. 726-729.

98. New York Times, 24 July 1963, p. 41.

99. Business Week, 27 March 1965, p. 141.

100. Morse, Foreign Policy and Interdependence, pp. 258-259;
     Karsten, "Should Europe Restrict U.S. Investments," p.
     245.

101. See R. W. Russell, "Transgovernmental Interaction in the
     International Monetary System," International Organization,
     Autumn 1973.

102. Interview with Francis Bator.

103. Roosa, Dollar and World Liquidity, pp. 27-28.

104. OECD, Working Party No. 3, The Balance of Payments Adjust-
     ment Process (Paris: OECD, August 1966), p. 28.

105. Business Week, 19 June 1965, p. 50.

106. The terms are here used to refer to (a) interactions
     between subunits of governments where a policy agreement
     is reached independently of the stated positions of the
     respective governments (transgovernmental interactions),
     and (b) causal influences on policy arising out of

international contacts where one of the actors is non-governmental. See Nye and Keohane, Transnational Relations, introduction and conclusion.

107. Wright and Molot, "Capital Movements and Government Control," p. 683.

108. Several French newspapers produced accounts of these BIS meetings; cited in New York Times, 3 January 1968, p. 74.

CHAPTER VIII

1. Weil and Davidson, The Gold War, p. 63.

2. New York Times, 3 March 1973, p. 46.

3. Statement of L. C. Hamilton, Treasurer, International Telephone & Telegraph; Joint Economic Committee, 1968 Economic Report, pp. 470-476.

4. For example, see Caterpillar Tractor's 1968 Annual Report, reprinted in House, Committee on Foreign Affairs, Foreign Direct Investment Controls, p. 148.

5. Quinn, New Euromarkets, p. 163; Business Week, 6 January 1968, p. 86, 13 January 1968, p. 97, 30 March 1968, pp. 58-59, 126.

6. The Economist, 21 September 1968, p. 99.

7. Rose, "Capital is Something That Doesn't Love a Wall," p. 102.

8. Testimony of J. D. Wheeler, Vice President, Westavco; House, Committee on Foreign Affairs, Foreign Direct Investment Controls, pp. 185-187.

9. Statement of C. E. Hopping, Chairman, Roberts Consolidated Industries, ibid., p. 138.

10. See Testimony of F. R. Milliken, President, Kennecott Copper, ibid., pp. 175-185.

11. Rose, "Capital is Something That Doesn't Love a Wall," p. 110.

12. See, for example, testimony of J. D. Layden, Vinnel Corporation; House, Committee on Foreign Affairs, Foreign

Direct Investment Controls, pp. 93-100.

13. U.S. Council of the International Chamber of Commerce, The Impact of U.S. Controls on Direct Investment (New York: mimeo., 1970).

14. Ibid., p. 5.

15. See, for example, OFDI, "Regulation of Foreign Direct Investment," and S. Pizer, "Capital Restraint Programs," in Commission on International Trade and Investment Policy, vol. I, pp. 100,138.

16. B. Geddes, "U.S. Direct Investment Overseas 1968-70," (D.B.A. dissertation, George Washington University, 1972), pp. 134-136.

17. S. Y. Kwack, "The Balance of Payments Effects of the U.S. Capital Controls," U.S. Treasury Conference on Capital Control Programs, December 1972 (mimeo.). Kwack suggests that the removal of the controls would result in a large outflow which would diminish over time.

18. J. Hewson and E. Sakakibara, "The Impact of U.S. Controls on the U.S. Balance of Payments," IMF Staff Papers, March 1975.

19. This possibility was noted by J. N. Behrman, "Assessing the Foreign Investment Controls," Law and Contemporary Problems, Winter 1969, p. 91 and F. Machlup, testimony in Joint Economic Committee, 1968 Economic Report, p. 406.

20. C. Wiesner, "A Theoretical Investigation into the Effects of an Interest Equalization Tax," (Ph.D., University of Tennessee, 1969), p. 121. Wiesner concentrates on real transfer effects. The IET also produces a balance of payments loss from potential debt servicing payments.

21. Lees, International Banking, pp. 222-223.

22. D. Morawetz, "The Effect of Financial Capital Flows and Transfers on the U.S. Balance of Payments Current Account," Journal of International Economics, November 1971.

23. Horst, "American Exports and Foreign Direct Investment."

24. Testimony of D. L. Commons, Senior Vice President,

Occidental Petroleum; House, Committee on Foreign
Affairs, Foreign Direct Investment Controls, p. 79.

25. New York Times, 21 September 1968, p. 49; 3 December
    1968, p. 61; 23 December 1968, p. 61.

26. Business Week, 21 December 1968, p. 25.

27. Ibid., 14 December 1968, p. 37.

28. Interview with Surrey.

29. See the Commission's report, Commission on International
    Trade and Investment Policy, vol. 3, p. 33. The member-
    ship included representatives of IBM, General Electric,
    First National Bank of Chicago, General Motors, Honeywell,
    Motorola, Merck, Utah Construction & Mining, Monsanto,
    Standard Oil (N.J.).

30. International Commerce, 21 April 1969 (published by the
    Commerce Department); quoted in House, Committee on
    Foreign Affairs, Foreign Direct Investment Controls, pp.
    100-101.

31. Statement of C. E. Fiero, Director of OFDI; Joint
    Economic Committee, Review of Balance of Payments
    Policies, 1969, p. 150.

32. U.S., President, Public Papers, R. M. Nixon, 1969, pp.
    265-267.

33. Bator, "Political Economics," pp. 62-64.

34. See, for example, U.S., Congress, Joint Economic Committee,
    Next Steps in International Monetary Reform, Report of
    the Subcommittee on International Exchange and Payments,
    90th Cong., 2d sess., September 1968. The report recom-
    mended wider bans around exchange parities. The final
    report of Johnson's CEA, in January 1969, recommended
    that flexible exchange rates be studied.

35. Bator, "Political Economics," p. 62.

36. Haberler has explained benign neglect in a number of
    articles; among these are U.S. Balance of Payments and
    the International Monetary System, reprint no. 9
    (Washington, D.C.: American Enterprise Institute, 1973);
    and "Prospects for the Dollar Standard," Lloyds Bank
    Review, July 1972.

318

37. The main lines of the report appeared in Business Week, 28 December 1968, p. 73; these were confirmed during the author's interview with H. S. Houthakker.

38. Statement of T. D. Willett; Joint Economic Committee, The Balance of Payments Mess, 1971, p. 385.

39. Interview with Houthakker; also see H. S. Houthakker, "Cooling Off the Money Crisis," Wall Street Journal, March 1973, reprinted in T. G. Evans (ed.), The Monetary Muddle (n.p.; Dow Jones, 1974), p. 36.

40. H. S. Houthakker, "Some Reflections on the International Monetary System," remarks delivered at the University of Bonn, 16 April 1969 (mimeo.). Houthakker also pointed out that what the United States wanted were parity changes (a crawling peg), not floating, since he believed the latter would result in a constriction of international trade and investment.

41. See Destler, Presidents, pp. 118-146.

42. Interview with Houthakker.

43. Quoted in The Economist, 7 October 1972, p. 53.

44. Statement of C. F. Bergsten; Joint Economic Committee, Balance of Payments Mess, p. 320. Also see C. F. Bergsten, The Dilemmas of the Dollar (New York: NYU Press, 1975), pp. 297-304.

45. Statement of C. F. Bergsten, ibid., pp. 320-323.

46. See C. F. Bergsten, "The New Economics and U.S. Foreign Policy," Foreign Affairs, January 1972.

47. See U.S., Department of State, "U.S. Trade and Investment Policy in an Interdependent World," in Commission on International Trade and Investment Policy, vol. I, p. 13; and Brandon, Retreat of American Power, p. 245.

48. The Economist, 22 May 1971, p. 53.

49. For example, W. L. Kohl, "The Nixon-Kissinger Foreign Policy System and U.S.-European Relations," World Politics, October 1975, pp. 39-40; and E. Stabler, "The Dollar Devaluations of 1971 and 1973," in Griffenhagen-Kroeger, pp. 247-248.

50. In the latter days of the Johnson Administration Treasury had put out "feelers" to foreign counterparts on the exchange rate question, and had received negative answers; see Rolfe and Burtle, Great Wheel, p. 85.

51. For example, statement of Undersecretary Deming, Joint Economic Committee, Balance of Payments Policies, 1969, pp. 178-179.

52. Statement of Undersecretary Volcker; U.S., Congress, Senate, Committee on Finance, Interest Equalization Tax Extension Act of 1969, Hearings on HR 12829, 91st Cong., 1st sess., p. 21.

53. Interview with Houthakker.

54. Statement of Martin; U.S., Congress, Senate, Committee on Finance, The International Financial Crisis, Hearings before the Subcommittee on International Finance and Resources, 93d Cong., 1st sess., 1973, p. 60.

55. Statement of Brimmer; Joint Economic Committee, Balance of Payments Mess, p. 14.

56. Testimony of C. E. Fiero; Joint Economic Committee, Balance of Payments Policies, 1969, p. 147.

57. New York Times, 26 January 1970, p. 84.

58. Interview with Houthakker.

59. Business Week, 3 August 1968, pp. 82-83. This effect was, of course, partly due to the three-fold schedule system of the FDIP.

60. Some of this inflow through the banking system was eventually limited by the imposition, by the Federal Reserve, in September 1969, of reserve requirements on Eurodollar borrowings of U.S. banks from their European branches; see J. S. Little, Eurodollars (New York: Harper and Row, 1975), pp. 226-230.

61. The Houthakker-Volcker mission reported this change of attitude to SDR's; New York Times, 2 April 1969, p. 63.

62. The Economist, 14 September 1968, pp. 17-18; 30 November 1968, p. 62.

63. Ibid., 6 January 1968, p. 42; New York Times, 2 January

1968, p. 16.

64. New York Times, 7 January 1968, p. 32.

65. Ibid., 3 January 1968, p. 74.

66. Hellman, Challenge to U.S. Dominance, pp. 133-134.

67. Statement of the Agency for Regional Planning, Business Week, 10 May 1976, supplement p. 2.

68. New York Times, 2 May 1968, p. 67.

69. Ibid., 3 February 1970, p. 65.

70. Testimony of Houthakker; Joint Economic Committee, Balance of Payments Mess, p. 259.

71. Houthakker, "Cooling Off the Monetary Crisis," in Evans, Monetary Muddle, p. 37.

72. The best account of the period August to December 1971 is in Brandon, Retreat of American Power, chapter 14. Also see E. Stabler, "The Dollar Devaluations of 1971 and 1973," in Griffenhagen-Kroeger.

73. For example, in a speech io the Bankers Association for Foreign Trade, cited in New York Times, 28 April 1971, p. 73.

74. R. A. Young, Instruments of Monetary Policy in the United States (Washington, D.C.: International Monetary Fund, 1973), p. 163.

75. New York Times, 28 December 1971, p. 41.

76. The Economist, 9 September 1972, p. 48.

77. Ibid., 5 January 1974, pp. 70-71, 2 February 1974, p. 70.

78. V. van Dine, "The U.S. Market After Controls," Euromoney, March 1974.

79. On the non-death of the Euromarkets, see H. Evers, "New York's International Revival," The Banker, September 1975; and "Banking in the Boom: A World Financial Survey," The Economist, 14 February 1975, pp. 10-14, 56.

CHAPTER IX

1. This theme is explored at greater length in Cooper, Economics of Interdependence and R. Gilpin, "The Politics of Transnational Economic Relations," in Keohane and Nye, Transnational Relations, pp. 48-69.

2. T. Baumgartner and T. R. Burns, "The Structuring of International Economic Relations," International Studies Quarterly, June 1975, p. 132.

3. The distinction between sensitivity and vulnerability is associated with the work of R. Cooper, The Economics of Interdependence and K. N. Waltz, "The Myth of National Interdependence," in Kindleberger, The International Corporation, pp. 205-226.

4. The term paradigm is here used to denote the ". . . entire constellation of beliefs, values, techniques shared by members of a given community. . .". See T. S. Kuhn, The Structure of Scientific Revolutions, 2d ed. (Chicago: University of Chicago Press, 1970), p. 175.

5. On the relationship between politicization and structural change, see R. O. Keohane and J. S. Nye, "World Politics and the International Economic System," in C. F. Bergsten (ed.), The Future of the International Economic Order (Lexington, Mass.: D. C. Heath, 1973).

6. R. Triffin "The Thrust of History in International Monetary Reform" Foreign Affairs, April 1969, p. 478.

7. G. W. Ball, "Cosmocorp: The Importance of Being Stateless," in C. C. Brown (ed.), World Business (New York: Macmillan, 1970), passim.

8. E. L. Morse, "The Transformation of Foreign Policies: Modernization, Interdependence and Externalization," World Politics, April 1970, passim.

SELECTED BIBLIOGRAPHY

Albin, R. "The Maturity Effect, Rates of Return and the
     Course of U.S. Foreign Investment." Journal of Inter-
     national Economics, February 1976.

Ackley, G. Recorded interview by J. Pechman. 1 August 1964.
     John F. Kennedy Library. Oral History Program.

Allison, G. T. Essence of Decision. Boston: Little, Brown,
     1971.

Aubrey, H. G. The Dollar in World Affairs, New York: Praeger,
     1964.

Baker, J. C. and Bradford, M. G. American Banks Abroad.
     New York: Praeger, 1974.

Ball, G. W. "Cosmocorp: The Importance of Being Stateless."
     In Brown, C. C., ed. World Business. New York:
     Macmillan, 1970.

"Banking in the Boom: A World Financial Survey." The
     Economist, 14 February 1975.

Barnet, R. J. and Müller, R. E. Global Reach. New York:
     Simon and Schuster, 1975.

Barr, Joseph W. Cambridge, Mass. Interview, 15 October 1975.

Bator, F. M. "The Politics of International Money." Foreign
     Affairs, October 1968.

_____. Cambridge, Mass. Interview, 24 June 1975.

Bauer, P. T. and Walters, A. A. "Economists and the Dollar
     Problem." Lloyds' Bank Review, April 1975.

Bauer, R. A.; de Sola Pool, I.; and Dexter, L. A. American
     Business Abroad. 2d edition. Chicago: Aldine, 1972.

Baumgartner, T. and Burns, T. R. "The Structuring of Inter-
     national Economic Relations." International Studies
     Quarterly, June 1975.

Behrman, J. N. "Assessing the Foreign Investment Controls." Law and Contemporary Problems, Winter 1969.

_____. "Foreign Investment Muddle: The Perils of Ad-Hocery." Columbia Journal of World Business, Fall 1965.

Bell, P. W. "Private Capital Movements and the U.S. Balance of Payments." In U.S. Congress. Joint Economic Committee. Factors Affecting the United States Balance of Payments. Compilation of studies prepared for the Subcommittee on International Exchange and Payments. Joint Committee Print, 87th Cong., 2d sess., 1962.

Beman, Lewis. "The Chastening of the Washington Economists." Fortune, January 1976.

Bergsten, C. F. The Dilemmas of the Dollar. New York: NYU Press, 1975.

_____. "The New Economics and U.S. Foreign Policy." Foreign Affairs, January 1972.

Birnbaum, E. A. "Changing the U.S. Commitment to Gold." Essays in International Finance, no. 63. Princeton University, 1967.

Boddewyn, J. J. "Western European Policies Toward U.S. Investors." The Bulletin, nos. 93-95, March 1974.

Brandon, Henry. The Retreat of American Power. New York: Delta, 1972.

Brash, D. T. "Australia as Host to the International Corporation." In Kindleberger, C. P., ed. The International Corporation. Cambridge, Mass.: M.I.T. Press, 1970.

Brittain, B. "Two International Monetary Decisions." In Griffenhagen-Kroeger, Inc. Cases on a Decade of United States Foreign Economic Policy: 1965-1974. 2 Volumes. San Francisco: n.p., 1974.

Brooks, J. The Go-Go Years: When Prices Went Topless. New York: Ballantine, 1974.

Bruck, N. K. and Lees, F. A. "Foreign Investment, Capital Controls and the Balance of Payments." The Bulletin, no. 48-49, April 1968.

Business Week. 1963-1974.

Cairncross, A. Control of Long-Term International Capital Movements. Washington, D.C.: Brookings Institution, 1973.

Caves, R. E. "International Corporations: The Industrial Economics of Foreign Investment." Economica, February 1971.

Caves, R. E. and Jones, R. W. World Trade and Payments. Boston: Little, Brown, 1973.

Cleveland, H. van Buren. The Atlantic Idea and Its European Rivals. New York: McGraw Hill, 1966.

Cohen, B. J., ed. American Foreign Economic Policy. New York: Praeger, Harper and Row, 1968.

_____. Balance of Payments Policy. Harmondsworth: Penguin, 1969.

_____. Vietnam: The Impact on American Business. A Study Commissioned by the Institute for Policy Studies for the Businessmen's Educational Fund, 1969. (Mimeographed.)

_____. "Voluntary Foreign Investment Curbs." Challenge, March/April 1967.

Cohen, S. D. International Monetary Reform, 1964-1969. New York: Praeger, 1970.

Commission on International Trade and Investment Policy. United States International Economic Policy in an Interdependent World. 3 Volumes. Washington, D.C.: Government Printing Office, 1971.

Committee for Economic Development. National Objectives and the Balance of Payments Problem. New York: CED, 1960.

_____. The International Position of the Dollar. New York: CED, 1961.

Cooper, R. N., ed. International Finance. Harmondsworth: Penguin, 1969.

_____. The Economics of Interdependence: Economic
Policy in the Atlantic Community. New York: McGraw
Hill, 1968.

Cutler, F. and Pizer, S. "U.S. Trade with Foreign Affiliates
of U.S. Firms." Survey of Current Business, December
1964.

Depres, E.; Kindleberger, C.P.; and Salant, W. S. "The
Dollar and World Liquidity: A Minority View."
The Economist, 5 February 1966.

Destler, I. M. Presidents, Bureaucrats and Foreign Policy.
Princeton: Princeton University Press, 1974.

Dillon, C. Douglas. Personal papers. John F. Kennedy
Library.

Dillon, Read and Company. Dillon, Read. New York:
n.p., 1974.

Dudley, L. and Passell, P. "The War in Vietnam and the
United States Balance of Payments." Review of
Economics and Statistics, November 1968.

Dunning, J. H., ed. International Investment. Harmondsworth: Penguin, 1972.

_____. "Technology, U.S. Investment and European Economic
Growth." In Dunning, International Investment.

Eckstein, Otto. Letter to the author, 15 July 1975.

The Economist. 1963-1974.

Ellsberg, D. "The Quagmire Myth and the Stalemate Machine."
In Ellsberg, D., ed. Papers on the War. New York:
Simon and Schuster, 1972.

Evans, T. G., ed. The Monetary Muddle. n.p.: Dow Jones,
1974.

Evers, H. "New York's International Revival." The Banker,
September 1975.

Farrer, L. L. "The Limits of Choice: July 1914 Reconsidered." Journal of Conflict Resolution, March
1972.

Fayerweather, J. The Mercantile Bank Affair. New York:
    New York University Press, 1974.

Federal Reserve Bank of New York. Annual Report, 1964.

Fielecke, N. S. Boston, Massachusetts. Interview, 9 June
    1975.

_____. "The Welfare Effects of Controls over Capital
    Exports from the United States." Essays in Inter-
    national Finance, no. 82. Princeton University, 1971.

Fleck, F. H. and Mahfouz, R. "The Multinational Corporation:
    Tax Avoidance and Profit Manipulation via Subsidiaries
    and Tax Havens." Swiss Magazine for Political Economy,
    no 2, 1974.

Freidel, F. FDR: Launching the New Deal. Boston: Little,
    Brown, 1973.

Galbratih, J. K. "The Balance of Payments: A Political
    and Administrative View." Review of Economics and
    Statistics, May 1974.

Geddes, B. "U.S. Direct Investment Overseas 1968-1970."
    D.B.A. dissertation, George Washington University, 1972.

Gilpin, R. "The Politics of Transnational Economic Relations."
    In Keohane, R. and Nye, J. S., eds. Transnational
    Relations. Cambridge, Mass.: Harvard University
    Press, 1972.

_____. U.S. Power and the Multinational Corporation.
    New York: Basic Books, 1975.

Golden, M. J. "The 'No-Tax Decision' of 1966." In Griffen-
    hagen-Kroeger, Cases on a Decade of United States
    Foreign Economic Policy.

Golden, S. "Johnson Administration Exonerated by New Study
    of Blame for Inflation." New York Times, 30 December
    1975.

Goldfinger, N. "A Labor View of Foreign Investment and Trade
    Issues." In Commission on International Trade and
    Investment Policy, volume I.

Gordon, K. Recorded interview by J. Pechman. 1 August 1964.
    John F. Kennedy Library. Oral History Program.

Green, D. S. "Government Organization for Policymaking and Execution in International Trade and Investment." In Commission on International Trade and Investment Policy, volume II.

Griffenhagen-Kroeger, Inc. Cases on a Decade of United States Foreign Economic Policy. 2 Volumes. San Francisco: n.p., 1974.

Grubel, H. G. The International Monetary System. Harmondsworth: Penguin, 1969.

_____, ed., World Monetary Reform. Stanford: Stanford University Press,1963.

"Guidelines for Banks and Nonbank Financial Institutions." Federal Reserve Bulletin, March 1965.

Haberler, G. "Prospects for the Dollar Standard." Lloyds Bank Review, July 1972.

_____. U.S. Balance of Payments and the International Monetary System. Reprint No. 9. Washington, D.C.: American Enterprise Institute, 1973.

Halm, G. N. "International Financial Intermediation: Deficits Benign and Malignant." Essays in International Finance, no. 68. Princeton University, 1966.

Harms, D. "An Analysis of the U.S. Voluntary Restraint Program: Its Effects on U.S. Balance of Payments and Private U.S. Industry." D.B.A. dissertation, George Washington University, 1968.

Harris, S. E. Economics of the Kennedy Years and a Look Ahead. New York: Harper and Row, 1964.

_____. Recorded interview by A. Schlesinger. 16 and 17 June 1964. John F. Kennedy Library. Oral History Program.

_____. "The U.S. Balance of Payments: The Problem and Its Solution." In Joint Economic Committee, Factors Affecting the United States Balance of Payments.

Heatherington, D. F. Remarks delivered to the Milwaukee World Trade Club, 3 December 1968. Reprinted in U.S. Department of Commerce News (n.d.).

Heller, F. M. "The Framework for Investigating Direct Manufacturing Investment Overseas." Law and Contemporary
Problems, Winter 1969

Heller, R. and Willatt, N. The European Revenge. London:
Barrie and Jenkins, 1975.

Heller, W. W. New Dimensions of Political Economy. New York:
W. W. Norton, 1966.

_____. Recorded interview by J. Pechman. 1 August 1964.
John F. Kennedy Library. Oral History Program.

Hellman, R. The Challenge to U.S. Dominance of the International Corporation. New York: Dunellen, 1970.

Hewson, J. and Sakakibara, E. "The Impact of U.S. Controls
on the U.S. Balance of Payments." IMF Staff Papers,
March 1975.

Hirsch, Fred. Money International. Revised edition.
Harmondsworth: Penguin, 1969.

Hogan, J. D. The U.S. Balance of Payments and Capital Flows.
New York: Praeger, 1967.

Horst, T. "American Exports and Foreign Direct Investments."
Discussion Paper no. 362, May 1974. Harvard Institute
of Economic Research. (Mimeographed.)

_____. "American Investments Abroad and Domestic Market
Power." In Bergsten, C. F.; Horst, T.; and Moran, T.
American Multinationals and American Interests.
Washington, D.C.: Brookings Institution, forthcoming.

Houthakker, H. S. "Cooling Off the Monetary Crisis." Wall
Street Journal, March 1973. Reprinted in Evans,
The Monetary Muddle.

_____. "Exchange Rate Adjustment." In Joint Economic
Committee, Factors Affecting the United States Balance
of Payments.

_____. Cambridge, Massachusetts. Interview, 3 July 1975.

_____. "Some Reflections on the International Monetary
System." Remarks delivered at the University of Bonn,
16 April 1969. (Mimeographed.)

_____. "The United States Balance of Payments: A Look Ahead." In Commission on International Trade and Investment Policy, volume I.

Hufbauer, G. C. "The Control of Capital Movements." U.S. Treasury Conference on Capital Control Programs. Discussion paper no. 5. 7-8 Decmeber 1972. (Mimeographed.)

Hufbauer, G. C. and Adler, M. Overseas Manufacturing Investment and the Balance of Payments. U.S. Treasury Department Tax Policy Research Study No. 1. Washington, D.C.: Government Printing Office, 1968.

Inkeles, A. "The Emerging Social Structure of the World." Paper prepared for presentation at the International Political Science Association Meeting in Montreal, Canada, August 1973. (Mimeographed.)

Jacobsson, Per. International Monetary Problems, 1957-1963. Washington, D.C.: International Monetary Fund, 1964.

Jasay, A. E. "The Social Choice Between Home and Overseas Investment." Economic Journal, volume 70, 1960. Reprinted in Dunning, International Investment.

Jervis, R. The Logic of Images in International Relations. Princeton: Princeton Univesrity Press, 1970.

Johnson, Brian. The Politics of Money. London: John Murray, 1970.

Johnson, H. G. "The Efficiency and Welfare Implications of the Multinational Corporation." In Kindleberger, The International Corporation.

_____. "The Monetary Approach to the Balance of Payments." Social Science Research Council. International Monetary Research Program. London: London School of Economics and Political Science, n.d.

_____. "Theoretical Problems of the International Monetary System." In Cooper, International Finance.

Johnson, L. B. The Vantage Point. New York: Holt, Rinehart and Winston, 1971.

Karsten, C. F. "Should Europe Restrict U.S. Investments." In Cohen, American Foreign Economic Policy.

Kelly, Janet. "American Banks in Britain." Ph.D. dissertation, Johns Hopkins University, 1975.

Keohane, R. "The Big Influence of Small Allies." Foreign Policy, no. 2, Spring 1971.

Keohane, R. and Nye, J.S. Transnational Relations. Cambridge, Massachusetts: Harvard University Press, 1971.

Keohane, R. and Nye, J. S. "World Politics and the International Economic System." In Bergsten, C. F., ed. The Future of the International Economic Order. Lexington, Mass.: D. C. Heath, 1973.

Kenen, P. B. "The International Position of the Dollar." In Cohen, American Foreign Economic Policy.

Kindleberger, C. P. American Business Abroad. New Haven: Yale University Press, 1969.

_____, ed. The International Corporation. Cambridge, Massachusetts: M.I.T. Press, 1970.

_____. Cambridge, Massachusetts. Interview, 9 June 1975.

_____. "The Politics of International Money and World Language." Essays in International Finance, no. 61. Princeton University, 1967.

_____. The World in Depression, 1929-1939. Berkeley and Los Angeles: University of California Press, 1973.

Knipe, J. L. The Federal Reserve and the American Dollar. Chapel Hill: University of North Carolina Press, 1965.

Knorr, K. Power and Wealth. New York: Basic Books, 1973.

Kohl, W. L. "The Nixon-Kissinger Foreign Policy System and U.S.-European Relations." World Politics, October 1975.

Koszul, J.-P. "American Banks in Europe." In Kindleberger, The International Corporation.

Kuhn, Loeb & Company. Kuhn, Loeb. New York: n.p., 1975.

Kuhn, T. S. The Structure of Scientific Revolutions. Chicago: University of Chicago Press, 1970.

Kuwayama, P. H. "Measuring the United States Balance of Payments." Federal Reserve Bank of New York. Monthly Review, August 1975.

Kwack, S. Y. "The Balance of Payments Effects of the U.S. Capital Controls." U.S. Treasury Conference on Capital Control Programs, December 1972. (Mimeographed.)

Larre, R. "Facts of Life About the Integration of National Capital Markets." Journal of Money, Credit and Banking, volume 1, 1969.

Lary, H. B. Problems of the United States as a World Trader and Banker. New York: National Bureau of Economic Research, 1963.

Lees, F. A. International Banking and Finance. London: Macmillan, 1974.

Little, J. S. Eurodollars: The Money Market Gypsies. New York: Harper and Row, 1975.

_____. "The Impact of the Euro-dollar Market on the Effectiveness of Monetary Policy in the U.S. and Abroad." New England Economic Review, March/April 1975.

Machlup, F. International Payments, Debts and Gold. New York: Scribner's Sons, 1964.

_____. Remaking the International Monetary System. Baltimore: Johns Hopkins Press, 1968.

_____. "The Transfer Gap of the United States." Reprints in International Finance, no. 11. Princeton University, 1968.

Magdoff, H. "Imperialism Without Colonies." In Owen, R. and Sutcliffe,B., eds.Studies in the Theory of Imperialism. London: Longmans, 1972.

Maisel, S. J. Managing the Dollar. New York: Norton, 1973.

Makin, J. H. "On the Success of the Reserve Currency System in the Crisis Zone." Journal of International Economics, February 1972.

Mandel, E. Europe vs. America. New York: Monthly Review Press, 1972.

332

Manning, R. "A Nash-Cournot Model of Taxation of International Capital Movements." Economic Record, March 1974.

Mayer, M. The Bankers. New York: Ballantine, 1976.

Michaely, M. The Responsiveness of Demand Policies to Balance of Payments. New York: Columbia University Press, 1971.

Modelski, G. "Some Continuities in the Structure of World Politics." Harvard University, November 1973. (Mimeographed.)

Morawetz, D. "The Effect of Financial Capital Flows and Transfers on the U.S. Balance of Payments Current Account." Journal of International Economics, November 1971.

Morse, E. L. Foreign Policy and Interdependence in Gaullist France. Princeton: Princeton University Press, 1973.

_____. "The Transformation of Foreign Policies: Modernization, Interdependence and Externalization." World Politics, April 1970.

Mundell, R. International Economics. New York: Macmillan, 1968.

Musgrave, P. B. "Direct Investment Abroad and the Multinationals: Effects on the U.S. Economy." Harvard Law School International Tax Program, 25-26 February 1975. (Mimeographed.)

_____. Taxation of Foreign Investment. Harvard University, 26 February 1975. (Mimeographed.)

Musgrave, R. A. "Tax Policy." Review of Economics and Statistics, May 1964.

New York Times. 1963-1974.

Nye, J. S. "Multinational Corporations in World Politics." Foreign Affairs, October 1974.

Okun, A. M. The Political Economy of Prosperity. New York: W. W. Norton, 1970.

Olsen, M. The Logic of Collective Action. Cambridge, Massachusetts: Harvard University Press, 1965.

Organization for Economic Cooperation and Development.
Working Party Three. The Balance of Payments Adjustment Process. Paris: OECD, August 1966.

Perroux, F. "The Domination Effect and Modern Economic
Theory." Social Research, volume 17, 1950. Reprinted
in Rothschild, K. W., ed. Power in Economics. Harmondsworth: Penguin, 1971.

Pierce, L. C. The Politics of Fiscal Policy Formation.
Pacific Palisades: Goodyear Publishing Company, 1971.

Pizer, S. "Capital Restraint Programs." In Commission
on International Trade and Investment Policy, volume
I.

Powrie, T. L. "Foreign Direct Investment in Canada." In
Rolfe, S. E. and Damm, W., eds. The Multinational
Corporation in the World Economy. New York: Praeger,
1970.

Quinn, B. S. The New Euromarkets. London: Macmillan,
1975.

Reuss, H. S. The Critical Decade. New York: McGraw
Hill, 1964.

_____. Recorded interview by R. J. Grele. 12 and 15
December 1965. John F. Kennedy Library. Oral
History Program.

Rivera, J. H. de. The Psychological Dimensions of Foreign
Policy. Columbus: C. E. Merrill, 1968.

Robbins, S. M. and Stobaugh, R. B. Money in the Multinational
Enterprise. New York: Basic Books, 1973.

Robinson, J. A. Congress and Foreign Policy Making.
Homewood, Illinois: Dorsey Press, 1962.

Robinson, S. W. Multinational Banking. Lejden: Sijthoff,
1972.

Rolfe, S. E. Capital Markets in Atlantic Economic Relationships. Boulogne-sur-Seine: Atlantic Institute, 1967.

Rolfe, S. E. and Burtle, J. L. The Great Wheel: The World
Monetary System. New York: Quadrangle, 1973.

Rolfe, S. E. and Damm, W., eds. The Multinational Corporation in the World Economy. New York: Praeger, 1970.

Roosa, R. V. "Assuring the Free World's Liquidity." In Joint Economic Committee. Factors Affecting the United States Balance of Payments.

_____. The Dollar and World Liquidity. New York: Random House, 1967.

_____. Monetary Reform for the World Economy. New York: Random House, 1965.

_____. "Movements of Long-Term Capital and the Adjustment Process." Review of Economics and Statistics, May 1964.

Rose, S. "Capital is Something that Doesn't Love a Wall." Fortune, February 1971.

Russell, R. W. "Transgovernmental Interaction in the International Monetary System." International Organization, Autumn 1973.

Salant, W. S., et al. The United States Balance of Payments in 1968. Washington, D.C.: The Brookings Institution, 1963.

Samuelson, P. A. "Economic Frontiers." In New Frontiers of the Kennedy Administration. Task Force Reports Prepared for the President. Washington, D.C.: Public Affairs Press, 1961.

_____. Cambridge, Massachusetts. Interview, 19 June 1975.

_____. Recorded interview by J. Pechman. 1 August 1964. John F. Kennedy Library. Oral History Program.

Scammell, W. M. International Monetary Policy. 2d edition. London: Macmillan, 1964.

Schlesinger, A. M. A Thousand Days. Boston: Houghton Mifflin, 1965

Schmiegelow, Henrik and Schmiegelow, Michele. "The New Mercantilism in International Relations." International Organization, Spring 1975.

Simon, H. A. "Rational Choice and the Structure of the
    Environment." In Emery, R. E., ed. Systems Thinking.
    Harmondsworth: Penguin, 1969.

Snider, D. A. "The Case for Capital Controls to Relieve the
    U.S. Balance of Payments." American Economic Review,
    volume 64, 1964. Reprinted in Dunning, International
    Investment.

Sorensen, T. C. Kennedy. New York: Harper and Row, 1965.

Stabler, E. "The Dollar Devaluations of 1971 and 1973."
    In Griffenhagen-Kroeger. Cases on a Decade of
    United States Foreign Economic Policy.

Stadnichenko, A. Monetary Crisis of Capitalism. Moscow:
    Progress Publishers, 1975.

Stein, A. A. "Balance of Payments Policy in the Kennedy
    Administration." Papers of the Peace Society Inter-
    national, volume 23, 1974.

Stern, R. M. The Balance of Payments. Chicago: Aldine,
    1973.

Surrey, Stanley S. Cambridge, Massachusetts. Interview,
    18 June 1975.

Takayama, A. International Trade. New York: Holt, Rinehart
    and Winston, 1972.

Tobin, J. The New Economics One Decade Older. Princeton:
    Princeton University Press, 1974.

_____. Recorded interview by J. Pechman. 1 August 1964.
    John F. Kennedy Library. Oral History Program.

Tonneden, R. L. Foreign Disinvestment by U.S. Multinational
    Corporations. New York: Praeger, 1975.

Triffin, R. Gold and the Dollar Crisis. New Haven: Yale
    University Press, 1961.

_____. "The Thrust of History in International Monetary
    Reform." Foreign Affairs, April 1969.

U.S. Congress. House. Interest Equalization Tax Act of
    1963. H. Rept. 1046 to Accompany H.R. 8000. 88th
    Cong., 1st sess., 1964.

U.S. Congress. House. Interest Equalization Tax Extension Act of 1965. H. Rept. 602 to Accompany H.R. 4750. 89th Cong., 1st sess., 1965.

U.S. Congress. House. Committee on Banking and Currency. Recent Changes in Monetary Policy and Balance of Payments Problems, Hearings. 88th Cong., 1st sess., 1963.

U.S. Congress. House. Committee on Banking and Currency. Recent International Financial and Monetary Developments, Hearings before the Subcommittee on International Finance. 91st Cong., 1st sess., 1969.

U.S. Congress. House. Committee on Foreign Affairs. Foreign Direct Investment Controls, Hearings before the Subcommittee on Foreign Economic Policy. 91st Cong., 1st sess., 1969.

U.S. Congress. House. Committee on Ways and Means. Interest Equalization Tax Act, Hearings on H.R. 8000. 88th Cong., 1st sess., 1963.

U.S. Congress. House. Committee on Ways and Means. Interest Equalization Tax Extension Act of 1967, Hearings on H.R. 3813. 90th Cong., 1st sess., 1967.

U.S. Congress. House. Committee on Ways and Means. Extension of the Interest Equalization Tax, Hearings. 92d Cong., 1st sess., 1971.

U.S. Congress. House. Committee on Ways and Means. Administration Request for Extension of the Interest Equalization Tax, Hearings on H.R. 3154. 93d Cong., 1st sess., 1973.

U.S. Congress. Joint Economic Committee. The Balance of Payments Mess, Hearings before the Subcommittee on International Exchange and Payments. 92d Cong., 1st sess., 1971.

U.S. Congress. Joint Economic Committee. Balance of Payments Statistics, Hearings before the Subcommittee on Economic Statistics. 89th Cong., 1st sess., 1965.

U.S. Congress. Joint Economic Committee. January 1963 Economic Report of the President, Hearings. 88th Cong., 1st sess., 1963.

U.S. Congress. Joint Economic Committee. January 1964 Economic Report of the President, Hearings. 88th Cong., 2d sess., 1964.

U.S. Congress. Joint Economic Committee. January 1965 Economic Report of the President, Hearings. 89th Cong., 1st sess., 1965

U.S. Congress. Joint Economic Committee. January 1966 Economic Report of the President, Hearings. 89th Cong., 2d sess., 1966.

U.S. Congress. Joint Economic Committee. The 1967 Economic Report of the President, Hearings. 90th Cong., 1st sess., 1967.

U.S. Congress. Joint Economic Committee. The 1968 Economic Report of the President, Hearings. 90th Cong., 2d sess., 1968.

U.S. Congress. Joint Economic Committee. The 1969 Economic Report of the President, Hearings. 91st Cong., 1st sess., 1969.

U.S. Congress. Joint Economic Committee. The 1970 Economic Report of the President, Hearings. 91st Cong., 2d sess., 1970.

U.S. Congress. Joint Economic Committee. The 1971 Economic Report of the President, Hearings. 92d Cong., 1st sess., 1971.

U.S. Congress. Joint Economic Committee. Factors Affecting the U.S. Balance of Payments. Compilation of studies prepared for the Subcommittee on International Exchange and Payments. Joint Committee Print, 89th Cong., 2d sess., 1962.

U.S. Congress. Joint Economic Committee. Foreign Economic Policy for the 1970's, Hearings before the Subcommittee on Foreign Economic Policy. 91st Cong., 1st sess., 1970.

U.S. Congress. Joint Economic Committee. Guidelines for International Monetary Reform, Hearings before the Subcommittee on International Exchange and Payments. 89th Cong., 1st sess., 1965.

U.S. Congress. Joint Economic Committee. New Approach to
United States International Economic Policy, Hearings
before the Subcommittee on International Exchange and
Payments. 89th Cong., 2d sess., 1966.

U.S. Congress. Joint Economic Committee, Outlook for the
U.S. Balance of Payments, Hearings before the Subcommittee on International Exchange and Payments.
87th Cong., 2d sess., 1963.

U.S. Congress. Joint Economic Committee. A Review of
Balance of Payments Policies, Hearings before the
Subcommittee on International Exchange and Payments.
91st Cong., 1st sess., 1969.

U.S. Congress. Joint Economic Committee. U.S. Payments
Policies Consistent with Domestic Objectives of
Maximum Employment and Growth. Report of the Sub-
committee on International Exchange and Payments. 87th
Cong., 2d sess., 1962.

U.S. Congress. Joint Economic Committee. The U.S. Balance
of Payments, Hearings. 3 volumes. 88th Cong., 1st sess.,
1963, 1964.

U.S. Congress. Senate. Interest Equalization Tax Extension
Act of 1965. S. Rept. 621 to Accompany HR 4750. 89th
Cong., 1st sess., 1965.

U.S. Congress. Senate. Committee on Banking and Currency.
Balance of Payments-1965, Hearings before the Subcommittee
on International Finance. 89th Cong., 1st sess., 1965.

U.S. Congress. Senate. Committee on Banking, Housing and
Urban Affairs. Extension of the Council on International Economic Policy, Hearings before the Subcommittee on International Finance. 93d Cong., 1st
sess., 1973.

U.S. Congress. Senate. Committee on Finance. Interest
Equalization Tax, Hearings on HR 8000. 88th Cong.,
2d sess., 1964.

U.S. Congress. Senate. Committee on Finance. Interest
Equalization Tax Extension Act of 1967, Hearings on
HR 6098. 90th Cong., 1st sess. 1967.

U.S. Congress. Senate. Committee on Finance. Extension of the Interest Equalization Tax, Hearings on HR 5432. 92d Cong., 1st sess., 1971.

U.S. Congress. Senate. Committee on Finance. Implications of Multinational Corporations for World Trade and Investment and for U.S. Trade and Labor. Report to the Committee on Investigation No. 332-69. Committee Print, 93d Cong., 1st sess., 1973.

U.S. Congress. Senate. Committee on Finance. International Aspects of the President's New Economic Policies, Hearings before the Subcommittee on International Trade. 92d Cong., 1st sess., 1971.

U.S. Congress. Senate. Committee on Finance. The International Financial Crisis, Hearings before the Subcommittee on International Finance and Resources. 93d Cong., 1st sess., 1973.

U.S. Council of Economic Advisors. Annual Report, 1967.

U.S. Council of Economic Advisors. Annual Report, 1969.

U.S. Council of the International Chamber of Commerce. The Impact of U.S. Controls on Direct Investment. New York, 1970 (Mimeographed.)

U.S. Department of Commerce. Records. John F. Kennedy Library.

U.S. Department of Commerce. Office of Foreign Direct Investments. "The Foreign Direct Investment Program and Its Relationship to the U.S. Balance of Payments." Remarks by C. F. Fiero (Director, OFDI) at a conference of the Tax Foundation, Inc., New York, December 1969. (Mimeographed.)

U.S. Department of Commerce. Office of Foreign Direct Investments. "Regulation of Foreign Direct Investment." In Commission on International Trade and Investment Policy, volume I.

U.S. Department of State. "Government Restrictions on the Outflow of Private Capital Employed by Principal Capital Exporting Countries." Reprinted in Joint Economic Committee, 1963 Economic Report.

U.S. Department of State. "U.S. Trade and Investment Policy in an Interdependent World." In Commission on International Trade and Investment Policy, volume 1.

U.S. Department of the Treasury. Maintaining the Strength of the United States Dollar in a Strong Free World Economy. January 1968.

U.S. President. Public Papers of the Presidents of the United States. Lyndon B. Johnson, 1965 and 1968.

U.S. President. Public Papers of the Presidents of the United States. John F. Kennedy, 1961 and 1963.

U.S. President. Public Papers of the Presidents of the United States. Richard M. Nixon, 1969.

Vanek, J. "Overvaluation of the Dollar: Causes, Effects and Remedies." In Joint Economic Committee, Factors Affecting the U.S. Balance of Payments.

Vernon, R. "The Economic Consequences of U.S. Foreign Direct Investment." In Commission on International Trade and Investment, volume I.

_____. "A Sceptic Looks at the Balance of Payments." Foreign Policy, Winter 1971-1972.

Young, R. A. Instruments of Monetary Policy in the United States. Washington, D.C.: International Monetary Fund, 1973.

Waltz, K. N. "The Myth of National Interdependence." In Kindleberger, International Corporation.

Weber, Max. The Theory of Social and Economic Action. New York: Free Press, 1964.

Weil, G. L. and Davidson, I. The Gold War. New York: Holt, Rinehart and Winston, 1970.

Wiesner, C. "A Theoretical Investigation of an Interest Equalization Tax." Ph.D. dissertation, University of Tennessee, 1969.

Williams, D. "Foreign Currency Issues in the European Securities Markets." IMF Staff Papers, September 1966.

Wilson, H. A Personal Record. Boston: Little; Brown, 1971.

Winch, D. M. Analytic Welfare Economics. Harmondsworth: Penguin, 1971.

Wright, G. and Molot, M. A. "Capital Movements and Governmental Control." International Organization, Autumn 1974.

For Product Safety Concerns and Information please contact our EU
representative GPSR@taylorandfrancis.com
Taylor & Francis Verlag GmbH, Kaufingerstraße 24, 80331 München, Germany

www.ingramcontent.com/pod-product-compliance
Lightning Source LLC
Chambersburg PA
CBHW070550270326
41926CB00013B/2265